PULP

Reading popular fiction

SCOTT McCRACKEN

Manchester University Press

Manchester and New York

Distributed exclusively in the USA by St. Martin's Press

The right of Scott McCracken to be identified as the author of this work has been asserted by him in accordance with the Copyright, Designs and Patents Act 1988.

Published by Manchester University Press
Oxford Road, Manchester M13 9NR, UK
and Room 400, 175 Fifth Avenue, New York,
NY 10010, USA

Distributed exclusively in the USA by
St. Martin's Press, Inc., 175 Fifth Avenue, New York,
NY 10010, USA

Distributed exclusively in Canada by
UBC Press, University of British Columbia, 6344 Memorial Road,
Vancouver, BC, Canada V6T 1Z2

British Library Cataloguing-in-Publication Data
A catalogue record for this book is available from the British Library

Library of Congress Cataloging-in-Publication Data applied for

20 0000⊦ 421

ISBN   0 7190 4758 7 *hardback*
        0 7190 4759 5 *paperback*

First published 1998

05 04 03 02 01 00   10 9 8 7 6 5 4 3 2

Typeset in Monotype Garamond by Lucy Morton, London SE12

Printed and bound in Great Britain by Biddles Ltd, *www.biddles.co.uk*

Contents

Acknowledgements

First thanks go to Anita Roy who encouraged me to submit the original proposal to MUP. Much of the writing of the book was completed while I was Visiting Scholar in the Program for Modern Thought and Literature at Stanford University and Visiting Professor at the University of the Pacific. A Fulbright Scholarship made both positions possible. I would like to thank the Fulbright Commission and all my colleagues at Stanford and UOP who provided a stimulating and comfortable atmosphere in which the book could develop. I would also like to thank Lucie Armitt, Avril Horner, Sally Ledger, Nickianne Moody, Stephen Owen, Antony Rowland and Steve Watts, who read parts of the manuscript in draft form. Special thanks go to Laura Chrisman and Brian Longhurst who read and commented on drafts of the whole manuscript and to David Glover whose help with the final revisions was invaluable. Last but not least, I am more than grateful to Georgina Waylen, who has lived with the project as long as I have and read through and offered advice on the manuscript at all stages. No one but myself, of course, can be held responsible for the final product.

introduction
World, reader and text

Some of my happiest experiences reading popular fiction have been on trains. There is something about the combination of being trapped yet going somewhere that is particularly conducive to the pleasures of pulp. While the popular narrative also traps in its predictability, despite, or maybe because of, that predictability, there is more scope for an escape into fantasy. Below, I look at two accounts of the experience of reading popular fiction: one about reading on the train, the other about reading in the airport lounge; but these are just two of the many contexts of a highly varied experience that can be an idle pursuit, a secret joy, a public pleasure, a liberation from the constraints of everyday life or a profound disappointment.

Studying popular fiction means getting to grips with every aspect of those experiences. In this book, I define popular fiction simply as fiction that is read by large numbers of people; but in the context of the late twentieth century that definition needs some refinement. Contemporary popular fiction is the product of a huge entertainment industry. Written fiction is only a part of that industry, which markets and sells popular narratives for film, radio, television and periodicals as well as in book form. To study popular fiction, then, is to study only a small part of popular culture. Nonetheless, written popular narratives can tell us much about who we are and about the society in which we live. The Russian writer Osip Mandelstam wrote: 'It is terrifying to think that our life is a tale without a plot or a hero, made out of desolation and glass, out of the feverish babble of constant digressions.'[1] Popular fiction, from folk tales and fairy tales to popular ballads to modern bestsellers, has always provided a structure within which our lives can be understood. Who we are is never fixed, and in modern societies an embedded sense of self is less available than ever before.[2] Popular fiction has the capacity to provide us with a workable, if temporary, sense of self. It can alleviate the terror described by Mandelstam. It can give our lives the plots and heroes they lack. While the same can be said for all fiction, narratives read by large numbers of people are indicative of widespread hopes and fears.

In this introductory chapter, I suggest three perspectives on the experience of reading popular fiction that might structure its study. These can be termed briefly, the world, the reader and the text.[3] No single one of these elements can be completely separated from the other two, they co-exist in a complex and dynamic relationship, but each is crucial to our understanding of the contemporary experience of popular fiction. Of the three, the first is the broadest. It describes the social context of popular fiction, but this context is never a given; it is always in dispute. Popular fiction is both created by and a participant in social conflict. An understanding of the second, the reader, in relation to the contemporary world requires an understanding of the construction of the modern self. Our view of the self determines whether we see the reader as active and critical or passive and uncritical. The third, the text itself, has been the traditional object of study for literary criticism, often to the exclusion of the world and the reader. In this book, I argue that the text should be considered in the context of the total experience of reading popular fiction.

Reading popular fiction

To demonstrate the importance of the relationship between world, reader and text, I begin with two different representations of the experience of reading popular fiction. The first is from an essay by Walter Benjamin entitled 'Detective Novels, Read on Journeys'. Benjamin was writing in Central Europe before the Second World War. His account attempts to capture the totality of the experience of reading a detective novel on a train.

Each traveller, at one time or another, has reached towards the suspended, swaying volumes [at the station bookstall], less out of the joy of reading than with an obscure feeling that he is making an agreeable sacrifice to the gods of the railway. He knows the coins, which he consecrates to this offertory box, commend him to the mercy of the boiler god that glows through the night, the smoke naiads that romp over the train, and to the stucco demon who is master of all lullabies. He knows them all from dreams and he is familiar with all the mythical ordeals and perils … and the vertiginous succession of innumerable thresholds of time and space that they move through, from the famous 'too late' of those left behind, the archetype of all loss, the loneliness of the compartment, the anxiety of missing one's connection, to the horror of entering the unfamiliar arrival hall. Bewildered he feels caught up in a giant machine and recognises in himself the speechless witnesses of the conflict between the railway gods and the station gods.[4]

Benjamin begins by describing the pleasures involved in the act of buying a work of popular fiction in a railway station, but he goes on to describe the purchase as a kind of ritualised act, made as much in fear as in pleasure. Since the nineteenth century, the railways have been used as a symbol of the alienation we feel in the face of the gigantic, anonymous systems of modernity. Benjamin's representation of the railway as a 'giant machine' can be seen as a metaphor for the world in which the reader of popular fiction exists. According to the sociologist Anthony Giddens, modern society is characterised by large, impersonal, 'self-referential systems'. These systems, like railways, are 'largely autonomous and determined by their own constitutive influences'[5] and within them the self loses its sense of agency and is beset by doubts and anxieties. This is not unlike what happens to Benjamin's traveller–reader. Caught up in the anonymity of the railway system, the self threatens to fragment into warring factions, and it is into the gap created by the fragmented self that the popular text enters. For Benjamin, the railway journey is the optimal site for travel reading; and, indeed, the 'railway novel' was an early description of a bestseller.[6] Benjamin suggests that the popular text supplies a regular, familiar pattern, but that this is not enough in itself. The whole process of purchasing and reading a detective novel on a train acts as a kind of ritual which allows the reader to maintain a workable sense of self throughout the disruptive experience of the journey. He describes how different types of popular narratives provide the opportunity to project or fantasise different kinds of potential selves.

In each case, the process of self-reinvention involves a transaction between world, reader and text.

Nowadays the setting for the experience of reading popular fiction is as likely to be the airport departure lounge as the railway station. The 'cyberpunk' science-fiction writer Pat Cadigan, has said that she wants to write novels that would fill the emptiness she experienced waiting for a plane in Wichita airport, Kansas, on a Sunday in the late 1970s.[7] My second extract is taken from Walter Nash's *The Language of Popular Fiction*. Nash also represents the experience of reading popular fiction in the context of the environment in which it is read, but he is more prescriptive than Benjamin about the limits of the text's influence.

> Here in the airport lounge, how becalmed we voyagers are, all spellbound and dreambound! How equable this climate – this mild, well-regulated air, untouched by frost or torrid heat, or the bite or chilling wind! Suspended between Somewhere and Elsewhere, we bask in the Light of Anywhere. It is a place where fantasies luxuriate. As our feet wander the mute and carpeted acres, our eyes flit speculatively among figures and faces. Look, now, at this man coming towards us. His neat blue suit proclaims the businessman, but who knows what underworlds of espionage, what services to a secret cause are implicated in that brief-case? Those policemen at the boarding gate are tensely waiting for the two drug-trafficking mafiosi to show up. That woman's elegance, ever so slightly ruffled – for her silk scarf hangs negligently, and she has just dropped a glove – tells us that she is on her way to meet her lover, the American neurosurgeon, who will never marry her as long as his demented wife (of whom she has no knowledge) still lingers on in the expensive Swiss clinic. Here we all are, in this Land of In-Between. We are characters in enjoyably bad books, it seems. We are in the right place for Popular Fiction.[8]

Nash also describes the pleasures of popular fiction, but unlike Benjamin, who attempts to engage with the totality of the experience of the world, the reader and the text, Nash argues that popular fiction is confined to the fantasy 'In-Between' world of the airport, and therefore outside the sphere of the critical, the rational and the cognitive. This view of popular fiction's role in the world has consequences for the way Nash reads popular texts. He quickly concludes that 'popfiction' has no 'merit': 'Popfiction, the disposable article, is committed to the simplest moralities, the crudest psychologies, and has few philosophical pretensions.'[9]

Nash's argument is that these simple texts bear no relation to the real and vital worlds from which we depart and in which we arrive, or what Nash calls 'the weathers of our destinations and the happenings of our ordinary lives'.[10] Benjamin, by contrast, sees the role of the popular text in relation to the world in which we live. In the following chapters, I argue that the context in which popular fiction is read is crucial to our understanding of it. Following Benjamin, my concern is with the relationship between the 'real' worlds of arrival and departure, and the textual, fantasy world of in between. The reader of popular fiction is always between destinations; however, I want to examine the connections that relate the *self who reads* to the *self of everyday life*. These connections make it more difficult than Nash admits to distinguish between the 'simplest moralities' and the 'crudest psychologies' of popular fiction and the 'lessons of serious literature', which he tells us are 'not quickly learned'. Instead, I suggest that popular fiction can only be easily dismissed if it is treated in isolation and not as part of the larger dynamic sketched out by Benjamin.

This raises the question of how we judge cultural value. In what follows I am wary of clear boundaries between so-called 'high' and 'low' cultures. While this opposition still has important symbolic value and while texts continue to be judged within its terms, it has little empirical worth. It is, for example, difficult in the late twentieth century to find a social class that prefers 'classic' to popular fiction.[11] As we shall see, the social groups that make up the audience for popular fiction are diverse and overlapping. What is of more interest to current criticism is the relationship between a particular audience (or coalition of reader groups) and a particular text or genre. Questions of cultural value posed in this way refuse the abstract categories of high and low, good and bad. Instead we need to ask about the kinds of values a particular audience has a vested interest in creating or sustaining. We need to know what kinds of social conflicts are being played out through the assertion of one set of values over another. Implicit in such questions is the role of the critic in defining and defending what John Frow calls 'regimes of value'.[12] By this he means the broad framework of values upon which a particular audience agrees. The critic's interests in disrupting or confirming a regime of value need to be analysed as part of the discussion of popular culture. To understand the kinds of frameworks within which such questions are asked, in the following sections I look in more detail at the broad concepts of world, reader and text.

The world

Popular fiction at the end of the twentieth century is a quintessential product of the modern world. The modern age or modernity is usually dated from the end of feudalism and gets fully underway with the rise of industrial capitalism. It is a time of rapid social change that brings contradictory results. In the words of Marshall Berman:

> To be modern is to find ourselves in an environment that promises us adventure, power, joy, growth, transformation of ourselves and our world – and, at the same time, that threatens to destroy everything we have, everything we know, everything we are ... To be modern is to be part of a universe in which, as Marx said, 'all that is solid melts into air'.[13]

Popular fiction emerges out of these contradictions, and its ability to articulate them in a way that the reader can relate to is central to its success. Popular fiction, we might say, mediates social conflict. In other words, it acts as a medium between reader and world through which the social contradictions of modernity can be played out. An understanding of the world of popular fiction means an understanding of its role in social conflict. Battles are fought across its pages, victories won and defeats suffered. If we do not exactly emerge bleeding, we may well return exhausted from the struggle over meaning that takes place in all popular texts.

The following passage from *A Tangled Web* by Judith Michael, a paperback bestseller in 1995, gives a typical representation of the contradictory world of modernity:

> Noontime crowds filled the streets of London, and Sabrina merged with them, a Londoner again, Sabrina Longworth again, free and independent, on her way to Ambassadors, the exclusive antique shop she had created after her divorce from Denton. She never thought of Denton except when she was in London, and she thought of him briefly now: his round rosy face, his fascination with himself and his pleasures, his love of women and gambling. He had been gambling in Monaco when Max Stuyvesant's ship went down; he was the one who identified the body of Sabrina Longworth. Max's body had never been found.
> ... She had planned her trip to Ambassadors for the end of October, while Garth gave a paper at the International Biogenetics Conference at the Hague; then they would meet in Paris for a week to themselves.[14]

The culture of modernity is made in the city, and was born in the large Western metropolises of the nineteenth and twentieth centuries.

Here, Sabrina is identified with the city – she is a Londoner; but the passage places that identity in the context of a much bigger, global culture. She has flown to London from Chicago, and the references to Monaco and The Hague suggest that she is part of an international network of connections. Contemporary popular fiction commonly sets its characters amidst the modern systems of international finance, and technological and political networks, which are part of the organisational power of modernity. Their identities are produced through the interaction of the personal and the impersonal. In Giddens's words: 'One of the distinctive features of modernity, in fact, is an increasing interconnection between the two extremes of extensionality and intentionality: globalising influences on the one hand and personal dispositions on the other.'[15] In fact, Sabrina's position is reminiscent of the reader in Benjamin's essay, who is stuck inside the railway system for the duration of the journey but forever within the modern institutions that organise our lives. However, the perplexing reference to Sabrina Longworth's 'body' introduces an element of mystery into the passage, as if her identity is not as clearly defined as my reading so far might suggest. Alternative readings of the passage, for example a gendered analysis like that explored in Chapter 3, might note that Sabrina's feminine identity is defined by international connections to men: Denton, Max and Garth. Her self-definition by what appear to be masculine networks of power indicates that her identity is not entirely in her control. The use of the word 'again' in the sentence, 'a Londoner again, Sabrina Longworth again', suggests rather that it is not fixed but is subject to change, a suggestion that comes closer to the postmodern idea that we have not one identity but multiple identities. This demonstrates that how we view the relationship between the reader and the representation of identity in the text depends very much on how we define the modern, or perhaps postmodern, self.

The reader and self-identity

While the modern self is presented by the defenders of modernity as a critical self, the reader of popular fiction has not, historically, been given such a glowing report. The philosopher G. W. F. Hegel saw individualism, the right to criticism and autonomy of action as three of the main characteristics of the modern subject.[16] Walter

Nash's account of the reader of popular fiction, by contrast, is as uncritical, non-autonomous and without individuality – lost, in effect, in the airport lounge. In this, he follows in a long line of literary criticism. In the eighteenth century how one read became a way to distinguish between the rational subject and those who could not reason: 'Men of the ruling class, so went the dominant mythology, read critically, read not to imitate but to engage productively with argument and with narrative.'[17] Women and working-class readers, on the other hand, could not be so trusted. They would identify uncritically with the characters and be swept away by the fantasy of popular romance.[18] As we have seen, Nash makes a similar distinction: the reader of popular fiction is, he implies, of less significance than the reader of serious literature.

Thus, the study of popular fiction calls into question the idea of the self as a critical agent. The critical and influential self fits well with the eighteenth-century view of 'men of the ruling class', but a contemporary account needs to be aware of the social conflicts which structured that view. It would question the idea that reason resided only amongst ruling-class men and would look at the thought processes of readers of popular fiction from other, less powerful social groups. One way to begin is to take Giddens's suggestion that the 'reflexive project of the self ... consists in the sustaining of coherent yet continuously revised, biographical narratives'.[19] This would allow a view of the popular text as supplying some of the material through which narratives of the self can be sustained and revised. However, such an account would have to allow for the various ways different readers use popular texts and the many different 'readings' they achieve. Pierre Bourdieu, who has made a study of how different social groups 'read' culture, has suggested that the kinds of interpretations arrived at depend upon the social, educational and cultural background of the individual.[20] As I discuss in Chapter 1, this would mean that we are not looking at one reader of popular fiction, but many, all engaged in the projection of different selves.

Some postmodernist accounts have taken this insight further and argued that the idea of the coherent, rational self is no longer sustainable in the late twentieth century. Not only are there multiple selves, but each self is divided into multiple parts. The self consists of fragments of gendered, class, ethnic and sexual identities: 'deconstruction, decentering, disappearance, demystification, discontinuity, *différance*, dispersion, etc. Such terms express an onto-logical rejection of the traditional full subject.'[21] Postmodern accounts of the fragmented self (or selves) can be seen as merely a shift in emphasis away from the idea of the rational self towards the process of dissolution and reconstruction that was already found in accounts of modernity. However, postmodernism's concern with the non-rational and the non-self is useful in that it allows the focus to switch to forms of identity that have been marginalised in modernist criticism: those of women, working-class readers, lesbians and gays and minority cultural groups, for example. The concept of postmodernism, when understood as a heightened consciousness of the modern/postmodern atmosphere, has created an extended and subtler account of identity.[22] The kinds of criticism (not all of which would welcome the label 'postmodern') which have contributed to these developments include feminist, postcolonial, gay, lesbian and queer criticism. I will return to the discussion of postmodernism in Chapters 1 and 4.

The idea of fragmented and changeable selves is explored in *A Tangled Web* through the device of two twin sisters, Sabrina and Stephanie, who swap places. Sabrina is a glamorous antique dealer in London, while Stephanie is the bored wife of a world-famous American geneticist. However, Sabrina finds it is easy to slot into Stephanie's role, because she finds that her identity is formed as much by other people's expectations as by Stephanie's own personality.

> By now she did not guard her tongue as she had in the beginning; if she spoke occasionally from Sabrina's background and experience, or did not know what they were talking about when they reminisced together, the others found ways to explain it away. They explained everything away; they always had, from her first night home when they were in the kitchen and she'd asked Garth and the children where they kept the pot holders. After that there had been dozens of mistakes and slips of the tongue, but no one was suspicious or even curious because, Sabrina realized, people see what they want to see and they find reasons for oddities to protect the comfortable order and predictability of their lives. (13)

Sabrina finds that people invent narratives that explain the inconsistencies in their lives as a form of self-protection. Sabrina has to find a new self in the context of becoming a wife and mother. For Stephanie, who loses her memory in an explosion, the experience of finding a new self is more traumatic.

Sabrina Lacoste. And he is … he is … Max. He said Max. Max Lacoste. Her shivering would not stop. That name meant nothing to her, either. She felt she was falling soundlessly through that terrible fog of nothingness, absolutely alone, unconnected to anything or anyone. She saw herself reaching out her hand, searching for someone to clasp it, but there was no one. Oh, help me, she cried silently, tears stinging behind her eyelids. Help me to find a place to belong. (55)

The idea of 'a place to belong' reflects the utopian pull of a secure identity in an insecure world. Stephanie's story is of her attempt to find a narrative that will explain her life, and it is to the analysis of such narratives that I now turn.

The text

The third and final part of the equation of world, reader and text is the popular narrative itself. According to Nash (for whom, we remember, the world of popular fiction is restricted to fantasy, which for him limits the reader's capacities for critical thought) the popular text is characterised by convention:

> All narratives employ conventions … but … in popular fiction the conventions are simplified and more or less fixed, whereas in writing of more advanced pretension the conventional game is free, diverse, endlessly modified … popfiction is nothing if not predictable.[23]

Nash's view here can be placed in a tradition of literary criticism which prizes innovation in form above all things. Only literature that handles 'convention unconventionally' can be taken seriously. This tradition tends to confine itself to the text alone, to the detriment of the study of the world and reader. A more anthropological or sociological view would be less dismissive of the role of conventional narratives in human affairs. In her study of fairy tales, *From the Beast to the Blonde*, Marina Warner writes: 'I began by investigating the meanings of the tales themselves, but I soon found that it was essential to look at the context in which they were told, at who was telling them and why.'[24] Like contemporary popular narratives, fairy tales work within familiar narrative patterns and like popular fiction they are derivative and unoriginal in the sense that they are reworkings of tried and tested formulae. However, in each case the teller of a familiar tale has to be aware of context and audience: 'the meanings they generate are themselves magical shape-shifters, dancing

to the needs of their audience.'[25] Clearly, there is a *world* of difference between the telling of a fairy tale to a small group of listeners
and the writing of a work of popular fiction, which must enter into
the maelstrom of the modern culture industry, where it is mass-
produced, marketed and stacked on supermarket shelves; but in each
case 'the tale must sense the aspirations and prejudices, the fears
and hungers of its audience.'[26]

Warner's argument complicates how we view popular narratives.
It is one thing to say that popular fiction consists of simple narratives, quite another to say that all simple narratives would make
successful popular fiction. Popular fiction may use simple forms,
but if these forms are to win an audience they must be able to
address that audience's concerns. The situation is complicated in
modern societies because, where originally narratives would be mediated through the spoken word, today popular fictions are received
not just through writing but through many other kinds of media as
well, including radio, television, film and information technologies.
For one theorist of postmodernity, Jean Baudrillard, this profusion
of 'texts' means that the distinction between reality and fiction has
been lost. We now live in a world of 'hyperreality'.[27] Such a view, at
the very least, decentres the written word as the 'authentic' form of
mediated experience and serious fiction as its proper place. While
'the printed word remains at the core of modernity and its global
networks',[28] contemporary popular fiction exists in the context of
the matrix of texts and codes from which a self must, somehow, be
created.

As we have seen, to be considered inauthentic, frivolous or trivial
is nothing new for popular fiction; what is new at the end of the
twentieth century is the decline of authoritative texts. In the maelstrom of the information age no single narrative appears to have
jurisdiction over any other.[29] Consequently, one of the major tasks
in the study of popular fiction is the definition of boundaries. In an
information age more than ever before the reader is constantly drawing a line between what makes sense in terms of her or his life and
what does not. Reading the texts available involves a search for
forms and structures that will give those texts meaning. The quest
for meaning in narratives gives the reader the opportunity to confront the opportunity of new and exciting selves and the threat that
they may dissolve as quickly as they appear.

Form

The analysis of how meaning is achieved in popular texts requires close attention to narrative form. While, as we have already seen, attention to form is not enough in itself, it is essential to the process of working out what a narrative actually does. A key concept in formalist criticism is genre. The term 'genre' in its simplest sense relates to the classification of narratives. Genre refers to particular formal characteristics that define a work of literature as belonging to a particular group that shares those characteristics. Traditional genres include epic, pastoral, tragedy and comedy. Chapters 2, 3, 4 and 5 of this book are devoted to the key genres of popular fiction. However, genre criticism is a provisional art, as genre boundaries are never absolutely fixed. Each new example of a particular genre may modify and change what is understood by the classification it comes under. It is notoriously difficult to isolate the basic elements of any particular genre and to produce a definitive version of what, for example, a detective story is. Attempts to do so are not likely to be final, but temporary statements about the ongoing development of a form. Chapter 1 attempts to define what is meant by a 'bestseller', a literary form which, at bottom, can only be defined as a text that sells well. However, as we shall see, it is possible to define some other common characteristics amongst this group. Genres are best understood, then, not in terms of basic elements, but as historical and relational. They are historical in that they define a form in terms of what has gone before and what might come after. They are relational in that they give a definition of a form that shows how it differs from other literary forms. In other words, genre is important as much because it shows what a detective novel or a bestseller is as what it is not: that it is not a popular romance or a classical tragedy, for example.

Contemporary society has produced some new genres and seen others die out. If we return to Benjamin's traveller, the importance of the genre he reads lies in its ability to supply a pattern or structure which mediates the relationship between self and society in a particular way.[30] In contemporary popular fiction, particular characteristics, including the cover, title and even the name of the publisher, alert the reader to the genre to which a particular work belongs. *A Tangled Web* has its title and the name of the author embossed in

silver on a bright pink and red design superimposed on a silver web
on a black background. The cover and the marketing of the book
set up certain expectations in its readers, even before they buy the
novel, alerting them to anticipate a certain kind of narrative.[31] The
success of *A Tangled Web* is signalled by the announcement that it
figured in the bestseller list of the *New York Times*, and we are told
that not only is the book itself a bestseller but it is a sequel to a
previous bestseller, *Deceptions*. Some readers may also be aware of
the television mini-series that was made of the first novel. Thus
modern popular genres are defined in relation not just to other
novels, but in relation to other 'texts' like newspapers, magazines,
television and film.

A bestseller like *A Tangled Web* may include several different genres.
In the first passage quoted it is possible to identify elements of the
thriller in the representation of Sabrina's relationship to organisational power, the romance in the questions raised about feminine
identity, and the detective novel in the mysterious identification of
her own dead body. The artful weaving of several popular genres
into one narrative can allow a more complex exploration of self-
identity, while still giving the reader familiar boundaries within which
to project his or her fantasies. While the popular text has to provide
a certain expected narrative structure, however, the fragility of the
self means that there can be no simple reflection of a pre-existing
identity. The different genres of detective fiction, popular romance,
horror and science fiction must supply a setting in which the
permeable boundaries of the self can be transgressed even if they
are then re-fixed.

Utopia

The potential for transgression contained in popular fiction creates
the possibility for new and different potential selves. This brings me
to a much-debated aspect of popular fiction, its utopian function
(this is discussed in more detail in Chapters 4 and 6). By utopianism,
I mean popular fiction's ability to gesture to a better world. In this
book, I argue that the negotiation between world, reader and text
does not simply smooth over the contradictions and conflicts of
contemporary society. It may well do the opposite and provoke a
feeling of dissatisfaction, a sense that 'something is missing'.[32] This

sense of lack often has the opposite of a sedative affect. It can prompt the reader to look for something different, something better. The pleasures and transgressions involved in the experience of popular fiction are a constant reminder that a better, more fulfilled life is a possibility. Popular fiction engages in modernity's need to colonise the future,[33] to project new worlds for ourselves. It engages with the modern sense of the ambivalent, indeterminate nature of the present, a sense that the past has not finished who we are and that the future is still open. In this vision, the world, its texts and we ourselves are incomplete and have the potential to be remade. As Marina Warner writes in her conclusion to *From the Beast to the Blonde*:

> For what is applauded and who sets the terms of recognition and acceptance are always in question … We the audience, you the reader, are part of the story's future as well, its patterns are rising under the pressure of your palms, our fingers too.[34]

The pulp in the title of this book, then, refers to two things. One is the fiction itself, which is cheap and disposable, but can be moulded to our fantasies and desires. The other is the self, which appears to be equally squashy and shapeless, but, equally and for that reason, can take up a multitude of new forms. If popular fiction turns the mind to mush, then that mush is also the fertile compost for new growth.

In the following chapters I take these issues further, involving some of the theoretical debates that surround contemporary culture. This introduction has already taken us into the realm of theory. Theory at its worst is an abstract jargon concerned with obscure debates, but at its best can provide the ideas we need to be able to understand the complex relationship between world, reader and text. This book is not a theoretical primer, but it does use the critical approaches of modern social and cultural theory to understand the transaction between world, reader and text. Critical theory drawn from several sources provides the analysis of contemporary society (the world) introduced above. However, my analysis of the texts of popular fiction also draws on literary theories, including structuralism and poststructuralism, to look at form. Marxist, psychoanalytic, feminist, lesbian and gay and postcolonial criticism are used to analyse the modern self and the accounts of fragmentation that characterise modernist and postmodernist cultural forms. The aim is to use theory to establish an understanding of the complexity of the reading strategies involved in our experience of popular fiction.

It would, however, be impossible to consider every approach to every form of popular fiction in one book. For this reason, I tackle no more than one or two methods in each chapter and encourage the reader to refer backward to concepts and theories introduced previously and apply them to subsequent material. Overall, there is a general movement as the book progresses: from context in Chapter 1, to narrative structure in Chapters 2–3, towards a more detailed discussion of different kinds of reader identity in Chapters 4–6. In the first chapter, 'Bestsellers', I look at the concept of the bestseller in relation to the theories and critiques of mass culture. This provides a context for the world in which contemporary popular fiction exists. In Chapters 2 and 3, I introduce two highly influential critical approaches to the 'formula' narratives of detective fiction and popular romance: structuralism and feminist psychoanalysis. Chapter 2 demonstrates a structuralist approach to the analysis of detective narratives and looks at the figure of the detective in relation to the ideas of the modern self introduced below. In Chapter 3, I explore the construction of a gendered self in romance and introduce feminist psychoanalytic cultural theory. The concept of fantasy provides a way of understanding the interaction between reader and text. While these approaches do not exhaust the many ways that detective fiction and romance have been interpreted, they serve to lay the necessary groundwork for further discussion: for example, the reading of Walter Mosley's detective fiction in Chapter 6. Chapter 4 continues the discussion of fantasy and utopianism in relation to science fiction. It considers modernist and postmodernist forms of science fiction and introduces the modern/postmodern debate in relation to the question of textual boundaries and the boundaries of the self. Chapter 5 continues this discussion in relation to horror. Freud's theory of the uncanny and Julia Kristeva's theory of abjection are used to examine this genre's exploration of the limits of the self. Chapter 6 looks at transgression and utopianism in popular fiction. Roland Barthes' ideas of pleasure and *jouissance* and Mikhail Bakhtin's concept of the carnivalesque are discussed in relation to the novels of Jilly Cooper. The notion of a transgressive identity is explored in Walter Mosley's detective, Easy

Rawlins, and the importance of a utopian 'yearning' is examined in Terry McMillan's bestseller, *Waiting to Exhale.*

A common theme in all the chapters is the importance of the situation of the reader. It would therefore be somewhat unfair (and, as I suggested above in relation to the question of cultural value, methodologically suspect) if I did not at times signal my own position as both reader of popular fiction and academic critic. Thus, while much of the book is written in an 'objective' style, I do make occasional appearances in both the roles of academic and reader. This is to make the point that my own subjectivity is as important a determinant on my reading as for any of the imaginary readers I create to make an argument. I began this introduction with my own experience of reading popular fiction. I signal my presence when I talk about the function of the study of popular culture in universities in Chapter 1 and I make a more personal appearance in Chapter 5 when I discuss horror. This seems appropriate, because, as I argue, horror is a genre that seeks to destabilise the sense of a rational self, the common disguise of the critic. I give full attention to the importance of pleasure in reading, including my own, in Chapter 6.

Conclusion

In this chapter, I have introduced the study of popular fiction as the study of the total experience of reading popular fiction, out of which I have abstracted three main elements: the world, the text and the reader. I have suggested that the modern world is a place of social conflict and that popular fiction must engage with its contradictions if it is to be successful. The reader has been discussed in terms of an active process of making selves through reading. The text has been discussed in terms of form and structure, genre and in the context of the information age. It is possible to summarise the relationship between the world, the reader and the text as follows. The text, the popular narrative itself, is produced in the world and becomes a part of the world. But a fictional narrative is more than just a part of the world; it is also a reflection upon that world. The relationship between text and world involves a two-way process that requires a reader to put into effect. The reader is also a product of the world, but, at the same time, she or he is an agent in that world, changing it through her or his actions. Despite the fact that it is often thought of as a passive and purely recreational activity, reading popular texts is part of this process of change. Popular fiction can supply us with the narratives we need to resituate our*selves* in relation to the world. The reader of popular fiction is actively engaged in the remaking of him- or herself and this act of remaking has a utopian potential.

Notes

1 Osip Mandelstam, *The Egyptian Stamp* [1928], quoted in Marshall Berman, *All That Is Solid Melts Into Air: The Experience of Modernity* (New York, Simon & Schuster, 1982), p. 174.
2 Anthony Giddens, *Modernity and Self-Identity: Self and Society in the Late Modern Age* (Cambridge, Polity Press, 1991), p. 20.
3 My starting point for this discussion is Edward Said's essay 'The World, the Text, and the Critic', although his 'critic' is a very particular kind of reader. See *The World, the Text, and the Critic* (Cambridge MA, Harvard University Press, 1983).
4 Walter Benjamin, 'Kriminalromane, Auf Reisen', in *Gesammelte Schriften*, vol. iv, ed. Rolf Tiedemann and Hermann Schweppenhäuser (Frankfurt am Main, Suhrkamp, 1972), pp. 381–2.
5 Giddens, *Modernity and Self-Identity*, p. 5.
6 The first recorded reference in the *Oxford English Dictionary* is 1871, but Charles Dickens mentions railway novels in *Dombey and Son* in 1848.
7 Pat Cadigan, Reading at Liverpool University, June 1995.
8 Walter Nash, *Language in Popular Fiction* (London, Routledge, 1990), p. 1.
9 *Ibid.*, p. 3.
10 *Ibid.*, p. 2.
11 See John Frow, *Cultural Studies and Cultural Value* (Oxford, Clarendon Press, 1995) for an extended discussion of this question.
12 *Ibid.*, pp. 144–55.
13 Marshall Berman, *All That Is Solid Melts Into Air*, p. 15.
14 Judith Michael, *A Tangled Web* (New York, Pocket Books, 1995), pp. 18–19 (henceforth page numbers given in text).
15 Giddens, *Modernity and Self-Identity*, p. 1.
16 Jürgen Habermas, *The Philosophical Discourse of Modernity* (Cambridge MA, MIT Press, 1987), p. 17.
17 Cora Kaplan, *Sea Changes: Essays on Culture and Feminism* (London, Verso, 1986), p. 124.
18 *Ibid.*, p. 122.
19 Giddens, *Modernity and Self-Identity*, p. 5.
20 Pierre Bourdieu, *Distinction: A Social Critique of the Judgement of Taste*

(Cambridge, MA, Harvard University Press, 1984).

21 Ibn Hassan, quoted in Richard Bernstein, *The New Constellation: The Ethical-Political Horizons of Modernity/Postmodernity* (Cambridge, Polity Press, 1991), p. 199.

22 Bernstein, *The New Constellation*, p. 225.

23 Nash, *Language in Popular Fiction*, pp. 3–4.

24 Marina Warner, *From the Beast to the Blonde: On Fairy Tales and their Tellers* (London, Chatto & Windus, 1994), p. xii.

25 *Ibid.*, pp. xix–xxi.

26 *Ibid.*, p. 408.

27 Jean Baudrillard, 'Simulacra and Simulations', in Mark Poster (ed.), *Selected Writings* (Stanford CA, Stanford University Press, 1988).

28 Giddens *Modernity and Self-Identity*, p. 24

29 Jean-François Lyotard, *The Postmodern Condition* (Manchester, Manchester University Press, 1984).

30 'Genres are essentially literary *institutions*, or social contracts between a writer and a specific public, whose function is to specify the proper use of a particular cultural artifact.' Fredric Jameson, *The Political Unconscious: Language as a Socially Symbolic Act* (London, Methuen, 1981), p. 106.

31 John Sutherland, 'Fiction and the Erotic Cover', *Critical Quarterly*, 33:2 (1991) 3–18.

32 'Something's Missing: A Discussion Between Ernst Bloch and Theodor W. Adorno on the Contradictions of Utopian Longing', in Ernst Bloch, *The Utopian Function of Art and Literature* (Cambridge MA and London, MIT Press, 1988).

33 Giddens, *Modernity and Self-Identity*, p. 111.

34 Warner, *From the Beast to the Blonde*, p. 411.

one
Bestsellers

Making the phenomenon of the bestseller my focus, in this chapter I consider popular fiction's relationship to mass culture. Central to my discussion will be the division between those critics who consider mass culture to have a negative influence on modern life and those who detail its positive as well as its negative aspects. The former see mass culture as an irresistible force, creating standard products for a standard consumer. They argue that it eliminates any spark of agency or creativity in its audience. The latter are more cautious, understanding mass culture as a contradictory phenomenon, open to intervention and affording the opportunity for critical engagement by its audience. This debate is, in effect, a continuation of the contrasting perspectives on popular fiction given by Benjamin and Nash in the Introduction and I resume the discussion of cultural value begun in that chapter. As before, while I recognise the important insights of the various negative critiques, I tend to favour more positive approaches: those that emphasise the importance of the reader's situation and response rather than seeing her or him as a passive recipient. The chapter ends with a case study of the bestselling titles in Britain in 1995.

A short history of popular fiction

The word 'popular' has a long and contested history, which is reflected in the word's changing meaning over the last three hundred years. Its original definition as 'of the people' developed an additional cultural dimension in the nineteenth century, when it began to be used to describe an easy, comprehensible style. By the beginning of the twentieth century, it was used to describe newspapers and fiction.[1] Yet the term has always been contested, signifying on the one hand the authentic voice of the people and on the other their ignorance, vulgarity and susceptibility to manipulation.[2] This conflict reflects not just two different versions of the same thing, but the fact that in the mass societies of modernity to be popular is also to be powerful and that power is fought for by political and economic interest groups.[3] Popular fiction, like other forms of popular culture, is subject to that contest.

Today the bestseller is the most familiar kind of popular fiction. It differs from previous forms in that it is entirely a product of the industrial age, mechanically reproduced alongside other goods, services and cultural artefacts. Earlier forms of popular culture had a much more direct relationship with their readers or listeners. Folk tales, ballads and even epic poems could expect and receive a direct audience response. Popular theatre in the seventeenth century might already have been a business, but there was still for Shakespeare a level of immediacy between the spoken word on stage and its reception in the pit. The nineteenth-century novels of Charles Dickens and Elizabeth Gaskell were serialised in popular periodicals and their distribution benefited from the steam press. Yet they were consciously aimed at a family audience. Whether or not the homogeneity of that audience was real or imaginary, such novels managed to be both high literature and part of popular culture. It was not until the end of the nineteenth century that a noticeable split occurred between a self-consciously difficult and elitist high culture and the mass culture it defined itself against. These changes were marked in Britain by the changing nature of publishing. The 1890s saw the decline of the circulating libraries that had guaranteed the respectability of the family novel. Shorter, single volumes began to be produced for sale rather than borrowing. Two of the key genres of popular fiction – detective fiction and science fiction – emerged towards the end of the nineteenth century. In the early twentieth century older genres like romance and gothic horror adapted to the mass market and began to assume their contemporary form. The growth of popular journalism and mass-circulation newspapers and magazines fed the taste for sensational stories; and popular novels supplied what the news could or would not. Emergent mass culture was made possible by the new technologies of industrial printing, radio, cinema, and eventually television and information technologies. These changed the relationship between art and audience, erecting barriers to a direct interchange between author and reader. At the same time, the ideal of an unmediated relationship between artist and audience began to be used by critics of mass culture in a nostalgic version of artistic production before the Industrial Revolution. The techniques and technologies for marketing bestsellers were honed in the interwar period and it was in the 1920s and 1930s (when the term 'pulp fiction' was originally used with reference to American magazines and paperbacks produced on low quality paper) that the first critiques of mass culture began to appear. Since 1945, the publishing industry has become thoroughly enmeshed, economically and generically, with the other major culture industries, which now include the music industry and video games as well as film and television. Developments over approximately the last quarter of the twentieth century have seen the circulation of texts through print, movies, journalism, television drama and chat shows in a process that has seemed to cut loose from any sense of social reality. In what has been described as postmodern culture, image seems to have become the reality. Yet despite some of the more apocalyptic prophecies, print culture continues to play a central part in everyday life.

The new conditions of contemporary culture make it difficult to compare bestsellers with earlier forms of popular culture. While it is true that Shakespeare's theatre was popular in its day and that the novels of Dickens were popular as well as accepted as part of Victorian high culture, the meaning and nature of what it is to be popular has changed over time. Thus, when a television production of George Eliot's 'classic' Victorian novel *Middlemarch* or a new film version of Jane Austen's *Sense and Sensibility* pushes the sales of those novels into the bestseller lists in Britain or the United States respectively, this is not just because readers had rediscovered the quality of the text through television or the big screen, but also because the text is being promoted as an image through postmodern marketing strategies. Similarly, in the United States in 1995 a poster advertising the film of Alan Paton's *Cry the Beloved Country* described it as 'from the bestselling novel'. Here 'bestselling' was being used to try to convince the potential audience that they would enjoy the film because it had already achieved popularity as a book. While Paton's liberal condemnation of apartheid does not correspond to the usual stereotype of the bestseller, an image of the film was promoted using sensational descriptions that might win an audience for the short period the film was on release. Contemporary bestselling fiction may include nineteenth- or twentieth-century classics, but such texts have to be remade and reinterpreted as a bestseller in the present, or what Walter Benjamin has called 'the time of now'.[4]

The bestseller

As I have already argued, the bestseller belongs to the industrial age. The book trade shares its basic features with other forms of enterprise in the modern capitalist economy: it relies for much of its income on mass production, distribution and consumption. In fact, the small-scale production of 'literary' novels is subsidised by popular fiction.[5] Produced in hundreds of thousands, the bestseller is distributed widely and sold and bought in newsagents, supermarkets, department stores and other chains, at railway stations, motorway service stations and airports, as well as in traditional bookshops. Timing is crucial to economic success. Publishers require a quick return on their investment and the term 'bestseller' usually describes high sales in the short term rather than enduring popularity.[6] If total sales over time defined the bestseller, then books like the Bible, the Koran, the works of William Shakespeare or John Bunyan's *Pilgrim's Progress* would figure high on the list. The novels of Tom Clancy, Jilly Cooper and Jackie Collins would not. The sociologist Robert Escarpit distinguishes between three speeds of selling: the 'fast-seller', which sells quickly, breaking even after three months, but sales of which then decline rapidly; the 'steady-seller', which has less spectacular sales but continues to sell well over a period of at least a couple of years; and the 'best-seller', which combines the early sales of the fast-seller, but then maintains high sales for a couple of years.[7]

As John Sutherland has pointed out, this definition of a bestseller differentiates it from the bestselling genre,[8] for example the detective novels, romances, science fiction and horror stories I discuss in Chapters 2–5. Thousands of books will be sold in these categories. Readers of romance fictions, for example, are estimated to read

20–40 books per month,[9] but only a few titles by well-known authors – for example, Patricia Cornwell (whodunits), Catherine Cookson (romance), Stephen King (horror) – will reach the top 100. Bestselling genres require different production strategies – for example, many romance and science fiction texts are given limited printings which sell out quickly – and are aimed at particular audiences, so require different forms of distribution and 'niche'-marketing. From a strictly economic view, however, it makes little difference to publishers whether they are producing a bestselling title or a bestselling genre as long as they can sell the copies printed at a profit. The use of researchers and assistants means the production of a novel by a bestselling author can eventually seem not to need the author at all.[10] In fact, in the case of one author, Virginia Andrews, the process has outlived the creator. Although she is dead, her novels are still produced 'in the style of' for a still-living audience. Production has to be geared to demand, and here speed is of the essence; in Marxian economics, 'the more the time of circulation is equal to zero, or approaches zero, the more does capital function, the more does its productivity and the self-expansion of its value increase.'[11] However, the world of the bestseller is about more than economics. It involves a complex combination of cultural processes.

The late twentieth century has seen a closer and closer intermeshing of politics, entertainment and promotional techniques: politicians appear with film stars on chat shows; film stars promote hamburger restaurants like Planet Hollywood; Burger King promotes Disney's film *Toy Story*; popular films like Oliver Stone's *JFK* and *Nixon* are made about politicians. Bestsellers are made in this world. They are publicised through advertisements in trade magazines, newspapers and posters. Articles and interviews appear in popular publications. Authors 'plug' their latest book on television. An appearance on *Oprah*, the most popular daytime show in the United States, has a huge significance for sales.[12] Film or television adaptations or 'tie-ins' also boost trade. Books may be reprinted to coincide with the release of the film, or a book version of a popular film may be published to cash in on the movie's success. In 1990, fourteen books of what Alex Hamilton calls 'mutanteen' made the top 100 on the back of the craze for the 'Teenage Mutant Ninja Turtles'.[13] In 1993, the film version of *Jurassic Park* by Michael Crichton (no. 43 in 1992)[14] took the book to the top of the bestseller list and hatched three other dinosaur texts.[15] In 1995, the popularity of the science-fiction television series *The X-Files* saw the mysterious appearance of two bestselling books; and Ann Rice's publisher sucked more sales out of the release of the film version of her novel *Interview with a Vampire*. In the same year Maeve Binchy widened her *Circle of Friends* with the movie of her book of that name.[16] This interlocking world of industry, politics and culture has led some theorists of mass culture to argue that twentieth-century culture forms a 'total system' which imposes a set of cultural and political norms on an increasingly passive populace.

The critics of mass culture

Critics of mass culture argue that it debases the value of art. The literary critics involved with the journal *Scrutiny* in the 1930s argued for the preservation of a canon of literary works, for example the 'great' English novelists, against the inroads of mass culture. Of Dorothy L. Sayers (discussed in Chapter 2), one of *Scrutiny*'s leading voices, Q. D. Leavis, said that her detective novels 'have the appearance of literariness: they profess to treat profound emotions and to be concerned with values', but are in fact, 'stale, second-hand, hollow'.[17] Theodor Adorno, who was associated with the Marxist Frankfurt School in Germany, argued with Max Horkheimer in 1944 that such debasement of art is a universal characteristic of what he called 'a totally administered society', by which he meant a world in which the culture industries had left little or no room for individual creativity.[18] However, despite their apparent agreement, the critics associated with *Scrutiny* and the Frankfurt School had quite different analyses of mass culture. Q. D. Leavis approached the question from a conservative, elitist position. Whereas Adorno's critique, while incorporating a preference for 'high' culture, was informed by his anti-capitalist perspective. In this section I explore the usefulness of a 'negative' critique of mass culture. In the following sections I go on to examine the more positive analyses that give greater credence to the role of the audience's interpretation of and intervention in mass culture.

Despite their differences, all theorists of mass culture agree that popular culture cannot be understood in terms of individual texts. Instead those texts must be read and interpreted in relation to the totality of production, distribution and consumption that organises the conditions of their reception. In 1964, when a negative theory of mass culture was the dominant mode of criticism for popular culture, Stuart Hall and Paddy Whannel proposed ten 'doctrines' that might be adhered to by an 'imaginary composite critic of mass culture':[19]

1 Power: power is concentrated in a few hands, and methods of maintaining it have been refined by the techniques of manipulation.
2 Mass production: cultural products are mass-produced to a formula that allows no place for creativity.
3 Consumers: people are not seen as participants in the society but as consumers of what others produce.
4 The pseudo-world: increasingly the media define our sense of reality and organise our experience into stereotypes.
5 The unambiguous world: mass culture makes us all alike, not merely by manufacturing standardised products but by trivialising the important things until they are reduced to the level of the commonplace.
6 The break with the past: mass culture destroys folk art, dehydrates popular art and threatens fine art; there is an obsession with fashion and novelty.
7 Corruption of feelings: the media exploit rather than satisfy our needs and desires; our worst instincts are appealed to and our best instincts are distorted.
8 The flattery of mediocrity: the age of the Common Man, the Ordinary Person, the Man in the Street.
9 The cult of personality: in an age of conformity, the mass replaces a community of publics, a substitute for pure individuality is found in the glorification of personality.
10 Escape from reality: the audience receives the products of the mass media, and is encouraged to receive them in a state of dream-like passivity.

The novels of Jackie Collins can be used to investigate the extent to which the bestseller corresponds to these ten doctrines. Collins's novels are written according to a successful formula. They are mass-produced and sold with glossy covers in supermarkets, airports and railway stations as well as in bookshops. Jackie Collins (sister of the actress Joan Collins) is a Hollywood personality in her own right. She appears on chat shows to market her books, where she is often interviewed not so much as a novelist but as an expert who knows the world of the stars from the inside. Her media personality, her novels and her performances can all be seen as part of an integrated strategy to sell the Jackie Collins product to the consumer. The texts themselves also provide evidence for negative theories of mass culture. There follow three extracts from Collins's *Hollywood Husbands* (no. 2, 1987), the second in the series that includes *Hollywood Wives* and *Hollywood Kids*. In common with many bestsellers, the novel is written in short sections, each of which forms a brief narrative, complete in itself. The text moves between the present and back-ground information which is given in short, italicised 'flashbacks'. The first passage is taken from a section less than two pages long describing the pre-party preparations of Poppy and Howard Soloman. The second two extracts are from the following section, which tells the reader of Howard's childhood and first sexual experiences.

Poppy Soloman was getting dressed, and when Poppy got ready for a party – watch out!

Howard repaired to his own bathroom, locked the door, and had his second snort of the day. Cocaine. A little habit he had been indulging in for a few months now.

Carefully he laid out the white powder on a special mirror-topped tray, coaxed it into two neat lines, and with the help of a straw, snorted it into his nostrils. One long, deep breath and the rush was incredible. Better than sex. Better than anything. Howard felt like he could own the world. He *did* own the world. He owned a fucking studio, for Christ's sake. Well, not exactly owned it, ran it. The same thing. It gave him the power he wanted, only to really enjoy the power he needed an occasional snort. Nothing habit-forming, mind you. Howard knew when enough was enough, and duly limited himself. Once in the morning to get off on the right foot. And once in the evening *only* if they were going out or enter-taining at home. Since they went out or entertained every night, he regularly snorted twice a day. Not such a terrible thing. Some actors, producers and studio people couldn't get through a meeting without vis-iting the john three times.[20]

Howard Soloman was born when he was sixteen, and his mother divorced his father, fled from Philadelphia to Colorado, and shortly after, married Temple Soloman. He couldn't wait to change his name from Jessie Howard Judah Lipski to the much more simple Howard Soloman. What an escape! (60)

It took Howard's first wife, the fierce black activist whom he married when he was nineteen, to teach him the joys of getting a woman off too. 'Just go for the button an' liiiiifit off, babee!' she instructed while clasping him around the back of the neck with ebony legs he thought might strangle him. (61)

These passages can be fitted neatly into Hall and Whannel's imaginary ten doctrines. The easily digested gobbets of text can be compared with the 'manipulation' practised by the rapid succession of images, music and text in television advertisements (1). *Hollywood Husbands* makes for a quick, uncomplicated read. It reproduces standard clichés, which do not challenge the reader to question or criticise (2). Thus, the reader is reduced to a consumer of what others produce (3). Some of the characters in *Hollywood Husbands* are recognisable characterisations of 'real-life' film actors so that the novel perpetuates the Hollywood myth, contributing to the 'pseudo-world' of tabloid news stories, magazine articles and gossip where stars are given extravagant and exciting personalities that continue and overlap with their roles on screen (4). The novel reproduces stereotypes (5). Howard Soloman is an assimilated Jew, desperate to forget his orthodox childhood. The move from a different cultural background to the mainstream is represented as a liberation: 'What an escape!' Howard's African-American ex-wife (who isn't even given a name here) is represented as aggressive, 'fierce', and sexually active (she is an 'activist') in comparison with his passive, white girlfriends. The text represents a series of rushes, reducing experience to sensations, and might therefore be said to corrupt authentic feeling (7). Howard's life becomes his enjoyment of power and his exhilaration after snorting cocaine, while his relationships with women are reduced to a series of orgasms. The sensational nature of the text makes the bestseller ephemeral, lasting only as long as it is a fashionable novelty (6). Its drug-like effects induce passivity in the audience (10).

While *Hollywood Husbands* seems to coincide with the ten doctrines, negative theories of mass culture have their limitations. At times they seems to reject popular culture simply because it is popular. The group associated with *Scrutiny* defended the 'high' art enjoyed by an educated elite at the expense of the cultural interests of the majority, while in the post-war period Richard Hoggart's *The Uses of Literacy* condemned mass culture in a lament for an older, mythologised version of working-class life.[21] In addition, several critics have noted such theories' persistent gendering of mass culture as feminine, where the fear of the masses is 'always also a fear of woman, a fear of nature out of control, a fear of the unconscious, of sexuality, of the loss of identity and stable ego boundaries in the mass'.[22] Huyssen relates this to the systematic exclusion of women from the institutions of high culture.[23] As we shall see (for example in Chapter 3) this gendering of mass culture leads to the prejudice that sees women as passive consumers of mass-produced narratives, and the elevation of 'masculine' genres over 'feminine' genres. Finally, negative theories assume that production determines consumption: the standard product creates a standard consumer. More recently, postmodernist cultural criticism has criticised this assumption and suggested that the mass-produced text has a degree of autonomy over and beyond its conditions of production.

Postmodernism

Despite the universal requirement for a quick return, the bestselling title needs to be distinguished from the bestselling genre because it has an *image* of uniqueness that allows it to participate in a postmodern 'economy of signs'. As Jean Baudrillard puts it: 'the advertising process of conferring value transmutes use goods (*biens d'usage*) into sign values'.[24] In other words, in the case of the bestselling title, it is the image of the product, not the product itself that counts. Thus, fast, high sales can be used by marketing departments to generate more sales. An appearance in the bestseller list of the London *Sunday Times* or the *New York Times Book Review* is used to convince potential readers that because so many other people have bought it, they should buy it too. The ability of the image of success to create more success suggests that in mass culture the popular text can cut loose from the conditions of its production and achieve a life of its own.

At the very least, this means that the bestselling text is open to several interpretations and this permits a more complex reading of *Hollywood Husbands*. Dana Polan has argued that 'one recurrent aspect of popular culture is its self-reflexive dimension – its pointed commentary on, and even pastiche or parody of, its own status as cultural item'.[25] From this perspective, Collins's novel could be read as an ironic, self-knowing reflection on the world of Hollywood. The technique of 'montage', where Collins 'cuts' from scene to scene, mimics and parodies the editing of Hollywood films. The representation of a world of sensations provides an ironic commentary on those films' content. Howard Soloman's use of cocaine signifies their ephemerality. The contradictions in his account about how much power he has and how much cocaine he uses signal the limits of his high. In the first moments he claims he owns a Hollywood studio, only to have to admit to himself that he merely manages it. He represents himself as a moderate user, but it becomes clear that he is a regular, twice-daily, drug-taker. A postmodernist commentary on *Hollywood Husbands* would also have to take into account its 'intertextuality', that is its relationship as a text to all the other multiple accounts of Hollywood available in mass culture. Thus, it is not possible to treat *Hollywood Husbands* as a discrete text. It exists as part of what Raymond Williams has called 'flow', the continuous stream of newspaper articles, advertisements, shows and commentaries that reach their peak in the experience of watching television, but which actually constitute the whole of our reception of mass culture.[26] All of these accounts contribute to the reader's fantasies about the Hollywood personalities, which overlap and extend beyond the actual texts. I discuss the question of fantasy at greater length in Chapters 3 and 6 and there is an extended discussion of postmodern science fiction in Chapter 4. For now it is enough to note that postmodernist criticism questions some of the more general claims of earlier theories of mass culture. It has been less successful at providing an alternative explanation for the power of popular texts. An understanding of the power of mass culture is best reached through the concepts of cultural hegemony and ideology.

Cultural hegemony and ideology

Following the Communist activist and theorist Antonio Gramsci (1891–1937), the term 'hegemony' has been taken up by Marxist cultural critics to describe the 'complex interlocking political, social and cultural forces' that maintain power in society.[27] The concept of cultural hegemony challenges the idea that dominance is total. Instead unequal power relations are the product of a continuing social process: they have to be made and remade over time. This contrasts with both negative theories of mass culture and postmodernist criticism, both of which play down the importance of culture as a site of contestation.

Given the importance of fashion and novelty in modern culture, struggles for cultural hegemony can be seen most clearly in the changing nature of the popular. Some trends reflect a changing world. John Sutherland has noted the increase in international themes in the bestsellers of the 1960s and 1970s.[28] Andrew Billon has observed the rise and fall of the 'sex and shopping' or 'bonkbuster' novel with the consumer boom of the late 1980s.[29] As we shall see in Chapter 3, feminist critics have charted the changes in the romance novel that accompanied 'second-wave feminism' in the 1970s, when heroines became less passive and began to challenge some of the earlier assumptions about a woman's role .[30] As Paul Kerr has pointed out in his essay 'The Making of (the) MTM (Show)', changes in society as a whole can stimulate changes in the production of popular culture and these changes may lead to more challenging products.[31] Often new oppositional trends, such as feminism, are absorbed and assimilated by the entertainment industry, changing its nature.

This means that timing is important not just to the economic success of the bestseller, but also to its success as a cultural intervention. In fact, the success of a particular text can never be guaranteed by the right distribution and marketing. What is a bestseller at one time may not sell well at another. Its intervention in mass culture has to be carefully calculated. The power of mass culture is not total and different kinds of cultural intervention may be possible. It is perhaps more accurate to talk of a tension between the text and the marketing image's particular interpretation of it. Once launched, the image of the bestseller is carefully controlled. Turnover is sustained by changing the marketing to match prevailing fashions. The paperback edition must follow the hardback at the optimum moment. New editions must be released with new covers, 'blurbs' and critics' 'quotes'. Marketing strategies effectively remake the image of the text, so that it will continue to appeal.[32]

A useful way of understanding the relationship between the text and its audience is through the concept of 'ideology'. Jane Woollacott writes: 'Works of fiction and specific genres are popular precisely because they articulate, work upon and attempt in different ways to resolve ideological tensions'.[33] Ideology can mean either a particular belief system or what Gramsci called 'common sense'.[34] By common sense he meant that in order to secure consent the ruling or hegemonic ideas must work within a framework that makes sense to those who are ruled. If we return to the triadic relationship between world, text and reader then ideology as common sense suggests the limits or horizons of meaning within which the self-identity of the reader is formed. According to Stephen Heath, it is through ideology that the reader constructs an imaginary relationship with the world:

> In ideology, it is said, is represented the imaginary relation of individuals to the real relations under which they live. It has also to be stressed, however, that this imaginary relation to ideology is itself real, which means not simply that the individuals live it as such (the mode of illusion the inverted image) but that it is effectively, practically, the reality of their concrete existence, the term of their subject positions, the basis of their activity in a given social order.[35]

The popular text enters into the imaginary relationship of the reader with the world; but the text itself allows the exploration of the limits of meaning available to the reader. It is easy to make a leap from this insight to a position that argues that in an unequal society subaltern (dominated) identities will always be impoverished, but the text's exploration of the limits of meaning can allow a number of different reader responses. It may even define our hopes for something better.[36] Harold Robbins's blockbuster, *Raiders* (no. 75, 1995) can be taken as an example. The novel is the sequel to an earlier, successful novel by Robbins, *The Carpetbaggers*. The relative lack of success of *The Raiders* underlines the point that repeating the same formula at a different time does not guarantee sales. Together the two novels tell the tale of three generations of the Cord family. The Cords control a large American corporation and have interests in broadcasting, electronics and gambling. *The Raiders* is set in the 1950s and focuses on the relationship between Jonas Cord, Jr., and his illegitimate son, Bat. The novel includes actual historical events and people. In the following passage the real-life leaders of the American Teamsters Union Dave Beck and Jimmy Hoffa meet the fictional Jonas and Bat and an intermediary, Chandler, in a Las Vegas hotel room. Beck and Hoffa threaten union trouble if the Cords do not agree to a partnership in their new casino and the situation becomes violent.

'Why bother?' asked Bat.

They stood, and Hoffa strode up to Bat. 'Who the hell are you, *sonny*?' he asked, his saliva spraying.

'I'll tell you who I'm not,' said Bat. 'I'm not a cheap little street punk. That's who I'm not.'

Hoffa danced like a boxer and threw a punch. It glanced off Bat's left cheek, stinging but not hurting. Hoffa danced some more, his fists up, ready to try again. Bat smiled faintly and kicked him sharply on the shin. Hoffa yelled and was distracted for the instant it took Bat to drive a fist hard into his solar plexus. Stunned, Hoffa dropped his hands, and Bat flattened his nose with a left jab, then broke his front teeth with a right cross.

'Open the door, Chandler!' Bat yelled. When Chandler hesitated, Bat yelled again.

Chandler opened the door. Bat grabbed the reeling Hoffa by the nape of the neck and seat of the pants and threw him into the hall. Hoffa rolled across the floor and against the elevator doors.

Dave Beck, crimson-faced, shrieked at Jonas, 'You'll regret this till the day you die!'

Jonas snapped a punch against his nose, splattering blood. 'That's just a sample of what you'll get if you try calling a strike on me, you sleazy tub of lard,' he said. 'You get out of town. I don't want to see you here again.'[37]

It is easy to pick out the conservative ideologies that are being propounded here: the superiority of capital over labour, the importance of masculine strength and competition, the use of violence as a resolution to conflict. At one level of meaning the passage is no more than a crude political message which paints unions as corrupt and underhanded while the owners of large corporations are heroic and efficient in response. Negative theories of mass culture might also pick out the relative poverty of the language. The insults used by Hoffa and Bat verge on the childish. The events are related through a series of familiar clichés. In this reading the text constructs an imaginary relation between reader and world which confirms his or her position as a passive consumer in the face of cultural hegemony. However, while this interpretation works, it is possible to delve further into the layers of meaning available and find other possible, more critical, reader responses.

As with many representations of violence in popular culture the action is highly symbolic. Even the insults exchanged by Bat and Hoffa signify a battle for supremacy that resonates with other themes in the book. Hoffa addresses Bat as 'sonny', a put-down that suggests he is not a real man, but which is also effective because of Bat's ongoing struggle for power with his father. Bat's insult, 'cheap little street punk', refers to Hoffa's working-class origins and is sufficiently effective to provoke his attack. The violence itself is represented in such a way as to mark a clear distinction between the two protagonists. Bat is portrayed as cool: Hoffa's blow glances off him and his faint smile indicates that he is in control. Hoffa by contrast lacks bodily control: his saliva sprays when he speaks and his boxer's dance appears somewhat ridiculous. He is not ready for Bat's street-fighting moves, which quickly disable him so that Bat can finish off with a display of textbook punching. Thus, the representation of these two characters defines their ideological limits or horizons. The antagonism between Cord father and son achieves a symbolic, if temporary, resolution when Jonas joins the fight. His engagement with the overweight Beck is a farcical repeat of the earlier battle. The victory is made complete when both union men are thrown out of the hotel room. Their ejection marks a symbolic resolution: unity amongst father and son and an end to the threat of labour trouble.

Even on this interpretation the passage appears to uphold the cultural hegemony of the large corporations which control mass culture. In so far as the passage gives pleasure to the reader it would appear to be through an identification with those who have power. However, a counter-argument might stress the importance of conflict in the affirmation of dominance. That the Cords have to engage with an opposing force demonstrates, at the very least, that their hegemony is not total. In this light, the representation of the fight can be seen to be testing the limits of the opposition it also constructs. This interpretation finds ammunition in that it is Bat, not Hoffa, who stoops to the low practices of shin-kicking and hitting below the belt. While a conservative reader response is one possibility, a transgressive reading is also available. In this reading the pleasure gained from the passage comes as much from the circus-style, slapstick nature of the violence, with its comic nose-splattering and clown-like protagonists, as from the victorious resolution. The possibility for two contradictory reader responses demonstrates the contradictory nature of power, which must transgress in order to affirm itself. Bat must stoop to conquer. The corporations have to use the intimidatory tactics the passage appears to ascribe to the unions in order to maintain their dominance. While overtly revering corporate and masculine power, *Raiders*, in common with many bestsellers, is actually full of transgressive moments. The role of transgression and the 'carnivalesque' is explored in more detail in Chapter 6. For now it is enough to note how the concept complicates the reader's response to the text. At the very least it demonstrates the complexity of Heath's 'imaginary relation of individuals to the real relations under which they live'. As I discuss in Chapter 3, the scene allows the reader to project into a fantasy setting where he or she can side with or against the defeated 'real-life' characters or the fictional heroes. Thus, while the ideology of the text provides the structures of meaning within which the reader's self-identity can be formed, the popular text may also provide the 'metaphors of trans-formation'[38] through which the reader can transgress those struc-tures and imagine a different world. However, to explore the posi-tion of the reader fully, we must turn to her or his actual situation.

Reader-identity

For the negative theories of mass culture, popular fiction disrupts the traditional function of genre, inserting itself between the reader and the text. In a more sophisticated argument, Fredric Jameson argues that in the modern period traditional genres do not so much 'die out, but persist in the half-life of the subliterary genres of mass culture, transformed into the drugstore and airport paperbacks lines of gothics, mysteries, romances, bestsellers and popular biographies'. In this process, the contract between writer and reader is disrupted by the commodification of the cultural product, where 'the older generic specifications are transformed into a brand-name system'.[39] However, while brand-name fiction like popular romance corresponds to this description, it would be wrong to draw the conclusion that its readers also conform to bland stereotypes. Often equally ignored by postmodernist theory, the reader's act of interpretation plays the crucial role in mediating between the popular text and the culture industry's marketing of that text within an economy of signs. The concepts of ideology and hegemony are helpful in that they create an understanding of the conditions and limitations within which the reader of popular fiction constructs his or her identity. We now need to go further and look at the role of the reader in more detail. Below I look at some of the theoretical approaches that are helpful

in exploring the distinction that can be made between the different
parts of mass culture and the different receptions that mass culture
encounters. A central question here will be identity. I am concerned
to examine what kinds of identities are available to the reader of
mass-market fiction. The work of the Frankfurt School provides a
useful starting point.

The Frankfurt School was founded in Germany in 1923. Those
members who were able escaped to the United States during the
Nazi period and the survivors returned to Germany after the war.
The School and those associated with it used Marxist and psychoanalytic criticism to analyse modern culture and society. As we have
seen, some of their work, for example the theory of the 'culture
industry' developed by Theodor Adorno and Max Horkheimer, shares
some common ground with Hall and Whannel's ten doctrines.
Adorno and Horkheimer argued that the world is increasingly
uniform and that entertainment is mass-produced in standard form.
They noted that film and broadcasting are now referred to as
'industries' and there are fewer and fewer differences between the
commodities on sale, while cultural products are manufactured
according to formulae which lack the distinctiveness of works of art.
However, the School also had a strongly developed sense of the
utopian potential inherent in modern capitalist society. With Marx,
they saw that, 'On the one hand the growth of economic productivity furnishes the conditions of a world of greater justice; on the
other hand it allows the technical apparatus and the social groups
which administer it a disproportionate superiority to the rest of the
population.'[40] In their essay 'The Culture Industry: Enlightenment as
Mass Deception', the *moral* disapproval often found in later theories
of mass culture is given a *political* inflection. Adorno and Horkheimer
argue that mass culture is the product of a 'totally administered
society'. The rational world-view that characterises modernity has
become a straitjacket. Reason has become instrumental: a means to
profit rather than a means for emancipation. Films are made with
budgets that run into millions of dollars, while the resources available to abolish hunger are not exploited.[41] Thus, the culture industry
reflects a social system that is racked with inequality. Modern
identities are made in the context of unequal power relations, where,
as for Howard Soloman in *Hollywood Husbands*, there is social pressure
to be like the norm, the mainstream: 'Life in the late capitalist era

is a constant initiation rite. Everyone must show that he fully identifies with the power that is belabouring him.'[42]

Consider the following passage from Julie Burchill's 'sex and shopping' novel, *Ambition*:

> On Madison Avenue, at the soft-tech, Italo-Japanese, black-beige Armani shop, she bought black label, and at Krizia she bought sportswear that would have had a nervous breakdown if one did anything more rigorous than hail a cab in it. She avoided Walter Steiger but did succumb to a pair of pewter, lace and plastic Vittorio Riccis for Zero. She snapped up a brace of six-hundred-dollar sweaters at Sonia Rykiel and half a dozen pairs of cashmere tights at $178 a throw at Fogal, thinking of their less extortionate cousins that David Weiss had wiped his velvet cosh on that night over the dustbins behind the Kremlin Club. She wondered what he was doing, then stopped. It hurt too much ...
>
> On Park Avenue she went to Martha, where all first ladies hope to go when they die for, and flicked through the Bill Blass, Galanos, David Cameron and Carolina Herrera before deciding she didn't want to look like any First Lady, living or dead, and ignoring Pope's advice she took a cab to West 56th Street where she bought a Norma Kamali dress as blue-black as a bruise and tighter than Nancy Reagan's smile.[43]

This orgy of consumerism appears initially to be unadulterated joy. However, closer examination reveals that Susan Street's unlimited spending is a response to desires that cannot be met. As she shops, Susan remembers her sado-masochistic relationship with David Weiss. It is not clear whether the sentence, 'It hurt too much', refers to emotional or physical pain. Later in the passage the violence in her sex-life is transferred to the purchases themselves when the Norma Kamali dress is described as 'blue-black as a bruise'. If, at first, Susan appears to be constructing her identity freely in the market-place, taking the fashions of the moment and assembling a self out of the ephemera of modernity, this darker aspect of the shopping experience reveals the power relations that constrain the kinds of self she can actually attain. If we return for a moment to our earlier example, *Hollywood Husbands*, it is interesting to note that behind the narrative of glitzy lives lies a story of child sex-abuse, as if there too the other side of glamour is violence and pain. The critical theory of Adorno and Horkheimer unearths this other side of culture, using what Adorno called a 'negative dialectic'. Dialectical thought in Marxist theory refers to the ability to reflect upon one's own consciousness: 'the attempt to think about a given object on one level, and at the same time observe our own thought processes as we do so'.[44] Dialectics can be used either to review the limitations of our situation, or to consider its hidden potential. Adorno tends to emphasise the denial of utopia rather than its possibility. His focus on the negative elements of popular culture helps us to build up a picture of the oppressive constraints on identity imposed by mass culture, but his work is less helpful for an analysis of the kinds of response this provokes.

Work on how culture is received has been developed further by the French sociologist Pierre Bourdieu in his book *Distinction: A Social Critique of the Judgement of Taste*. Writing against the view that taste is the ability to appreciate high art, Bourdieu argues that taste is formed in relation to what he calls educational, cultural and social capital. Using extensive surveys in France in the 1960s and 1970s he finds, for example, a taste in '"light" music or classical music devalued by popularization … is most frequent amongst the working classes and varies in inverse ratio to educational capital.'[45] He concludes that a taste for particular forms of culture is the product of the social milieu in which one grows up (cultural capital) and of the education one receives (educational capital): 'To the socially recognized hierarchy of arts, and within each of them, of genres, schools or periods, corresponds a social hierarchy of consumers.'[46] Where negative theories see interchangeable, mass-produced commodities, Bourdieu sees the almost superficial details between, say, drinks or cars, as 'distinctive features' which allow the consumer almost endless possibilities for different tastes.[47] These tastes are 'a systematic expression' of a distinctive lifestyle[48] and are created in what Bourdieu calls the 'habitus': the relationship between the dispositions of the consumer and her or his place in economic and social space.[49] Thus Bourdieu's more nuanced analysis of the culture of modernity permits a view of popular fiction as productive of the kinds of distinctive selves I argued for in the introduction.

No generalisations can be made about the reader of popular fiction. Bourdieu argues that factors like gender and class create different relationships to culture. Taste is not a matter of free choice. Rather choice is a privilege of class: 'Economic power is first and foremost a power to keep economic necessity at arm's length.'[50] The absence of necessity creates the time and distance to cultivate an appreciation of high art. Gender also plays a part in the making of taste. Women's relationship to culture is different to that of men. They have traditionally been characterised as having a less aesthetic disposition because they are constructed as closer to nature: 'the refusal to surrender to nature, which is the mark of dominant groups – who start with self-control – is the basis of the aesthetic disposition'.[51] The way in which we read popular fiction, then, will be a product of our distinctive social circumstances, and, as we shall see in the case study that concludes this chapter, gender is a crucial defining category.

Bourdieu's emphasis on the situation of the consumer has a special consequence for the study of popular fiction. He suggests that the aesthetic appreciation of what has been classified as low culture, for example popular fiction, can be related to the production of new kinds of taste by new social classes: 'science fiction or detective stories are predisposed to attract the investments of those who have entirely succeeded in converting their cultural capital into educational capital or those who, not having acquired legitimate culture in the legitimate manner, maintain an uneasy relationship with it.'[52] This means that, for example, one's position in an academic institution will effect how one reads. The recent introduction of courses on popular fiction into universities might be explained by the waning of an older elite system and its replacement by academics who wish to make a broader definition of culture respectable. It could be argued that academics like myself have an interest in creating a new taste that challenges the old so that we can put ourselves forward as its promoters and judges. Bourdieu warns of two dangers that may emerge from an academic taste for popular culture. The first is that 'popular' taste is defined simply as the opposite or the negation of high art and, as a consequence, there is no real attempt to study its conditions of production, forms and reception.[53] The second is the mirror image of the above where 'popular' taste is celebrated uncritically because it is supposed to stem from a mythical version of the 'people'. This is a fundamentally conservative view akin, as Bourdieu points out, to the idealisation of the peasantry by the declining aristocracy before the French Revolution. It romanticises a static view of society where the relationship of the classes never changes. Thus, one of the dangers of studying popular fiction is that the texts become a vehicle for a particular form of academic theory.

Ironically, Bourdieu himself comes close to this kind of idealisation in his claims that working-class culture is characterised by a hostility to formal experimentation and a preference for narrative order and realism: 'In theatre as in cinema, the popular audience delights in plots that proceed logically and chronologically towards a happy end, and "identifies" better with simply drawn situations and characters than with ambiguous and symbolic figures and actions.'[54] This claim contradicts Bourdieu's later argument that the same text will be interpreted differently by different social groups and by fractions within that group.[55] In fact, as we shall see in the following chapters, many narratives that proceed chronologically deploy metaphor and symbolism in ways that complement or contradict the texts' overt realism. What is considered realistic is subject to change and processes of identification shift over time. In addition, in the late twentieth century contemporary popular culture is saturated with non-realist forms, from the use of images in advertising[56] to the editing processes involved in film, television drama and pop videos and the uses of surrealism, dreams, madness and fantasy in soap opera.[57] As we have seen, the bestselling novels of Jackie Collins and Harold Robbins are composed of short passages of prose that leap from character to character, so that the narrative is built up from internally coherent fragments which invite the reader's imaginative intervention. Fantasy is a vital part of popular romance, science fiction and horror stories. These elements should make us wary of simplifying the formal elements of the texts or of positing an idealised reader of popular fiction.

While Bourdieu argues that the consumer has a certain 'competence' but sticks to a conservative view of mass culture itself, Walter Benjamin argued that all consumers bring a certain amount of expertise to mass culture.[58] Their active engagement is facilitated by the way that the mass reproduction of cultural products strips them of their 'aura': 'the technique of reproduction detached the reproduced object from the domain of tradition'.[59] This has the remarkable result of allowing the cultural artefact 'to meet the beholder or listener in his own particular situation', which 'reactivates the object reproduced'. Consequently, in the age of mass culture, everyone can be an expert: 'It is inherent in the technique of film as well as that of sports that everybody who witnesses its accomplishments is somewhat of an expert.' For Benjamin, writing in the 1930s, the mass reproduction of culture opens up two stark possibilities. On the one hand, for humanity, 'self-alienation has reached such a degree that it can experience its own destruction as an aesthetic pleasure of the first order. This is the politics which Fascism is rendering aesthetic.' On the other, 'Communism responds by politicizing art.'[60] In the late twentieth century the politics of culture do not present such clear alternatives. However, the broad thrust of Benjamin's argument has been developed towards a criticism that examines the degree of control that mass culture exerts over its consumers: to the forms of self-identity fashioned in modernity. The idea that the consumer has some kind of expertise allows a less pessimistic version of the culture of modernity than that given by negative theories of mass culture. As Janice Radway has put it: 'If we can learn, then, to look at the ways in which various groups appropriate and use the mass-produced art of our culture ... we may well begin to understand that although the ideological power of contemporary cultural forms *is* enormous, indeed sometimes even frightening, that power is not yet all pervasive, totally vigilant, or complete.'[61] To get a better sense of the variety of bestselling texts, I finish this chapter with an analysis of the bestsellers of 1995.

Bestseller texts

A study of bestseller texts, as opposed to the machinery of their production and marketing, reveals both diversity and continuity. While some forms like the thriller, the romance and the family saga claim a large proportion of sales, bestselling titles are often hybrid genres, combining several elements of popular narrative. Every year since 1979, Alex Hamilton of the *Guardian* has compiled a list of the top 100 paperback 'fastsellers'. A snapshot, the list includes only books published in the previous year. In it Hamilton classifies according to his own system of genre definition, which, like all systems of classification, is to some extent subjective. For 1995, he lists 26 thrillers, 7 crime, 6 romances, 5 sagas, 5 autobiographies, 4 humour, 4 fantasy, 3 television tie-ins, 3 film tie-ins, 2 horror, 2 science, 2 gardening, 1 collection of short stories and 1 each of biography, adventure, psychology, drink, suspense, juvenile, travel. This leaves 23 texts that he categorises as 'novels'.

It is possible to squeeze some of the 'novels' into genre categories: 1 could be described as a thriller, 1 crime, 8 romance/family sagas, 1 gothic horror, 2 blockbusters, and 1 humour. Of the film tie-ins, 1 is gothic horror, 1 romance, and 1 science fiction. Of the television tie-ins, 2 are science fiction. I would reclassify one of Hamilton's romances (Jackie Collins's *Hollywood Kids*) as a blockbuster (see below). Adapting Hamilton's classification to my own (also subjective) classification would therefore produce the following figures for 1995: 27 thrillers, 8 crime/detective, 18 romance/family saga, 6 science fiction/fantasy, 4 gothic horror/suspense, 3 blockbusters, 13 non-fiction, 21 other. However, a more accurate picture of the popularity of different genres is given by their percentages of the total sales of 26 million books. This breaks down as follows: thriller 33.2 per cent, crime/detective 8.3 per cent, romance/family saga 27.6 per cent, science fiction/fantasy 5.8 per cent, gothic horror/suspense 5.5 per cent, blockbusters 3 per cent non-fiction 10.9 per cent, other 5.7 per cent.

Significantly, this division gives roughly one-third thrillers, usually associated with a male readership, and one-third romance/saga, usually associated with a female readership. It is clear that one of the most important categories differentiating readers is that of gender. Women have different reading habits to men and historically they have read more fiction. In a study of the British reading public, 47 per cent of women claimed to have finished a book in the previous fortnight, while only 30 per cent of men could say the same.[62]

Genre classification in the analysis of bestsellers is useful up to a point. It can help track trends in sales. For example, following Hamilton's categories we see that in the 1990s the thriller occupied most space in the top 100: twenty-five places in 1992, and twenty-three in 1993 and 1994. Over the last ten years, the thriller has usually occupied between a fifth and a quarter of the places, and its share is increasing. Occasionally, as in 1986, the romance/saga category outsells the thriller, with 23.3 per cent of sales in 1986 to the thrillers 20.5 per cent; but no other genre comes close. Detective fiction normally makes a small showing. It did unusually well in 1995. Science fiction, despite huge sales as a genre (some US chain bookstores devote more shelf space to science fiction than to general fiction) has no one author who can guarantee a title in the top 100. Only authors like Ann Rice and Stephen King keep gothic horror in the list. However, genre categories are misleading because so many bestsellers do not fit neatly into them. In fact a better definition of the formal characteristics of the bestselling title, as opposed to the bestselling genre, is its ability to integrate several popular genres.

The biggest category in the top 100, the thriller, is best described as a hybrid. As we shall see in Chapter 2, the critic Tzvetan Todorov includes the thriller as a variant of the detective novel, but the thriller can also be traced back to the masculine adventure romance of the late nineteenth century.[63] Today the category includes a variety of forms. John Grisham's popular tales make use of the legal world, but the thriller includes spy novels, like Ian Fleming's James Bond series, Frederick Forsyth's tales of international intrigue, and Elmore Leonard's complex plots of heists and stings. Traditionally written by men for a male audience, the thriller functions to construct a masculine identity in the midst of the powerful institutions of modernity: the law, organised crime, big business, national or international politics. One of the reasons the category does well in the bestseller lists is because of its ability to adapt the role of the male hero to current trends. For example, Tom Clancy's *Debt of Honour* (no. 4 1995) spins a compelling paranoid fantasy around fears of a weakened United States in the 'new world order' threatened by the imperialist economic and military ambitions of Japan and China. The central hero is Jack Ryan, national security adviser to the president, but who in early Clancy works was a protagonist in the Cold War. This time Ryan stitches up a deal with his old rival in the former KGB and the new alliance allows the West to win again.

The much more nebulous category, the blockbuster, is also a hybrid genre. The term has become attached to novels like those of Alex Hailey and Harold Robbins, which are not usually thrillers, but which have plots that are structured around big business, airports, hotels and large corporations. Blockbusters often contain elements of the saga, a history of a particular family. Jilly Cooper's novels, for example, include romance and comedy. A novel like *Polo* (no. 1, 1992) is structured around a traditional romance narrative, the tale of the appropriately named Perdita, who does not know who her father is. However, that narrative is embedded in the modern world of polo, which links it to networks of power in Britain, American and Latin America. The mystery of Perdita's father combines elements of the detective narrative, but is also related to the search for herself, a quest that is conducted, in the tradition of popular romance, through several love affairs. Cooper's novels contain a vast range of characters, many of whom overlap with her earlier block-busters, *Riders* (no. 10, 1986; about the world of show jumping) and *Rivals* (no. 5, 1989; about the world of television). They are full of rumpacious sex and merge into the category of the 'bonkbuster', a category that was almost invented by Jackie Collins. A variant on the bonkbuster that emerged in the late 1980s was the 'sex and shopping' novel (for example, Julie Burchill's *Ambition*, no. 18, 1990, discussed above), which tended to take the act of consumption as its defining field. In contrast to the 1970s, these tended to be authored by women rather than men.

Perhaps surprisingly, the hybridity of the bestseller is also evident in non-fiction texts. In 1995, Hamilton noted that 'in the past two years the non-fiction quota has doubled'.[64] This meant that, in that year, there were thirteen non-fiction books in the top 100. However, much non-fiction borrows and gains its popularity from genres of popular fiction. Of the two science books, Richard Preston's *The Hot Zone* (no. 57), about the Ebola virus, capitalises on Michael Crichton's science-fiction work *Congo* and its film adaptation. Stephen Hawking's *A Brief History of Time* (no. 13) surprised commentators with its popularity when it was first released in hardback; yet it speculates on subjects like black holes and time travel which are the raw material for science fiction. Another explanation is that *A Brief History of Time* or Richard Dawkins's *The Selfish Gene* are 'trophy' books. That is, they are bought to look good on the bookcase, but are not actually read.[65] Here the act of consumption is made to create a specific environment (equivalent to Bourdieu's concept of the habitus) that constructs an identity for the purchaser as someone who reads that kind of book.

Biographies and autobiographies (often written by 'ghost' writers) form the bulk of non-fiction sales. The second most successful book overall of 1993 was Jung Chang's *Wild Swans*. Significantly, despite its status as a 'true story', *Wild Swans* conforms to one of the genres of popular fiction; it is a family saga, telling the tale of a Chinese family over three generations from a domestic, feminine point of view. The Asian-American writer Amy Tan writes similar fictional accounts, for example *The Joy-Luck Club*, which have great success. While the use of the family saga in autobiography is a relatively new development, according to Bourdieu, 'The titles and authors favoured by the best-seller readership will vary from country to country, but in each case there will be a preponderance of the life-stories and memoirs of exemplary heroes of bourgeois success or "non-fiction" novels.'[66]

Popular biographies raise three points in relation to the bestseller. First, like astrology and self-help books that often reach the top 100, biographies offer exemplary narratives that provide structures for potential forms of self-identity. Second, they demonstrate why Bourdieu puts inverted commas around the word 'non-fiction'. It is difficult to distinguish between fact and fiction in biographies that, as in the case of *Wild Swans* cited above, mimic the narratives of popular fiction. Third, the ability of bestselling texts to construct or sustain a sense of self illustrates the power of the popular.

The buying and reading of bestsellers is thus a contradictory process. Readers are at once complying with the laws of the culture industry and performing an act which creates a distinct identity: they may purchase 'trophy' books like *A Brief History of Time* to mark a distinction or claim a solidarity between their cultural identity and that of their peers; they may read bestsellers for reassurance; or they may read in conscious dialogue with a group to form 'links and bonds with significant others'.[67]

Conclusion

In this chapter, I have suggested that while negative theories of mass culture give us a broad understanding of the power of the culture industry, their definition of mass culture as mass-produced, standard products needs to be qualified. A significant, postmodern characteristic of contemporary bestsellers is their self-reflexive qual-ity. In fact, they commonly take as their subject matter the industry of which they are a product. Hollywood, large corporations, tele-vision, hotels, retail, airports, casinos and horse-racing are frequent settings in the novels of Jackie Collins, Harold Robbins, Jilly Cooper, Danielle Steel and Dick Francis.[68] These reflect the extent to which culture is a powerful force in maintaining hegemony in contempo-rary society, as important as the worlds of law or politics that provide the background for the novels of writers like John Grisham or Jeffrey Archer.[69] The bestseller's abiding concern with powerful institutions gives us a clue as to what puts it in demand. It is not just the ability to reflect and perpetuate the powerful ideologies that govern our lives. The successful bestseller must also relate those generalised and impersonal structures to the personal life and self-identity of the reader. Even in bestsellers that appear to focus on personal issues, like Michael Crichton's *Disclosure* (no. 14, 1994), which is about sexual harassment, or Danielle Steel's *Mixed Blessings* (no. 18, 1993), which is about couples who have fertility problems, personal issues are treated in relation to the impersonal institutions that constitute the self-referential systems of modernity discussed in the Introduction. In *Disclosure*, the setting is a software company and the case involves legal proceedings and corporate politics as well as the personal consequences for the man who is the 'victim'. His search for evidence involves international contacts and he even enters the science-fiction world of virtual reality (discussed in Chapter 4) when he explores his company's high-tech database. In *Mixed Blessings* the impersonal institutions are the worlds of medicine and the legal process of adoption, each of which creates a context for the personal hopes and fears of the parents involved. Thus, the bestseller performs the difficult and impressive job of relating the personal to the institutional. Although the bestseller is a commodity, it is not just a commodity. It must also answer some of the needs of its consumers, so that it can, as Paul Gilroy describes a twelve-inch single, come to 'anticipate, even demand, supplementary creative input'.[70] Equally, the narrative of the bestseller must be available for appropriation by its readers.

In the next four chapters I look at different bestselling genres and the kinds of identity constructed in the transaction between reader, text and world. In the final chapter, I will look more closely at the kinds of alternative audiences and reader-identity created both by transgressive readings of the bestseller and by particular reader constituencies within the popular audience.

Notes

1 Morag Shiach, *Discourse on Popular Culture: Class, Gender and History in Cultural Analysis, 1730 to the Present* (Oxford, Basil Blackwell, 1989), p. 27.
2 *Ibid.*, p. 30.
3 Raymond Williams, *The Politics of Modernism*, ed. Tony Pinkney (London, Verso, 1989), p. 109.

4 Walter Benjamin, 'Theses on the Philosophy of History', in *Illumina-tions* (New York, Schocken, 1969), p. 263.

5 John Sutherland, *Fiction and the Fiction Industry* (London, Athlone Press, 1978), p. xiii.

6 In this it corresponds to the characteristics of modernity identified by the nineteenth-century French poet, Charles Baudelaire, 'the transient, the fleeting, the contingent': quoted in Jürgen Habermas, *The Philo-sophical Discourse of Modernity* (Cambridge MA, MIT Press, 1987), p. 8.

7 Cited in John Sutherland, *Bestsellers: Popular Fiction of the 1970s* (London, Routledge & Kegan Paul, 1981), p. 7.

8 Sutherland, *Bestsellers*, pp. 7–8.

9 Joan Schulhafer, 'Embracing the Niche', *Publishers Weekly*, 14 June 1993, 43.

10 See the description of the production of a Barbara Cartland novel in Rosalind Brunt, 'A Career in Love: The Romantic World of Barbara Cartland', in Christopher Pawling (ed.), *Popular Fiction and Social Change* (London, Macmillan, 1984), pp. 137–9.

11 'The expansion and contraction of the time of circulation operate therefore as negative limits to the contraction or expansion of the time of production or of the extent to which a capital of a given size functions as productive capital. The more the metamorphoses of cir-culation of a certain capital are only ideal, i.e., the more the time of circulation is equal to zero, or approaches zero, the more does capital function, the more does its productivity and the self-expansion of its value increase. For instance, if a capitalist executes an order by the terms of which he receives a payment on delivery of the product, and if this payment is made in his own means of production, the time of circulation approaches zero.' Karl Marx, *Capital* vol. 2. (Moscow, Progress Publishers, 1967), p. 128.

12 Victoria Griffith, 'The Power of the Plug', *Financial Times*, 1 April 1996, p. 19.

13 Alex Hamilton, 'Adrift on a Sea of Turtles', *Guardian*, 10 January 1991, p. 24.

14 Number and year in brackets refers to the book's place in Alex Ham-ilton's annual paperback 'fastseller' list, published in the *Guardian*. See below for more details.

15 Alex Hamilton, 'Clogs by the Aga', *Guardian*, 11 January 1994, p. 7.

16 Alex Hamilton, 'Titans and Terrors in a Troubled Industry', *Guardian*, 19 January 1996, p. 21.

17 Q. D. Leavis, 'The Case of Miss Dorothy Sayers', in Bob Ashley (ed.), *The Study of Popular Fiction: A Source Book* (London, Pinter, [1937] 1989), pp. 71–2.

18 Theodor W. Adorno and Max Horkheimer, *Dialectic of Enlightenment* (London, Verso, [1944] 1979).

19 Stuart Hall and Paddy Whannel, 'The Popular Arts', in Ashley (ed.), *The Study of Popular Fiction*, p. 60.

20   Jackie Collins, *Hollywood Husbands* (London, Pan, 1987), p. 59 (henceforth page numbers given in text).

21   Q. D. Leavis, *Fiction and the Reading Public* (London, Chatto & Windus, 1932); Richard Hoggart, *The Uses of Literacy: Changing Patterns in English Mass Culture* (Fair Lawn NJ, Essential Books, 1957).

22   Andreas Huyssen, *After the Great Divide: Modernism, Mass Culture, Postmodernism* (Bloomington and Indianapolis, Indiana University Press, 1986), p. 52.

23   *Ibid.*, p. 62.

24   Jean Baudrillard, 'For a Critique of the Political Economy of the Sign', in *Selected Writings*, ed. Mark Poster (Stanford CA, Stanford University Press, 1988), p. 58.

25   Dana Polan, 'Brief Encounters: Mass Culture and the Evacuation of Sense', in Tania Modleski (ed.), *Studies in Entertainment: Critical Theories of Mass Culture* (Bloomington and Indianapolis, Indiana University Press, 1986), p. 175.

26   Raymond Williams, 'An Interview with Raymond Williams' by Stephen Heath and Gillian Skirrow, in Modleski (ed.), *Studies in Entertainment*, pp. 15–16.

27   Raymond Williams, *Marxism and Literature* (Oxford, Oxford University Press, 1977), p. 108. See also Antonio Gramsci, *Selections from the Prison Notebooks* (London, Lawrence & Wishart, 1971), p. 12.

28   Sutherland, *Fiction and the Fiction Industry*, p. 56.

29   Andrew Billon, 'Getting Up on the Wrong Side of Bed', *Observer Review*, 3 January 1993, pp. 2–3.

30   See Ann Rosalind Jones, 'Mills and Boon Meet Feminism', in Jean Radford (ed.), *The Progress of Romance: The Politics of Popular Fiction* (London, Routledge Kegan Paul, 1986).

31   Paul Kerr, 'The Making of (the) MTM (Show)', in Tony Bennett (ed.), *Popular Fiction* (London, Routledge, 1990), pp. 315–42.

32   For a case study of the marketing of a bestseller, see Avril Horner and Sue Zlosnik, '"Extremely Valuable Property": The Marketing of *Rebecca*', in J. Simons and K. Fullbrook (eds), *Writing: A Woman's Business. Women, Writing and the Market Place* (Manchester, Manchester University Press, 1997).

33   Jane Woollacott, 'Fictions and Ideologies: The Case of Situation Comedy', in Tony Bennett, Colin Mercer and Jane Woollacott (eds), *Popular Culture and Social Relations* (Milton Keynes, Open University Press, 1986), p. 215.

34   Gramsci, *Prison Notebooks*, pp. 325–43.

35   Stephen Heath, 'On Screen, in Frame: Film and Ideology', in Tony Bennett (ed.), *Popular Fiction*, p. 23.

36   Fredric Jameson, *The Political Unconscious: Narrative as Socially Symbolic Act* (London, Methuen, 1981), p. 287.

37   Harold Robbins, *Raiders* (New York, Pocket Books, 1995), pp. 249–50.

38   See Stuart Hall, 'For Allon White: Metaphors of Transformation',

      introduction to Allon White, *Carnival, Hysteria and Writing*, ed. Stuart
      Hall *et al.* (Oxford, Oxford University Press, 1993).
39   Jameson, *The Political Unconscious*, p. 107.
40   Adorno and Horkheimer, *Dialectic of Enlightenment*, p. xiv.
41   *Ibid.*, p. 139.
42   *Ibid.*, p. 153.
43   Julie Burchill, *Ambition* (London, Corgi, 1990), pp. 252–3.
44   Fredric Jameson, *Marxism and Form* (Princeton, Princeton University
      Press), p. 340.
45   Pierre Bourdieu, *Distinction: A Social Critique of the Judgement of Taste*
      (Cambridge MA, Harvard University Press, 1984), p. 16.
46   *Ibid.*, p. 1.
47   *Ibid.*, p. 226.
48   *Ibid.*, p. 175.
49   *Ibid.*, p. 101.
50   *Ibid.*, p. 55.
51   *Ibid.*, p. 40.
52   *Ibid.*, p. 87.
53   *Ibid.*, p. 57.
54   *Ibid.*, p. 32.
55   *Ibid.*, p. 194 (Bourdieu is here quoting Voloshinov, a member of the
      Bakhtin school whose work will be discussed in Chapter 6).
56   Huyssen, *After the Great Divide*, p. vii.
57   For example, the famous series in *Dallas* that later turned out to be a
      dream, or the depiction of religious mania and sexual obsession in
      Brookside.
58   In line with his refusal to acknowledge the competence of the average
      consumer, Adorno explicitly rejected this theory. Theodor Adorno,
      Letter to Walter Benjamin, 18 March 1936, in Theodor Adorno *et al.*
      Aesthetics and Politics (London, New Left Books, 1977) p. 123.
59   Walter Benjamin, 'The Work of Art in the Age of Mechanical Repro-
      duction', in *Illuminations*, p. 221.
60   *Ibid.*, p. 242.
61   Janet Radway, *Reading the Romance: Women, Patriarchy and Popular Litera-
      ture* (Chapel Hill and London, North Carolina University Press, 1984)
      p. 222.
62   Marianne Macdonald and Michael Streeter, 'The Joy of Reading Leaves
      Men on the Shelf', *Independent*, 2 January 1997, p. 3.
63   For a full discussion of the genre, see Jerry Palmer, *Thrillers* (London,
      Edward Arnold, 1978).
64   Hamilton, 'Titans and Terrors in a Troubled Industry', p. 21.
65   Macdonald and Streeter, 'The Joy of Reading', p. 3.
66   Bourdieu, *Distinction*, p. xii.
67   Brian Longhurst and Mike Savage, 'Social Class, Consumption and the
      Influence of Bourdieu: Some Critical Issues' in S. Edgell, K.
      Heatherington and A. Warde (eds), *Consumption Matters* (Oxford,
      Blackwell, 1996), p. 295.

68 See examples of bestselling novels by these authors above, and in addition Danielle Steel, *Jewels* (London, Corgi, 1993); and Dick Francis, *Driving Force* (New York, Fawcett Crest, 1992).

69 See, for example, John Grisham, *A Time to Kill* (London, Arrow, 1992); Jeffrey Archer, *First Among Equals* (London, HarperCollins, [1984] 1993).

70 Paul Gilroy, *The Black Atlantic* (Cambridge MA, Harvard University Press, 1993), p. 105.

two
Detective fiction

The intriguing mystery that marks the beginning of all detective fiction has been the subject of endless speculation. It has been claimed that the detective story has been theorised more extensively than any other form of popular fiction.[1] In this chapter I begin my own investigation with an analysis of the detective narrative as form. A formalist approach to popular fiction can be criticised for paying too little attention to the relationship between textual form and meaning in the world;[2] but much popular fiction is formulaic and an understanding of how the formula works is an essential starting point in its study.[3] In the first part of the chapter I use formalist and structuralist criticism to show the basic workings of the detective narrative. In the second part I show how the narrative form provides an interpretative framework from within which the reader can position him or herself in relation to the modern world. I argue that the mystery's solution supplies a temporary sense of self through which the reader is offered an apparatus for negotiating the boundaries that define identity. This negotiation need not be limiting. More often than not, we read for the uncertainties provoked by the mystery rather than the security given by the solution. More questions are raised in the narrative than are answered by its formal closure. This excess or surplus makes for the paradoxical productivity of the detective formula: its contemporary ability to produce new detective identities – the feminist detective, the gay detective, the black detective – as well as the older, more traditional figures like Sherlock Holmes or Lord Peter Wimsey.

Some of the grander claims for the detective story make it difficult to tie down to a particular historical period. At a basic level, the process of discovery might be said to be a universal function of narrative: all narratives proceed by way of revelation and explanation. Detective fiction has been compared with the myth of original sin, the first loss of innocence in the Garden of Eden, and the myth of Oedipus, whose discovery of his origins is also a discovery of his crimes.[4] Thus, the detective narrative can be seen as a new form of an old story: the narrative that attempts to explain what has gone before, to find a beginning or origin. The history of the contemporary genre is closely linked with the history of the modern legal process. One of the characteristics of modernity is the use of the law instead of arbitrary power. The detective narrative emerged at a time when the collection of evidence and the presentation of a case were replacing the extraction of a confession by torture.[5] The modern detective story is a narrative about collecting evidence by following up clues: the story of the legal conviction of the modern criminal. In societies governed by the rule of the law, the judicial process plays an important role in securing the consent required for hegemony. Detective fictions play out the social contradictions the law is designed to resolve. These are mediated through the figure of the detective, who represents the contradictory nature of the disciplined, modern self.

The first modern detective story is usually cited as 'The Murders in the Rue Morgue' by the American short story writer, Edgar Allan Poe. Published in 1841, Poe's short story contains many important elements of later detective narratives. The detection process is described both as a form of logic and of pleasure:

> As the strong man exults in his physical ability, delighting in such exercises as call his muscles into action, so glories the analyst in that moral activity which *disentangles*. He derives pleasure from even the most trivial occupations bringing his talent into play. He is fond of enigmas, of conundrums, of hieroglyphics; exhibiting in his solutions of each a degree of *acumen* which appears to the ordinary apprehension praeternatural. His results, brought about by the very soul and essence of method, have, in truth, the whole air of intuition.[6]

In the model later taken up by Arthur Conan Doyle in his Sherlock Holmes stories, the explanatory narrative gradually emerges as it is revealed to the detective's less astute friend. The brilliant but eccentric C. Auguste Dupin solves a mysterious murder by interpreting a number of clues. Where at first there only appears to be the fact of an unexplained, violent death, Dupin perceives in the clues a significance that reveals an explanatory logic.

Significantly, the short story is set in a modern city, Paris. Dupin's character fits his world. He might be described as urbane in the senses of both sophisticated and of the city. However, He has a contradictory identity. His friend describes him as having a 'Bi-part soul ... a double Dupin – the creative and the resolvent'.[7] His method of detection is both artistic and scientific, and in this he foreshadows the later generic detectives of the twentieth century, who combine a bohemian artistic intuition and a disciplined rigour, the rational and the irrational. The solution to the tale reveals a modern world that also contains elements of reason and unreason. The murders were committed by an escaped orang-utan: an explanation that is both perfectly logical and at the same time bizarre, revealing the presence of irrational, natural forces in modern society. (There is a comparable solution to the Arthur Conan Doyle mystery 'Silver Blaze', where a horse is found to be the culprit.) The modern detective tale negotiates between an idea of modern life as ordered and comprehensible and the fear that such an order is fragile, and that a pre-existing disorder will break through.

The first full-length detective novel is *The Moonstone* (1868) by Wilkie Collins. The mystery here is not a murder but the theft of an Indian diamond, which was originally set in a Hindu idol. The narrative is skilfully composed of a series of statements by various witnesses, all of whom are bound by legal rules of evidence. They must report only what they themselves have seen and heard, not relate hearsay, or use hindsight to interpret the events. The novel introduces perhaps the second classic fictional detective, Sergeant Cuff. Cuff combines professional analysis with an amateur creative bent. He is prepared to discourse for hours about growing roses, and during the narrative he retires to a small cottage outside London to pursue his hobby. Sherlock Holmes, similarly, retires to take up beekeeping, an activity he pursues with scientific rigour. In *The Moonstone*, the mystery is again related to ideas of the irrational in so far as the representation of the jewel is an example of what the postcolonial critic Edward Said calls 'orientalism'.[8] Its connection to the East gives it a mystic, religious significance that is represented as inferior and the opposite of Western rationalism.

Both Dupin and Cuff are precursors of the most famous detective, Sherlock Holmes, and Holmes inherits many of their characteristics. The first Sherlock Holmes story was published in 1887 in *The Strand*, a popular illustrated monthly, and the short stories as well as the 'Long Stories' were republished in a series of collections. By the time the last collection was published in 1927, the detective story was fully established and was going through what is often known as its 'golden age'. The novels of Agatha Christie and Dorothy L. Sayers created the classic English 'whodunit', and with some exceptions, like the short stories of G. K. Chesterton, established the longer detective novel as the dominant form. The English whodunit still featured a distinctive detective, but was often set in the English countryside rather than the modern city.

The period after the golden age is characterised by a diversification of the detective story into whodunits, thrillers and suspense novels. In contrast to Britain, the United States saw the development of 'hard-boiled' detective fiction; for example, writers like Raymond Chandler and Dashiell Hammett. A full account of this evolution would require a book in itself, so this chapter will concentrate on the development of the mystery novel, where the mystery is usually a murder. The classic detective story has persisted in England in the work of writers like P. D. James, Colin Dexter and Ruth Rendell. However, since the 1970s the idiosyncratic character of the detective has also been used to explore different and subversive identities. Since the resurgence of feminism in the 1960s and 1970s, writers in the United States like Sue Grafton, Marcia Muller and Sarah Paretsky have created independent, feminist detectives in the hard-boiled tradition. More recently, in the novels of Barbara Wilson, Mary Wings and Joseph Hansen, lesbian and gay detectives have sustained and developed the genre. In the 1990s, Walter Mosley has used the genre to write a history of African-American experience in the post-war period. Mosley's use of the transgressive qualities of detective fiction is discussed in Chapter 6. These recent novels, combined with the rapid development and success of detective fiction over the last 150 years, indicate the flexibility of the detective story, its ability to adapt and mediate the rapidly changing modern world. The multiple versions of the detective now available suggest that the role is paradigmatic of the possible selves available in the modern world. However, as formula fiction, the detective novel has been the target of mass-culture critiques. It is to its form that I now turn.

Narrative and form

The structuralist critic Tzvetan Todorov has discussed the detective genre in terms of a classification he calls a typology.[9] Todorov divides the genre into the three types mentioned above: the whodunit, the thriller and the suspense novel. He argues that the structure of all detective fiction can be understood as two stories. In the whodunit, the first story is that of the murder and is finished before the novel begins. The second is the story of the investigation, and this is the story that the novel actually relates. The thriller suppresses the first story and vitalises the second. The crime no longer comes before the action; rather the narrative coincides with the action: it is prospective (forward looking) rather than retrospective (looking backward). The suspense novel keeps the mystery of the whodunit and the two stories, but the second is not reduced to the simple detection of truth; the detective him- or herself is vulnerable to danger, and may even be a suspect in the investigation.

Todorov relates the detective narrative's two stories to the distinction made by the Russian formalist critic Viktor Shklovsky between the *fabula* and the *sjuzet*, where the *fabula* is the events 'as they happened', their chronology, while the *sjuzet* is the way in which the events are told, the formal devices that enliven the narrative.[10] In the case of the detective novel, the *fabula* is the mystery revealed: the crime itself and the events that led up to it. The *sjuzet* is the narrative of the investigation, which gradually pieces together the events that led up to the crime from the cles that are left behind. In the following example, I show how this structure works in a classic detective story: Conan Doyle's 'The Red-Headed League'.

The events (or *fabula*) in 'The Red-Headed League' are as follows. One of London's most notorious criminals, John Clay, takes a job with Mr Jabez Wilson, a pawnbroker, at half pay. Apparently an enthusiastic photographer, he spends a great deal of time in the cellar, which he pretends he is using as a dark room, but from where he is actually tunnelling into the vaults of a neighbouring bank. Requiring more time, he places an advertisement in the paper stating that there is a vacancy in the Red-Headed League and draws his red-headed employer's attention to it. The advertisement offers £200 a year, and, on being interviewed, Mr Wilson is offered the salary if he spends several hours each day copying out the *Encyclopaedia Britannica*. The tunnelling is brought to completion and Mr Wilson is told, summarily, that the League has been dissolved. Clay and his partner then wait until Saturday night to commit the robbery in order to give themselves time to get away.

The way 'The Red-Headed League' is narrated (its *sjuzet*) is to represent these events as an unfathomable mystery. The story begins when the narrator, Dr Watson, arrives at Sherlock Holmes's Baker Street rooms to find the red-headed Mr Jabez Wilson relating the strange events from his puzzled point of view. To him, of course, and to the reader, the whole episode appears inexplicable. The explanatory narrative is told through Watson's observations of Holmes's investigative technique. Thus, the *sjuzet* makes strange the facts of the crime, which are not fully revealed until the last few pages when Holmes finally explains his reasoning to Watson. Having correctly interpreted the clues, the detective's deductions lead him to arrange to wait on the Saturday night in the bank vault with Watson, the banker and the police for the unfortunate John Clay.

Shklovsky's opposition between the *fabula* and the *sjuzet* relates to the debate about formula fiction mentioned above. Using an argument we have already encountered in the introduction from Walter Nash, Shklovsky claimed that it is formal innovation that is the valuable element in literary texts – that is, the *sjuzet* not the *fabula*. Innovation performs the function of 'making strange' or defamiliarising (*ostranenie*) that which, through convention, has become normal.[11] Using Shklovsky's critical approach, it is possible to argue that defamiliarisation is an inherent part of the structure of the detective story. The method of detection provides a form through which the original events of the crime are made strange. As Shklovksy sees defamiliarisation as a function of art, this would appear to legitimate the detective story's aesthetic value, or what Walter Nash would call its literary merit. But a formalist approach can also be turned against the detective novel. In fact, two of the most common accusations levelled against it are formal and social conservatism. It is argued that the conventional structure of the detective novel, the way in which the murder and the investigation are repeated in each novel, means that there is no formal innovation. In fact, the contrary is the case: the shock of the murder is defused by the investigation, which seeks to reorder the mayhem back into a conventional, safe form. According to Franco Moretti: 'The *fabula* narrated by the detective in his reconstruction of the facts brings us back to the beginning; that is, it abolishes narration ... In this sense, detective fiction is anti-literary. It declares narration as a mere deviation.'[12] For Moretti, the complexity of narration, which Shklovsky sees as the essence of literature, is destroyed by the detective novel.

It is important to note that, while both these formal arguments focus on the text, both have implications for the text's relationship to the world beyond. In the next section I examine a structuralist approach to narrative; yet, as we will see, the formal characteristics of the narrative have an ideological dimension. Those who argue that the detective narrative is formally conservative usually also see it as socially conservative. For now, it is enough to note that the meaning of the detective story depends on how much emphasis we give to the critical, speculative aspects of the investigation and how much to the finality of the solution. Moretti assumes that the ending negates the investigation. This corresponds to the common argument that no one ever reads a detective story twice. But this contradicts many people's experience, including my own. I often cannot remember the solution, which turns out not to be the most important part, because the story of the investigation raises more questions than the solution can ever answer.

Narrative structure

Terence Hawkes describes structuralism as founded on the idea that 'the world is made up of relationships rather than things ... it claims that the nature of every element in any given situation has no significance by itself, and in fact is determined by its relationship to the other elements involved in that situation.'[13] A structuralist approach to narrative is, therefore, concerned with the ways in which the parts relate to the whole. Structuralist critics understand narrative as composed of two related structures, which can be most simply described as the horizontal and the vertical. The horizontal structure relates to the syntagma: the way in which the narrative is ordered syntactically as a sequence. Within the sequence each part achieves its meaning in relation to the order of the other parts. This is sometimes described using the term 'metonymy'. Metonymy is the rhetorical trope whereby a part of something is used as an equivalent to the whole. For example, the word 'Yard' is often used instead of the phrase 'the headquarters of the London police at Scotland Yard', as in 'Sergeant Jones of the Yard'. The word achieves its meaning in the context of a structure already known to the receiver of the message. The following passage, from Wilkie Collins's *The Moonstone*, can be used as an example:

> I looked where she pointed. The tide was on the turn, and the horrid sand began to shiver. The broad brown face of it heaved slowly, and then dimpled and quivered all over. 'Do you know what it looks like to *me*?' says Rosanna, catching me by the shoulder again. 'It looks as if it had hundreds of suffocating people under it – all struggling to get to the surface, and all sinking lower and lower in the dreadful deeps! Throw a stone in, Mr Betteredge! Throw a stone in, and let's see the sand suck it down!'[14]

The metonymic structure can be understood here as the way each narrative part fits into the structure of the whole. For the structuralist critic, the point of such an analysis is to show that meaning is achieved not just by the accumulation of the parts (or individual narrative units) of such a passage, but by how they are related to one another. Rosanna's question, '"Do you know what it looks like to me?"', achieves its full meaning in relation to the previous description of the sand and to her own answer. This structure mimics the structure of language itself, which, according to the linguist Ferdinand de Saussure, is made up of signs which refer not directly to anything outside themselves but to each other.[15] Meaning, then, is achieved out of the structural relationships of signs, where the key opposition is between *langue*, the total language out of which meaning can be formed, and *parole*, the 'word' or use of language in a particular instance.[16] The solution to the murder mystery relies on the assumption of a metonymic structure: that each part of the narrative, no matter how trivial, will achieve meaning in the context of the whole investigation.

The vertical structure of narrative refers to its associative or paradigmatic features. The way in which, when we read, we are interested in not just the horizontal relationship of signs or narrative units but in the vertical associations they spark off. The rhetorical trope for this process is metaphor, where one thing is substituted for another. For example, it is common in poetry to compare a lover with a rose, 'my love, a rose'. Here the relationship between the signs is not defined horizontally, but vertically or associatively. The rose is a metaphor for love, but we can extend the vertical axis to one's lover, the similarity between the brevity of temporal love and the short life of a flower (as in the phrase 'gather ye rosebuds while ye may'), the gift of roses, and so on for as far as we might wish to go. In the case of the passage above, to read paradigmatically would be to analyse not so much the combination of narrative units, but their associations. For example, the quicksand described in the passage above might be understood to represent the impenetrable mystery that is at the centre of the novel. Rosanna's image of people suffocating and her request to watch a stone sinking might then signify the extraordinary way the missing gem seems to draw people under its spell. There is no end to the number of associations possible. Where the solution to the mystery assumes a metonymic structure, the crime as metaphor defers a final truth, suggesting a complexity that needs to be constantly reinterpreted.

It is important to note at this point that a formal characteristic of the narrative like its horizontal or syntagmatic structure cannot be easily disentangled from other formal characteristics like the genre or the vertical structure. The sands are read today in the context of a retrospective knowledge that *The Moonstone* is a precursor of the modern detective novel, and the associations that the passage sparks off are ordered by the way the narrative units are combined in a certain sequence. As we have already seen in the introduction, the experience of reading popular fiction must be understood in its totality.

The somewhat confusing terminology of structuralist analysis can be summarised as follows:

the horizontal	*the vertical*
syntagm	paradigm
sequence	association
metonym	metaphor

The horizontal structure of the detective story allows us to reduce it to recognisable functions. Structuralist critics analyse narrative in this way. They argue that the basic narrative structure stays constant across a popular genre and that the characters from different texts are interchangeable.[17]

In the detective narrative we might enumerate five spheres of action related to characters: (1) the detective; (2) the helper; (3) the victim; (4) the witness; (5) the criminal. Each sphere of action may contain more than one character, and characters may perform actions in more than one sphere. Thus, in 'The Red-Headed League' the characters who correspond to these spheres are: (1) Sherlock Holmes; (2) Dr Watson, the police, the banker; (3) Mr Jabez Wilson, the banker; (4) Sherlock Holmes, Mr Jabez Wilson, the banker; (5) John Clay, his partner. Sherlock Holmes, for example, enacts the investigation, but he is also a witness to clues that solve the crime. Both Mr Jabez Wilson and the banker are victims of the crime; and the banker, Mr Merryweather, is helper, victim and witness.

The advantage of studying popular fiction using this kind of syntagmatic analysis is that it works well for formulaic narratives.[18] It allows the critic to look at its parts in relation to the whole and to look at individual works in relation to an understanding of a generic form. In Saussure's terminology, this is to look at the speech-act in terms of the total language. It gives a sense of how particular units of meaning, like formula narratives, are often structured in relation to larger structures of meaning. However, a syntagmatic analysis pays little attention to the second list – to the paradigmatic or associative features of the detective story. As I will show in the next section, it is these features which allow the text as form to be interpreted in relation to the world and reader.

Detective fiction and modernity

As we have already seen, the formalisation of judicial processes based on evidence and argument is a necessary precondition for the detective story. Detective narratives are constructed in relation to one of the most important self-referential systems of modernity: the law. The character of the detective is the contradictory product of that relationship and, in this, he (I refer here to early male detectives) is a fine example of the modern self. Detectives like Sherlock Holmes and Dupin are the epitome of the modern individual. On the one hand, they are supremely rational and able to engage expertly with the modern institutions and structures that confront them. On the other, they are introspective and alienated from the rest of society, to the point where they are considered abnormal by conventional standards. While scientific in his methods, the detective's self-identity also incorporates aspects of the modernist artist or bohemian. Thus, the detective stands on the cusp of one of the contradictions of modernity. Able to use reason, the detective's ideas of logic and rationality define him as a moderniser in the field of criminology; but his eccentricities and the work in which he engages make us aware of the limits and contradictions of reason.

Feminist critics of detective fiction have highlighted the way in which the mystery is often related to a masculine, Eurocentric version of rationality. Catherine Belsey has pointed out that women are always mysterious in the Sherlock Holmes stories.[19] In two narratives about stolen gems, Conan Doyle's 'The Sign of Four' and Wilkie Collins's *The Moonstone*, non-Europeans appear as superstitious and barbaric, even though both gems have been stolen in the context of the brutal repression of Indian resistance to conquest. These criticisms of the (male) detective's ideology can be related to Franco Moretti's argument, cited above in the context of structuralist analysis, that the detective narrative is anti-literary. He argues that the detective narrative is a function of modern mass culture, which abolishes originality and produces standard products.[20] The implications of this thesis are that the genre is socially conservative. The solution will always reflect the dominant ideology of the period. However, the argument that the detective rationalises and imposes a rigid, modernising view on the world is contradicted by the detective's role as artist. The bohemian side of the detective is open to the new possibilities opened up by modernity. A comparison of the metonymic and metaphoric structures of the detective narrative show how each metonymic narrative function corresponds to an interpretable metaphoric structure which gives it meaning in the world.

	Horizontal (*metonymic*)	*Vertical* (*metaphoric*)
1	the detective	the detective as modern self
2	the helper	the detective's world
3	the victim	the murder mystery
4	the witness	the process of detection
5	the criminal	the solution

As we have already seen in Chapter 1, the relationship between form and meaning is not fixed. Meaning will be effected by changes in the world and by the situation of the reader. Nonetheless, form does condition, if not determine, response. The successful formula narrative must be able to both satisfy in its predictability and mediate changes in the world. I now turn to the metaphoric structure and examine each of the vertical categories in turn to illustrate how the detective narrative copes with the contradictions of modernity.

The detective as modern self

The character of the detective provides a focus of interest in the detective novel at least as interesting as the murder mystery. The detective is a distinctive, modern individual, but one whose identity is defined in relation to his or her world. As the place in which the culture of modernity was made, that world is often, although not always, the city. When the detective moves to the countryside, it is a countryside viewed from the perspective of the city. For the detective, there is no place of original innocence, untouched by modernity. In 'The Adventure of the Copper Beeches', Holmes pronounces gravely: 'It is my belief, Watson, founded upon my experience, that the lowest and vilest alleys in London do not present a more dreadful record of sin than does the smiling and beautiful countryside.'[21]

The detective's self-identity cannot be disentangled from the world in which he or she lives. Holmes, like Dupin, is an urban individual and part of his identity is created through the ambience of his rooms in Baker Street, a bachelor pad in the centre of the capital. In contemporary detective fiction, Sarah Paretsky's V. I. Warshawski is defined by her relationship to Chicago, as Marcia Muller's Sharon McCone is by San Francisco. Detectives in these narratives signify something about modern urban life: a lifestyle, a way of being. As distinctive individuals, they are out of the ordinary, and may even verge on the pathological. The narrator of 'The Murders in the Rue Morgue' admits that Dupin's skill may be the result of a 'diseased intelligence', while Watson notes how Holmes appears to require a mystery in order to stay healthy. Deprived of the opportunity to detect, Holmes resorts to obsessive behaviour, taking cocaine as a substitute.

Detectives are loners. It is rare for passionate or romantic love to figure in their lives. They are defined not so much by their relationship to other people, but by their habits. They are often hard drinkers, and attention is paid to their particular tastes: V. I. Warshawski drinks whisky, while Ruth Rendell's Inspector Wexford and Colin Dexter's Inspector Morse are fond of real ale. The more health-conscious Warshawski follows a rigorous exercise programme, but her modern sense of what is healthy conflicts with the tastes in food she has inherited from her Italian mother.

> Since Loring still hadn't shown, I made coffee and a snack. After fried eggs at six this morning it was time to get back to a healthier regimen. I sautéed tofu with spinach and mushrooms and took it into the living room with the Smith & Wesson.[22]

The homes, cars, cooking and dress-sense of the detective define her or his individuality through a distinctive lifestyle. All these personal preferences can be read as signs that the detective lives in a certain type of society. The detective is a consumer, and exists in a society of mass consumption, where the self is defined by the kinds of distinctive tastes described in Chapter 1. At the same time, despite their individuality, their understanding of the modern world means that detectives have the ability to fit in. They have a style and a knowledge that allows them to be a part of their world. Sherlock Holmes is master of disguise. V. I. Warshawski often changes her car in order to deceive her pursuers, and in the novel *Guardian Angel* she rents and stays in the room formerly inhabited by the murder victim in order to find out more about his life and social world.[23]

Walter Benjamin has compared the detective to what he called the *flâneur*. The *flâneur* represents the new urban individual who is anonymous in the city crowd, who observes not only what the city has for sale but also his (for Benjamin the *flâneur* is male) fellow citizens:

> He only seems to be indolent, for behind this indolence there is the watchfulness of an observer who does not take his eyes off a miscreant. Thus the detective ... develops forms of reaction that are in keeping with the pace of a big city. He catches things in flight; this enables him to dream that he is like an artist.[24]

The bohemian artist is only one of the detective's identities, and, as we have seen, it contradicts another one, which is at least as important. At the same time she or he represents and participates in modernity by being a scientist. Sherlock Holmes writes monographs on types of tobacco ash and soil types. His deductions are based on logic and reason. His, apparently miraculous, ability to tell the profession of an unknown visitor or to describe where they have come from that morning is shown to have firm roots in skills of observation and deduction. He uses clues to explain mysterious events as if the world is a rational ordered place in which every effect will always have a clear and explainable cause. All detectives use a mixture of logical-rational and intuitive-artistic methods of deduction. If, then, we are to see the detective as a product of modern consumer culture, it is difficult to see him or her as simply obeying the anonymous, standard logic of that culture. The creative and critical aspects are equally important.

Thus, the detective's self is contradictory and cannot be said to consist of a single, defined identity. Instead, the detective operates by transgressing the boundaries that make up identities. He or she is able to cross the boundaries of class, 'race' and gender that normally define the self in a way that other people cannot. This brings the detective dangerously close to the criminal, but allows him or her to guide the client and, crucially, the reader through uncharted areas of modern society. In this sense, the detective facilitates a transgressive act, but it is matter of debate whether the narrative of detection confirms or disrupts the social boundaries transgressed.

The detective's world

While the natural world of the first fictional detectives was the modern city, archetypally the fog-filled streets of Sherlock Holmes's London, the English detective novel of the 'golden age' often takes the countryside as its setting. As in 'The Copper Beeches', the detective's adventures in the countryside are an exploration of the contradictions of modernity, an exploration that can be related to the contradiction already discussed between the detective as bohemian artist and the detective as rational scientist. Much as the term 'rational' requires its opposite in its definition, in the modern period the rural and the urban define one another: 'The widespread use of *country* as opposed to *city* began in the [late sixteenth century] with increasing urbanisation and especially the growth of the capital,

London.'[25] The rural setting relates to the artistic, romantic side of the detective, providing a space in which she or he can reflect on the modern world. Thus, Agatha Christie's Miss Marple is as much a *flâneur* as her urban counterparts. She is able to play the part of the innocent old lady, an anonymous type, and consequently to observe what others do not see.[26] Moreover, in the classic whodunit, the English countryside is part of a modern and progressive nation-state. Far from being cut off and isolated, the rural setting is linked to the city by railway, telegraph or telephone, while the characters who occupy that world are often cosmopolitan or accustomed to foreign travel.

A good example of a detective novel set in the countryside, but fully engaged with the modern, is *The Nine Tailors* by Dorothy L. Sayers (1934). Given the mutually defining relationship between detective and world, the character of the detective, Lord Peter Wimsey, is important. As an aristocratic man of leisure, Wimsey is close to being a *flâneur*. No particular residence is described in the novel, but his lifestyle is sufficiently communicated by his man-servant and helper, Bunter, and his Daimler. When he arrives in the small, snowbound village of Fenchurch St Paul's in the fens of East Anglia, he is clearly marked as distinctive by these signs of his class, yet he is able to fit in almost immediately, filling the gap left by one of the bell-ringers, who is ill. At first, Fenchurch St Paul appears to be the archetypal rural backwater, and the fact that the dead body is found in the churchyard seems to fix the narrative in a context of tradition and traditional values. As the narrative progresses, however, the unexplained body is gradually linked to a network of characters and events that places the village in the context of a much larger, modern society, which includes an earlier unsolved robbery, London's criminal underworld and the First World War. The investigation involves travelling to France, and one important witness, who is in the merchant navy, extends the novel's scope across the world.

Two important metaphors mediate the contradiction between modernity and tradition that runs through *The Nine Tailors*. The first is the practice of change-ringing church bells. Change-ringing is both a science and an art. It requires knowledge and skill in its perform-ance, but is so mathematically intricate that the Rector of Fenchurch St Paul's has written a treatise about it. In a foreword to the novel,

change-ringing is represented as peculiarly English and as antithetical
to modern understanding:

> From time to time complaints are made about the ringing of church bells.
> It seems strange that a generation which tolerates the uproar of the in-
> ternal combustion engine and the wailing of the jazz band should be so
> sensitive to the one loud noise that is made to the glory of God. England,
> alone in the world, has perfected the art of change-ringing and the true
> ringing of bells by rope and wheel, and will not lightly surrender her
> unique heritage.[27]

Bell-ringing is central to the investigation and the solution of the
murder mystery. On the one hand it represents the irrational nature
of the mystery, on the other the possibility of its logical solution.

The other key metaphor is the drainage system of the fens. As
much of the fens lie below sea level, they are in constant danger of
flooding. The drainage system is a modernising project that dates
back centuries, but which has fallen into decline. The novel ends
with Fenchurch St Paul's surrounded by water. The disrepair of the
drainage system and the inadequate restoration work reflect the
decline of the village, once with a large enough population to fill the
enormous church, but which now consists of 'three hundred and
forty souls, no more'.[28] Taking a metaphoric reading further, it is
possible to interpret these images of decline as signifying the decline
of England itself in the inter-war period. Such an interpretation
demonstrates how the detective narrative negotiates ideas of modernity and tradition; and, as we shall see below, through the relationship between the detective and his or her world, these ideas create
a sense of place for the modern self.

The murder mystery

The relationship between the murder mystery and modernity has
been understood in a number of different ways. The similar positions
of the reader and the detective have been noted from Sherlock
Holmes onward.[29] We have seen how Walter Benjamin described
reading a detective novel as kind of ritual performed by the reader.
Like Benjamin, Bertolt Brecht read the detective story as both a
product and critique of mass culture. For Brecht, the murder represents a logical puzzle, which *can* be solved, while mass society
presents us with an unknowable world where cause and effect do

not seem to operate as logical laws. He argued that the murder mystery operates in the same way as the mass media, which initially represents the world as a catastrophe, only then to reveal the 'inside story', initially provoking fear, only to allay that fear with a rational solution.[30] But whereas negative theories of mass culture would argue that the detective story is a conservative genre that evades proper criticism, for Brecht it involves enjoyable intellectual activity, stimulating social criticism.

For Ernst Bloch, another critic associated with the Frankfurt School, the murder represents an original catastrophe, the original loss of innocence that marks our entrance into the modern world.[31] Certainly, mortality is one aspect of life that does not fit comfortably with modernity.[32] The traditional rituals that were used to come to terms with death in the past are rendered old-fashioned and are seen as belonging to an older, obsolete set of values. Detectives are often conscious of their own mortality. Inspector Wexford in *Murder Being Once Done* is on holiday in London because of his heart condition.[33] In *Guardian Angel*, V. I. Warshawski is aware of how the ageing process is slowing her down, preventing her from escaping from violent antagonists as well as she used to. Sherlock Holmes is in danger of killing himself through drug-abuse and his medical adviser, the stolid Dr Watson, often expresses concern for his mental and physical health. The murder mystery, then, provides a context within which the detective's own mysterious self can be related to the modern world, and through the narrative the reader is offered the apparatus for negotiating the boundaries that define identity. Whether the crime is regarded as a banal, normal event or as a shocking incident, it supplies a narrative event through which questions about the self and society can be worked. The initial shock of the murder is usefully provocative, but it is not enough on its own. The narrative of detection is needed to complete the work of estrangement or of comprehending the crime in conventional terms.

The process of detection

Most of the detective novel is taken up with the process of detection and deduction, the recognition and interpretation of clues. In many detective novels the heterogeneity of the city creates the world in which false trails can be left. If we continue to see the detective's methodology as characterised by the rational-scientific and the intuitive-artistic, then within the first interpretive framework the clues leave a trail of abnormality in the midst of a normal world;[34] in the second interpretive framework the clues provide an opportunity to contemplate and reflect on that which goes beyond the rational-scientific model. Those critics, like Franco Moretti, who argue that popular fiction is essentially a function of mass culture serving to contain and subdue creative or speculative reflection tend to concentrate on the rational-scientific deductive process. Those critics, like Ernst Bloch, who see popular fiction as prompting an active participation and even utopian possibilities tend to emphasise its creative potential. Bloch writes of the surplus or excess of meaning that detective fiction provides, going beyond limited ideologies of what is rational.[35] Both analyses allow different accounts of the pleasures the text offers up to the reader. The former account can be used to argue that providing a clear account of causality creates pleasurable thought in a world where most people feel they do not understand how mass society works. Brecht talks of reading the detective novel as an intellectual habit. He emphasises the enjoyment provided by logical thought.[36] The latter account is more speculative, arguing that the detective narrative prompts thought beyond the formal puzzle, and it is this 'beyond' that provides the opportunity for the reader's pleasurable interaction with the detective story.

A moment in the Inspector Morse mystery *Last Bus to Woodstock* exemplifies both forms of pleasure. Morse has retired to a pub to think about the unsolved problem.

> if alcohol was dimming Lewis's intellectual acumen, it had the opposite effect on Morse. His mind began to function with an easy clarity. He ordered Lewis to take the weekend off...
>
> Morse, not an addictive smoker, bought twenty king sized cigarettes and smoked and drank continuously until 2.00 p.m. What had really happened last Wednesday evening? He was tormented by the thought that a sequence of events, not in themselves extraordinary, had taken place; that each event was the logical successor of the one before it; that he knew what one or two of these events had been; that if only his mind could project itself into a series of naturally causal relationships, he would have it all. It needed no startling, visionary leap from ignorance to enlightenment. Just a series of logical progressions. But each progression landed him at a dead end, like the drawings in children's annuals where

one thread leads to the treasure and all the others lead to the edge of the page. Start again.

'I'm afraid I shall have to ask you to drink up,' said the landlord.[37]

In this passage, the real ale and the cigarettes act as an aid to the detection process. If the mystery stands for the puzzle of modernity, which makes no sense, then Morse creates a sense for himself out of a personal ritual, one which can be compared with the space provided by the rural setting in the English murder mystery, but which is here the carefully chosen situation of the pub with good beer and a supply of cigarettes (Ernst Bloch describes an armchair, tea, rum and tobacco as the appropriate circumstances for reading detective fiction[38]). According to Theodor Adorno and Max Horkheimer, 'all ritual includes the idea of activity as a determined process which magic can nevertheless influence.'[39] The nostalgia that characterises the Inspector Morse novels can be seen as part of a ritual creation of a self in the context of modernity. In the process of detection, Morse creates a modern self that is characterised by the divide between a nostalgic aesthetic and the murder mystery that requires a logical solution. The thought processes he goes through in the passage are analogous to those of solving a crossword puzzle, one of Morse's favourite pastimes, where the solution is 'a series of logical progressions'. This would seem to characterise the problem as a rational one, but the situation of the pub also suggests Bloch's notion of 'excess', where the detection process involves a surplus over and above the limits of reason. In the case of Morse, we might see this utopian principle emerging in the difference between the formal, rational puzzle versus the ritual of beer and cigarettes. In the Morse novels, the crossword functions for Morse in the same way as the deductive process in the detective novel does for the reader, as a formal, logical problem, with rules and a learnt structure. It represents a formal, scientific evaluation of what is; an acceptance of a rationalised framework of explanation that leaves no room for reflection or speculation. The cigarettes and beer, on the other hand, are stimuli to thought beyond the formal puzzle – the, as yet unknowable, mystery of the murder itself; but, as stimuli, they are unpredictable, providing an excess of thought that draws into question the legitimacy of any formal enquiry.

This might be referred back to the double-sided figure of the detective: on the one hand a cool rationalist, certain of his or her identity, on the other the modern, angst-ridden subject, the artist, bohemian or *flâneur*. It is this doubleness that permits the dialectic (the ability described in Chapter 1 to reflect upon one's own consciousness) of detective fiction, where the utopian moment is at the same time the knowledge of limitation. To know that you want to transcend the boundaries imposed by the modern self, you must be aware that those boundaries are powerfully enforced.[40]

The solution

No detective story is complete without a solution. Clearly, in terms of a metonymic analysis of the detective story, the detection narrative and the solution are mutually sustaining. In terms of a metaphoric analysis, however, the solution provides the reader with an interpretative framework, from within which he or she can position him- or herself in relation to modernity. For example, the solution to *The Nine Tailors* reveals that the murdered man was a thief, a murderer and a blackmailer. He had been imprisoned in the belfry by someone he was trying to blackmail, where he was killed by the noise of the bells. This suggests that the English values referred to in the Foreword have had their revenge. The bells here signify a tradition that has defeated the negative values of modernity as represented by the thief. This interpretation is given historical legitimacy by the fact that the bells have murdered before, killing another representative of modernity, a Parliamentary soldier who was trying to rob the church during the Civil War. However, this interpretation cannot be seen as final. If the mystery contains an excess that cannot be solved, then equally, for the reader, there is a gap between the experience of reading the detective narrative and the experience of living within modernity that throws into doubt the legitimacy of the fictional solution, which must perform an artificial closure. This is not to deny the value of the processes of thought that accompany reading detective fiction or any popular text. Reading detective fiction ritualises the fear of modernity. In so doing it provides the reader with an identity. The consciousness remains, however, that such identity is a submission, a recognition of modernity's power, from which the railway carriage or the armchair or the Oxford pub can only protect us temporarily. According to Theodor Adorno, it is that power that prompts 'the need in thinking': 'the need in thinking is what makes us think'.[41] Morse's thought process in the pub forms, then, a complex moment which might be compared to the active mental process that is a part of reading popular fiction. This involves both the possibilities of closure and of new creative thought, the possibility of forming a single, limited identity or of multiple identities. It is understanding the complexity of this mental process that make studying popular fiction such an important critical task.

The postmodern detective?

The productivity of the detective formula has given rise to new kinds of detective at the end of the twentieth century. One version of the postmodern condition sees it as a more pluralist world, where feminist, lesbian and gay and non-white voices are now heard. These challenge a Eurocentric, middle-class, masculinist rationality. It could be argued that the detective narrative has always had a postmodern dimension in that both the mystery and the artistic-intuitive side of the detective represent the other side of modernity. But, in the late twentieth century, detectives operate within a larger constellation of possible identities. For example, new feminist detectives like V. I. Warshawski and Sharon McCone negotiate an identity in the context of the new possibilities created by women in the post-war period. They have a different, gendered perspective on the contradictions of modernity than male detectives like Dupin or Holmes. However, this does not necessarily make them postmodernists. Susan Rowlands has argued that, while V. I. lives in a postmodern city characterised by 'fractured values and communities', the process of detection resists postmodern fragmentation through a feminist critique of society.[42]

Mary Wings operates a similar dialectic by mixing the detective form with other genres. In *Divine Victim* she incorporates elements of the gothic, rewriting Daphne Du Maurier's *Rebecca*.[43] By transgressing genre boundaries, Wings is able to create a space for new transgressive identities; but the identity of the detective remains the starting point for her investigations. The flexibility of the detective formula allows the development of new identities both for new kinds of detectives and for new kinds of readers. It is not a case of using the detective story as a 'vehicle'. The detective form already has within it the critical framework for the kind of new narratives used by Paretsky and Wings or, as I will show in Chapter 6, Walter

Mosley's African-American detective, Easy Rawlins. The detective was often a transgressive figure; but in the 1980s and 1990s the form has broadened to include critical perspectives on gender, sexuality and 'race'.

Conclusion

This chapter has demonstrated some (certainly not all) of the methods by which the detective narrative can be understood. The critical approaches characterised by formalism and structuralism allow a clear view of the narrative itself and provide important concepts and techniques that are vital to the study of the text. The concept of modernity has been used to supply a context for the detective narrative: the world from which it emerges and upon which is reflects. The philosopher Jürgen Habermas has said that the philosophers of modernity are like 'detectives on the trail of reason in history, [they] seek the blind spot where the unconscious nests in consciousness, where forgetting slips into memory, where regression is disguised as progress, and unlearning as learning process'.[44] I would suggest that the reverse is also true: detectives are the philosophers of modernity. This is the case in both senses of philosophy described by Antonio Gramsci. First, in the sense that everyone is a philosopher, because 'even in the slightest manifestation of intellectual activity whatever, in "language", there is contained a specific conception of the world.' Second, in the sense that detectives are critical of the world in which they live. They pursue what Gramsci calls the 'second level' of philosophical enquiry: 'that of awareness and criticism'.[45] Thus, while most detectives move in the sphere of everyday life rather than (with a few exceptions) the rarefied air of academe, the murder mystery is precisely the kind of blind spot of which Habermas speaks, a moment when the narrative of modernity as progress is thrown into doubt by the violence that is its other side. In an ambivalent position between criminality and the law, the detective is someone who must construct a critical 'conception of the world' that takes into account both sides of the contradictions of modernity. In consequence, far from representing the hardened identity of a rational, modernist self, the boundaries of the detective's personality are permeable. His or her position is transgressive, and her or his identity is constantly in process. I have argued that the detective narrative helps to construct new identities: the murder, the detective's self-identity and the world in which the investigation takes place map out an area within which the relationships between identity and society are constructed. It is, therefore, possible to begin to argue that the act of reading detective narrative can itself be a creative process, where the reader inserts her- or himself into the definitions provided by the text as part of a process of experimentation which measures their adequacies and inadequacies. The next chapter takes this exploration further by introducing the concept of fantasy as a way of understanding the relationship between reader-identity and text.

Notes

1 David Trotter, 'Theory and Detective Fiction', *Critical Quarterly*, 33:2 (1991), 66–79.
2 Stephen Knight, *Form and Ideology in Crime Fiction* (London, Macmillan, 1980), pp. 5–6.
3 See J. G. Cawelti, *Adventure, Mystery and Romance: Formula Stories as Art and Popular Culture* (Chicago, Chicago University Press, 1976).
4 Ernst Bloch, 'A Philosophical View of the Detective Novel', in *The Utopian Function of Art and Literature* (Cambridge MA and London, MIT Press, 1988), pp. 255–61.
5 *Ibid.*, pp. 245–7; Franco Moretti, 'Clues', in *Signs Taken for Wonders* (London, Verso, 1983), pp. 138–9.
6 Edgar Allan Poe, 'The Murders in the Rue Morgue', in *Selected Tales*, ed. Julian Symons (Oxford, Oxford University Press, [1841] 1980), p. 105.
7 *Ibid.*, p. 109.
8 Edward Said, *Orientalism: Western Conceptions of the Orient* (Harmondsworth, Penguin, 1991).
9 Tzvetan Todorov, 'The Typology of Detective Fiction', in *The Poetics of Prose* (Oxford, Basil Blackwell, 1977), pp. 42–52.
10 *Ibid.*, p. 45. Terence Hawkes, *Structuralism and Semiotics* (London, Routledge, 1977), pp. 65–6.
11 Hawkes, *Structuralism and Semiotics*, pp. 62–3.
12 Moretti, 'Clues', p. 148.
13 Hawkes, *Structuralism and Semiotics*, pp. 17–18.
14 Wilkie Collins, *The Moonstone* (London, Bantam Classics, [1868] 1982), p. 25.
15 Hawkes, *Structuralism and Semiotics*, pp. 19–28.
16 'the dominant opposition is between *langue*, which is to say the ensemble of linguistic possibilities of a given moment, and the *parole*, or the individual act of speech, the individual and partial actualization of

some of these potentialities'. Fredric Jameson, *The Prison-House of Language* (Princeton, Princeton University Press, 1972), p. 22.

17 For an example of this approach, see Vladimir Propp, 'Morphology of the Folk Tale', in Bob Ashley (ed.), *The Study of Popular Fiction: A Source Book* (London, Pinter, [1928] 1989), pp. 92–6.

18 Examples of studies using this approach include Umberto Eco, *The Bond Affair* (London, Macdonald, 1977); and W. Wright, *Sixguns and Society: A Structural Study of the Western* (Berkeley, California University Press, 1975).

19 Catherine Belsey, 'Critical Practice', in Ashley (ed.), *The Study of Popular Fiction*, pp. 32–4.

20 Moretti, 'Clues', pp. 155–6.

21 Arthur Conan Doyle, 'The Adventure of the Copper Beeches', in *The Complete Adventures of Sherlock Holmes*, ed. C. Morley (Harmondsworth, Penguin, [1892] 1985), p. 270.

22 Sara Paretsky, *Guardian Angel* (Harmondsworth, Penguin, 1992), p. 395.

23 *Ibid.*, p. 249.

24 Walter Benjamin, *Charles Baudelaire, A Lyric Poet in the Era of High Capitalism* (London, Verso, 1983), p. 41.

25 Raymond Williams, *Keywords* (London, Fontana, 1976), p. 81. See also the reference to the city, pp. 55–7.

26 Cora Kaplan, 'An Unsuitable Genre for a Feminist', in Ashley (ed.), *The Study of Popular Fiction*, pp. 199–200.

27 Dorothy L. Sayers, *The Nine Tailors* (London, Coronet, [1934] 1988), p. 5.

28 *Ibid.*, p. 12.

29 Belsey, 'Critical Practice', p. 231.

30 Bertolt Brecht, 'Über die Popularität des Kriminalromans', in *Gesammelte Werke* vol. 8 (Frankfurt am Main, Suhrkamp Verlag, 1967), pp. 450–7.

31 Bloch, 'A Philosophical View', p. 258.

32 'In the socialized society … death is felt exclusively as external and strange. Men have lost the illusion that it is commensurable with their lives. They cannot absorb the fact that they must die.' 'The present society still tells us lies about death not having to be feared, and it sabotages any reflection upon it' Theodor Adorno, *Negative Dialectics* (London, Routledge, 1990), pp. 369, 396.

33 Ruth Rendell, *Murder Being Once Done* (London, Hutchinson, [1972] 1991).

34 Moretti, 'Clues', p. 135.

35 Bloch, 'A Philosophical View', p. 255.

36 Brecht, 'Über die Popularität des Kriminalromans', p. 450.

37 Colin Dexter, *The Last Bus to Woodstock* (London, Pan, 1977), p. 39.

38 Bloch, 'A Philosophical View', p. 245.

39 Theodor Adorno and Max Horkheimer, *Dialectic of Enlightenment* (London, Verso, 1979), p. 8.

40 'Only he who always submits survives in the face of the gods. The

awakening of the self is paid for by the acknowledgment of power as the principle of all relations.' *Ibid.*, p. 9.

41 Adorno, *Negative Dialectics*, p. 408.

42 Susan Rowlands, 'Detecting Society in the Novels of Sarah Paretsky', paper given at conference, 'Detective Fiction: Nostalgia, Progress and Doubt', Liverpool John Moores University, November 1996.

43 For a discussion of her methods, see Mary Wings, 'Rebecca Redux: Tears on a Lesbian Pillow', in Liz Gibbs (ed.), *Daring to Dissent: Lesbian Culture from Margin to Mainstream* (London, Cassell, 1994). For a critical commentary on lesbian detective fiction, see Paulina Palmer, 'The Lesbian Thriller: Transgressive Investigations', in Pete Massent (ed.), *Criminal Proceedings: The Contemporary American Crime Novel* (London, Pluto, 1997).

44 Jürgen Habermas, *The Philosophical Discourse of Modernity* (Cambridge MA, MIT Press, 1987), pp. 56–7.

45 Antonio Gramsci, *Selections from the Prison Notebooks* (London, Lawrence & Wishart, 1971), p. 323.

three
Popular romance

Romance is the original form of popular fiction. Its primary function of wish-fulfilment is the characteristic element of narratives that propel the reader into a fantasy world where a full and complete identity can be imagined. Yet romance is also the genre which has been taken least seriously in literary studies. It has been compared disadvantageously with more 'serious' literary forms. In the ancient world, the epic narrative of martial valour towers over tales of love. In the Middle Ages, the popularity of the chivalric romance was accompanied by associations of frivolousness. In the modern era, romance has been given a lesser place than the realist novel.[1] In the twentieth century, two additional factors have contributed to its marginal status: first, an association from the 1930s onwards of popular romantic fiction with mass-market formula publishing; and second, the identification of that market with women readers and their supposed concerns – love, desire, fantasy and imagination.

This chapter focuses on contemporary popular or mass-market romance. In Britain the market leader is the publisher Mills & Boon; in North America it is Mills & Boon's sister company, Harlequin. Since the 1930s, demand for the group's fictions has expanded enormously and annual sales now exceed 180 million copies internationally. Although the contemporary formula romance needs to be distinguished from earlier forms of romance, I begin this chapter with a discussion of two elements which are a common feature of the genre throughout the ages: the representation of desire and the importance of a fantasy setting. Contemporary popular romance is aimed specifically at women. Until recently, critics neglected it, but since the early 1980s feminist critics have conducted a revaluation of the form. Using a 'gendered' analysis and psychoanalytic criticism, they have discussed the nature of the appeal of romantic fiction to women in the context of a male-dominated society. I use these insights to examine the construction of a gendered reader-identity in contemporary formula romance. Just as the structuralist analysis developed in Chapter 2 is relevant beyond the detective novel, feminist psychoanalytic criticism has applications to the study of popular fiction as a whole. In particular, the concept of fantasy is crucial to an understanding of the partial and incomplete identifications the reader makes with the popular text. At the same time, an important criticism of psychoanalysis is its tendency to universalise to the detriment of historical specificity. I argue that the most successful uses of psychoanalytic criticism relate psychological structures to historical moment. To show how this might be done, in the final part of the chapter I move from formula romances to the family saga. In a discussion of Catherine Cookson's *The Golden Straw* (1993), I suggest that whereas changes within the 'formula' romance occur over years, the family saga can be read as charting those changes through several generations in one narrative.[2]

The history of the romance genre is longer and more complex than that of the detective story. In the Introduction, I defined the concept of genre in two ways: as works of literature that share particular formal characteristics and as literary forms that satisfy certain expectations in a delimited readership. However, these definitions are complicated by the longevity of the romance form and its extraordinary adaptability. While its most common manifestation is the love story, the prospect of love can be replaced with a more abstract hope for riches, fame or adventure. The audience of contemporary popular romance is overwhelmingly female, but romance has not always been a form for or about women. Women play a small, if symbolically important role in medieval romance, while in the modern period the masculine romance has persisted in the form of adventure stories,[3] spy novels and thrillers. In fact, the only clear element that unites all romance narratives is their concern with desire and the prospect of its satisfaction.

For example, the ancient Greek romance takes place in the free zone that the critic Mikhail Bakhtin calls 'adventure time'.[4] Adventure time in the Greek romance is the time of desire, where nothing matters except the passion of two young lovers. During that time, the lovers encounter numerous adventures, may visit four or five countries, and discourse on several topics; but as these events and conversations take place within adventure time, they do nothing to change the real world or what Bakhtin calls 'everyday time'.[5] The separation of the everyday and the world of adventure is extreme in the Greek romance, but it represents a dialectic between desire and the real or everyday which persists in contemporary popular romance.

The representation of desire requires a setting or scene of fantasy on to which desire is projected. In the Greek romance that setting is the world of adventure. In the next major stage in the history of the genre, the chivalric romance, the fantasy setting is developed further. Chivalric romances were enormously popular in the Middle Ages, when they were often read aloud to largely illiterate audiences.[6] They involve a more complex interaction between desire and the real than that found in the Greek romance: incorporating 'a casual interplay between history and miracle ... The writers could encompass the marvellous and the everyday without a change of key.'[7] The scene of fantasy is an enchanted world in which the life of adventure is portrayed by a gallant knight, and love by his devotion to an aristocratic lady. An important form of chivalric adventure is the quest for a precious prize, buried treasure for example.[8] During the quest, the hero encounters some kind of monster, which represents for Northrop Frye the ultimate form of lack, 'the sterility of the land itself'; while finding the prize is the 'victory of fertility over waste land'.[9] Thus, the narrative charts the history of a desire from its beginnings to fulfilment or satisfaction. Frye describes the stable and destabilising elements of the genre as the twin components of aristocratic ideology and proletarian hope.[10] The upper-class world holds an appeal beyond its social confines, as a scene on to which the non-aristocratic reader/listener can project his or her desires. The idea of a better world, whose inhabitants are more prosperous, happier or live more exciting lives, remains a common scene of fantasy in contemporary popular romance.

I introduced a structuralist approach to popular narratives in Chapter 2. A structuralist analysis can also be applied to romance, which repeats narrative patterns or archetypes. For example, Northrop Frye points to the common use of images that are derived from the womb as a place of safety, against which are contrasted the trauma of separation from mother, and the desire to return to an original, protected and unified state.[11] Structuralist accounts play an important role in contemporary critical accounts of romance texts. As we shall see below, ideas of archetypes or recurring patterns re-emerge in psychoanalytic approaches which emphasis the importance of early infantile development in identity formation. However, despite the obvious applicability of structuralism to the romance form, the important role of the extra-textual world in the dialectic between desire and the real cannot be ignored. While the *fabula* of the romance narrative is structured around the object of desire (whether a loved one or a utopia), the *sjuzet* tells of the difficulty of satisfying that desire. The true path of love never runs smooth in romance, nor is utopia easily, if ever, gained. The physical, temporal and social barriers that impede satisfaction signify the world.

The formula romance

In contemporary formula romances the conflict between historical reality and desire manifests itself in a series of archetypal situations. Yet despite the apparent similarity of these situations, the formula romance has been gradually updated since its inception in the early twentieth century. In the 1930s, while the economic context for most readers was the Depression, Mills & Boon fictions told tales of high society. In the 1940s, the context of the war led to a breaking down of class barriers and to more realism. The 1950s saw a shift back to fantasy worlds of international travel. From the 1960s onwards, heroines became more independent and in the 1970s gradually absorbed feminist ideas. Mills & Boon now offer a variety of different formulas, including 'Temptation', 'Legacy of Love' (historical romances), 'Favourites' (reprints of popular titles).[12] Silhouette, part of Mills and Boon, publishes a hybrid genre of formula romance/thrillers, with an 'action-heroine'. The heroine of Saranne Dawson's *In Self Defence* saves the hero instead of the other way round.[13] In the 1980s, the obstacles to desire became more a question of emotions than social situation or opportunity.[14]

For example, in Penny Jordan's *Valentine's Night* (1989) Sorrel reluctantly agrees to accompany her Australian cousin, Val, whom she has never met before, to an isolated Welsh farmhouse, because there is no room at home. To her surprise, Val turns out to be a man, Valentine, and they are forced by bad weather to spend three days alone together, snowbound in the farmhouse, which has only one bed. During this ordeal, Sorrel finds her desires contradict what she believes to be her true or real self. She is a virgin, thinks of herself as uninterested in sex, and is engaged to be married to the less-than-exciting book dealer, Andrew. However, the enforced presence of Val arouses hitherto unsuspected emotions. In the following passage, she tries to distract herself from these feelings by talking about her work, a tapestry.

> 'I've done the first three seasons,' she heard herself telling him, in a voice that was suddenly, for no reason at all, slightly breathy. It couldn't be because he had bent his head over her work, just in the direction she was pointing, so that his dark hair brushed against her wrist, causing tiny tingling sensations to race along her veins, heating her entire body, could it? No, of course not. It was unthinkable ... ridiculous ... impossible that she should react to this abrasive Australian in a way that she had never reacted to Andrew, the man she had agreed to marry.[15]

Valentine's Night illustrates the way in which the romance form operates to blur the boundaries between fantasy and reality. On the one hand, the cottage is a real place. On the other, it acts as a fantasy setting for Sorrel's unconscious desires. With Valentine's arrival, a real aspect of her life, her engagement, turns out to be the most easily changed. Later, when Valentine and Sorrel finally make love, Sorrel imagines at first that it is a dream, only realising the truth when she wakes up later. The romance narrative probes the nature of the heroine's identity by exploring the interaction between her unconscious and reality. Whereas the solution to the murder mystery suggests that the world is knowable, romance narratives represent a more ambivalent relationship between the world, the text and the reader. The representation of desire in romance means that there can be no direct or unmediated experience. In the romance text, desire and fantasy disrupt the reader's perception of a knowable world that might supply a secure sense of self-identity. In its representation of the heroine's desires, the text describes an identity that is not fixed, but in the process of change. As she tries to make sense of her situation, the heroine is constantly turning her experience of the world into explanatory narratives in the hope of coming to terms with her desires; but, until the narrative resolution, these narratives always fail fully to comprehend her situation. Thus two processes can be identified which historicise the formula romance. First, the heroine's situation is updated over a period of years. Second, each narrative charts the heroine as she goes through a period of personal transformation. Both these factors mean that there is no easy or straightforward identification of the reader with the heroine. The reader must adapt her expectations over time, while the individual narrative provides no fixed point on which to project herself.

Feminist criticism

The situation of the heroine in popular romance is inextricably bound up with her position as a woman in the modern world. It has been suggested that there may be a connection between the parallel rise of 'second wave' feminism in the post-war period and the increase in the popularity of popular fiction.[16] Following this argument it might be possible to draw a parallel between the shift from social to emotional obstacles in formula romances and the growing influence of feminist and psychoanalytic ideas in the late twentieth century. Both are factors in what Anthony Giddens calls the 'transformation of intimacy'.[17] Over the last thirty years, it is feminism that has contributed most to our understanding of gender relations. There are many kinds of feminist criticism and it would be wrong to suggest that they share a common approach. However, most recent feminist theory has made a distinction between biological *sex*, and *gender* roles – which are understood to be a product of social and cultural conditioning.[18] This distinction has been articulated by using the terms 'male' and 'female' to refer to sex, and 'masculine' and 'feminine' to refer to gender. Feminists have argued that masculinity and femininity are constructed by social and environmental factors rather than being innate or essential characteristics that accompany biological make-up. The distinction between sex and gender is central to a critique that sees women's subordination as a consequence of social structure and cultural conditioning.

A 'gendered critique' has been used by feminist critics to pioneer several different approaches to popular romance. Some critical feminist accounts see popular romance as complicit with the social norms of women's subordination to men. According to this analysis, the heroine is represented as no more than a longing. Her 'soft' identity is moulded through her relationship to her male lover.[19] From this perspective, popular romance is a conservative form, where femininity is defined in relation to a fixed point, masculinity. The following passage from *Valentine's Night* can be interpreted in this way:

> She stood still in the street as the pain hit her, clutching her dress-box in her arms, oblivious to the angry glower of the woman who almost walked into her, her eyes wild with anguish.
> She loved him. She loved Val. She loved him, and if he asked it of her she would throw all her caution and her fear to the four winds, and give him whatever he should desire from her.
> But he wouldn't ask. To him, she was simply a brief diversion to amuse him for a moment out of time. She tried not to think of the beautiful girls in Australia who must flock round him … tried not to allow herself to imagine how dull he must find her in comparison. (138–9)

A feminist critique of this passage that employed a sex/gender distinction might interpret Sorrel's realisation that she loves Val as the heroine defining herself as uncertain and confused in contrast with the more certain and attractive masculine figure. The answer to her confusion can only be the recognition she desires from him. In other words, femininity as a subordinate position is defined and confirmed through her relationship with his more secure masculine identity. This view would suggest that the text provides an uncritical representation of women's socialisation into a male-dominated society. Instead of being made or gendered, women's subordination is presented as natural to her sex.

By contrast, Janice Radway, in her detailed study of a group of women romance readers, finds evidence that the romance reader has an active, critical role. She argues that, for her study group, reading romances is a 'highly desirable and useful action'.[20] The readers discriminate between the texts they like and those they dislike. They are guided through the huge quantities of popular romances the industry produces by an advisor, 'Dorothy Evans', who gives guidance to readers in the bookshop where she works and publishes a newsletter directing subscribers to the best stories. Not only do the readers in Radway's study have preferences between different types of 'formula' romances – for example, between historical romances, gothics or family sagas – but also titles by favourite authors are sought out and disfavoured authors avoided. Radway does a structuralist analysis of the narrative functions of the romances read. However, Radway's account needs to be distinguished from a purely formal approach in that she gives central place to the reader of popular fiction. The 'good' romance narrative is one that is favoured by its readers; the 'bad', one that is not. The 'desirable and useful action' of romance is discovered by a focus on the historical or 'real' situation of the women who read the texts: their response to them rather than the formal properties of the narratives themselves.

Radway's critical approach is part of the more general reassessment of romance from a feminist perspective. Radway's focus on the reader involves a gendered critique, and she seeks to make some connections between the romance form and the position of women in a male-dominated society, which she, in common with many feminists, terms 'patriarchy'. She suggests that romance narratives provide a way for women who occupy traditional feminine roles in society to understand their lives. Reading popular texts amounts to a positive choice: 'Romance fiction, as they experience it, is … *compensatory literature*. It supplies them with an important emotional release that is proscribed in daily life because the social role with which they identify themselves leaves little room for guiltless, self-interested pursuit of individual pleasure.'[21]

Using Radway's findings, it is possible to argue that the woman reader may not automatically identify with Sorrel's feminine position, or, if she does, that identification may provide for a more critical perspective on gender relations than is immediately obvious from the text itself. Critical accounts that see the reader of popular romance as identifying unproblematically with the heroine not only assume a passive reader; they also simplify the relationship between representation (the text) and reality (the world), the problematisation of which, as we have seen already, is intrinsic to the romance form. In order to explore this further, it is necessary to look at the different ways feminist critics have used psychoanalysis to understand popular romance.

Feminism and psychoanalysis

More recently, some feminists have used psychoanalytic ideas to argue that the sex/gender distinction pays too little attention to questions of cultural representation. They contend that the idea of a biological sex that exists before culture is not useful because we all come to the body already culturally conditioned to understand it in terms of a masculine/feminine divide. Even the body is 'read' according to a preconceived set of binarisms (for example, male/female, strong/weak, hard/soft, active/passive), which are constructed within what the French psychoanalyst Jacques Lacan calls the 'symbolic order' – that is, the laws and conventions of a particular culture.[22] In Western culture, the symbolic order is structured around the symbolism of male power, in which the most important symbol is that of the 'phallus'. As a symbol, the phallus does not refer directly to the biological (flesh and blood) penis; rather, it signifies the power attributed to men in society.[23]

The psychoanalytic concept of sexuality adds a more complex understanding of desire to the question of gender difference. The fixed binarism of masculine/feminine tends to assume an equally fixed desire by men for women and by women for men. In psychoanalysis, there is no presupposition that sexual desire is limited to heterosexual relations. Rather, the adaptable nature of desire is stressed and an important role is given to fantasy in the choice of sexual object. In the words of the feminist psychoanalytic critic, Juliet Mitchell:

> The psychoanalytic concept of sexuality confronts head on all popular conceptions. It can never be equated with genitality nor is it the simple expression of a biological drive. It is always psycho-sexual, a system of conscious and unconscious human fantasies involving a range of excitations and activities that produce pleasure beyond the satisfaction of any basic physiological need. It arises from various sources, seeks satisfaction in many different ways and makes use of many diverse objects for its aim of achieving pleasure. Only with great difficulty – and then never perfectly – does it move from being a drive with many component parts – a single 'libido' expressed through very different phenomena – to being what is normally understood as sexuality, something which *appears* to be a unified instinct in which genitality predominates.[24]

According to feminist psychoanalytic criticism, the context in which feminine sexuality develops is different to that of masculine sexuality. Men and women enter into different relationships with the symbolic order through the Oedipus complex. The Oedipus complex arises through the primary identification of both boys and girls with their mother. Paradoxically, it is the mother who first occupies the 'phallic' position of authority. The discovery that the mother does not hold as powerful a position in society as the father (it is the father who symbolises the phallus) creates the crisis through which the boy and the girl receive a gendered identity. The boy accepts his 'inferior phallic powers', sometimes known as 'the castration complex', but with the promise that he will later occupy as powerful position in relation to women as his father does. The girl learns of her subordinate position in relation to the symbolic order, her castration complex, but for her there is no promise of full entry to the symbolic order; consequently her feeling of lack persists as a sense of exclusion.[25]

The Oedipal crisis is often dramatised in the formula romance as some kind of childhood trauma. In *Valentine's Night*, such a trauma explains Sorrel's virginity and her fear of sexual contact. At the age of eleven, she saw a couple making love in the open air, an experience that awakened unsettling emotions: 'It frightened me. She was so … so vulnerable. I ran away then. I couldn't bear to see any more. The whole thing terrified me, and I felt guilty because I knew I should never have watched, but I couldn't seem to help myself' (71). This corresponds to what Freud called a 'primal scene'. The term is used 'to connote certain traumatic infantile experiences which are organised into scenarios or scenes'. Freud attributed particular importance to a scene in which the child sees sexual relations between its parents. He argued that the primal scene is understood by the child 'as an act of aggression by the father in a sado-masochistic relationship'.[26] Sorrel perceives the scene she witnessed as an act of violence by a man against a woman. Dramatised in the formula romance, the primal scene serves to represent the feminine position as lacking power, as outside the symbolic order. The masculine position, by contrast, is powerful and has an identifiable place within it. This is emphasised when Sorrel's experience is contrasted with Val's, who, 'with certain experiences of his own making love out in the open beneath a summer sky, hid his own amusement'. Val's sexual identity, here at least, appears secure.

Women's marginal position in modernity is often represented on the opening pages of the formula romance. The following passage from *The Seed of Vengeance* by Elizabeth Power is typical in its representation of exclusion:

Erica didn't know how much longer she could bear it, watching her father being treated like a criminal.

Now that the afternoon session was in progress, he was sitting, hands clasped tensely on the table he shared with his defence counsel, that shock of white hair and the gaunt line of his face making him look more like an old man, Erica thought sadly, instead of the leading force behind Witney Laboratories. So much for English justice. Dear God! Could his heart stand it?

Unable to help herself, unobtrusively, she slipped out of the stuffy courtroom, welcoming the cooler air in the lobby. Beyond the windows, London throbbed and roared and hooted, lights cutting through the murk, prompting a glance towards her slim wrist. Hardly half-past three, and already it was getting dark![27]

Erica's marginal position in relation to the symbolic order is represented by her relationship to the judicial system that administers society's laws. She enacts her exclusion by walking out of the 'stuffy courtroom', but it is important to note that her attitude is characterised by both a sense of powerlessness – she is 'unable to help herself' – and a sense of resentment and resistance to the way things are, 'So much for English justice'. It is not insignificant that Erica's father has lost his authoritative position in society, 'the leading force behind Witney laboratories'. The lack of a powerful male protector leaves Erica as a lonely individual figured against the backdrop of the modern city, London. It is a position in some ways comparable with that of the figure of the detective discussed in Chapter 2. Here, however, gender is the primary signifier of identity, and the description emphasises her femininity. Her body acts as the site which displays her gender, her 'slim wrist' contrasts with the threatening darkness of the city, and in the next paragraph her back is described as 'stiffening beneath a creamy white coat'. The narrative opens, then, with Erica's identity constructed as both marginal and having lost the fixed bearings that should structure her desires. At this moment, her sexuality appears to lack a unifying principle and is the 'drive with many component parts' described by Juliet Mitchell. The subsequent paragraphs introduce an authoritative male figure who quickly displaces her father in the narrative and in Erica's life, Rafe Cameron.

He was all she remembered and more, from his splendid height and that self-assured way he held his dark head, to those strong features moulded with hard arrogance – that striking authority in that determined jaw and cheekbones, in the sensual, yet uncompromising mouth. (5)

The view that argues that formula romances are a conservative form might take this as a powerful intervention; one which serves to shape the unformed nature of the feminine character's desires into a unified feminine sexuality, subordinate to the masculine symbolic order figured by Rafe's 'striking authority'. However, Ann Barr Snitow argues that the genre reverses the dominant perspective in society to focus on women's subjectivity;[28] and for Tania Modleski, the heroines of contemporary romances engage in a "continual deciphering of the hero's behaviour. The Harlequin heroine probes for the secret underlying the masculine enigma, while the reader outwits the heroine in coming up with the "correct" interpretation of the puzzling attitudes and actions of the man.'[29] The action of 'deciphering' is comparable to the position of the reader/detective in detective fiction. Here again, however, the key factor is the working out of identity in relation to gender relations. The enigma is not just modernity, but the gender of the symbolic order that structures modern cultures. Modleski locates an unconscious 'latent' fear of male violence in romance narratives: 'the desire to be taken by force (manifest content) conceals anxiety about rape and longings for power and revenge (latent content)'.[30] By making a distinction between the literal meaning of the text and its metaphoric meaning, Modleski suggests that popular romance does not simply direct its reader towards an uncomplicated identification with the heroine and her desire for the hero. Rather, the narrative enacts a dialectic, where a feminine identity is produced in the context of the antagonistic relationship between femininity *as it is defined* within culture and *as it is lived* by women. Thus, reading romance can produce a sense of resistance to the symbolic order, and even a desire for vengeance against it.

Evidence for this argument can be found in the common device whereby the hero has to show his vulnerability before the heroine will admit her love for him. For example, the plot of *Seed of Vengeance* is as follows. Erica's father, Sir Joshua who runs Witney Laboratories, has been put on trial for stealing the formula for a new wonder drug that prevents migraine. Rafe Cameron has the evidence that could prove his innocence, but he resents the family because he thinks Erica rejected his offer of marriage because he is from a lower class. In fact, Erica rejected him because she thought (incorrectly) that he was having an affair with her father's new young wife.

Rafe refuses to hand over his evidence unless Erica agrees to marry him and have his children. She, in desperation, agrees, but hides her revenge (her seed of vengeance) in the knowledge that she cannot get pregnant. She hopes to fool him into giving up the evidence before he discovers her secret. Thus, her ostensible position is resistance against Rafe's power. However, despite everything, she cannot help desiring his 'raw animal vitality' and finds she enjoys their sexual relationship. She even starts to become jealous of another woman, Vikki, whom she suspects has a prior place in Rafe's affections. The key moment occurs after they have first made love on their honeymoon. The encounter is described in violent, but passionate terms which reflect Modleski's dynamic between the apparent desire to be taken by force and a fear of male violence. Afterwards, Erica turns away and Rafe's voice becomes 'husky' (60). Erica does not realise, but the reader can deduce, that Rafe is crying. Despite appearances, sex is not enough and he wants Erica to show affection towards him. As the narrative proceeds, Rafe's vulnerable side becomes clearer to Erica, until the point where she is able to recognise his feelings as genuine. The final scene shows Rafe as a 'new man' of the 1980s, getting up to look after their baby – for, despite her belief in her infertility and despite a serious car accident after she becomes pregnant, Erica does manage to give birth. A similar moment, revealing Val's vulnerability to feeling, occurs in *Valentine's Night* when Sorrel nearly dies in the snow: 'She opened her eyes and looked at him, shocked by the colour of his skin. Beneath his tan he looked haggard ...' (105). Such moments suggest that feminine and masculine positions define each other in the formula romance. Romance narratives are as much about a man finding his place in a feminine world as a woman finding her place in a man's world. Rafe's conversion to a perfectly socialised husband is further evidence of the changes feminism has brought about in the formula romance.

The idea that romances represent a feminine view of the world is further developed in Radway's study. We have already seen how Northrop Frye's structuralist analysis raised the importance of archetypes that signify the womb. Radway uses Nancy Chodorow's psychological study of mothering to understand the kinds of utopia figured by the popular romance. According to Chodorow, the girl's 'incomplete Oedipal resolution' means women have a continuing need and desire for the mother: 'This finally produces in women a continuing wish to regress into infancy to reconstruct the lost intensity of the original mother–daughter bond.'[31] Thus, popular romance answers a peculiarly feminine nostalgia for infantile pleasures. It is possible to find numerous examples in popular romance where the heroine is reduced, through circumstance or illness, to a position of total dependency. In *Valentine's Night*, the cottage represents a warm, womb-like, safe area, in contrast with the cold and dangerous exterior. After Val rescues Sorrel from the snow he assumes a maternal role, although one which is not without its own sexual *frisson*:

> He carried her upstairs to the bedroom, where the fire still glowed and the air was so warm that her body was attacked by pins and needles driving out the freezing chill of the snow.
> ... holding her gently, he proceeded to undress her, far more deftly and capably than she could have done, all the time keeping up a calming flow of conversation, talking to her in the same kind of gentle voice he might have used to a terrified child. (105–6)

A comparable moment occurs in Emma Richmond's *A Wayward Love*.[32] The heroine, Paris, is reduced to nervous exhaustion through overwork, but the hero, Oliver Darke, catches her on the point of collapse and then takes care of her, calling a doctor and cooking her meals until she recovers. In Catherine Cookson's historcal romance *The Golden Straw* the heroine, Emily, is similarly reduced to illness, first by exhaustion, nursing her employer and running her business, and later by a violent attack that causes a miscarriage. On each occasion she is cared for and brought back to health by the hero, who is a doctor. An interesting aspect of these examples is that the man plays the part originally played by the mother. After the Oedipal crisis when the mother has lost her 'phallic' authority, only a man has sufficient power in the symbolic order to provide the necessary care.

The idea of a regression to infantile sexuality has led some critics to compare romance to pornography. According to Ann Barr Snitow, 'In pornography all things tend in one direction, a total immersion in one's own sense experience, for which the paradigm must certainly be infancy.'[33] As women's sexual satisfaction is, however, usually dependent on a stable social situation, the heroine of the formula romance is constantly trying to mediate between an overpowering sense of her own sexual feeling and the need to control that feeling so that a secure relationship can be formed.[34] The outcome of the popular romance is almost always a successful heterosexual relationship – usually marriage – and it is this closure which is most liable to accusations of conservatism. However, as I argued in Chapter 2, to judge a narrative in terms of closure is to limit the analysis unnecessarily to textual form. Such a limitation is particularly problematic in the case of formula romances, which are commonly read one after the another. The experience of reading is thus not of a single text, but of multiple texts in series, where each closure is just a prelude to another opening. Helen Taylor argues that the relationship between reader and text is not between a 'fixed book and a generalised universal reader', but a 'relationship between an active, critical reader, and a text, with all its literary, historical and cultural references, not to mention the way it has been produced, packaged and marketed'.[35] In the case of popular romance the relationship is between an active reader and a series of texts, creating a complex dynamic between those texts, a changing world and a changing reader. One key concept that emerges from psychoanalytic criticism which helps to understand this process of exchange (sometime called the difference between a 'text in use' and 'a text in itself'[36]) is fantasy.

Fantasy

I have already used the term 'fantasy' to describe an essential element in romance, the scene or setting of fantasy on to which desire is projected. The Freudian understanding of fantasy suggests that a fantasy involves a complex relationship with the scene or setting.[37] If we take the formula romance as an example of a fantasy text, then Freudian psychoanalysis complicates the idea that there is a simple identification between the female reader and the feminine heroine. Fantasy in psychoanalytic theory is an essential part of psychic life,[38] which emerges early in a child's development. The infant's realisation that it is separate from the mother induces a sense of lack that includes just a trace of the memory of satisfaction.[39] The gap is filled by fantasy (sometimes spelt 'phantasy', to distinguish it from the everyday meaning of fantasy), which provides the means by which the child can imagine a sense of wholeness. Juliet Mitchell describes this process as follows: 'Phantasy is the setting for the desire (wish) which came into being with its prohibition (absence of object)', where the absence of object indicates a form of lack. 'The baby, or any human subject of whatever age, places himself as actor somewhere in the scene … The place the subject occupies is unfixed or even invisible being de-subjectivised as often in dreams. Phantasies are scripts capable of dramatisation, usually in visual form.'[40] The most radical Freudian psychoanalysts suggest that the role of fantasy in psychic life means that the subject can never achieve a permanent fixed identity.[41]

Given the centrality of both desire (which presupposes some form of lack) and fantasy in romance, these insights are important. If the romance is understood as the setting of desire, then that setting will not supply the opportunity for total identification. Let us take *Valentine's Night* as an example of a text that might be understood as a setting for desire. The Welsh farmhouse is, as I have already argued, both a 'realistic' and a fantasy setting. The realistic or metonymic mode depicts the building as kind of trap, in which Sorrel is caught with her unwelcome male cousin. Only the bedroom and the kitchen are heated, so that they are forced to spend day and night together. In the fantasy, however, the cottage can be understood in a number of different ways. Reading in the metaphoric mode described in Chapter 2, the kitchen and the bedroom are symbolic of two traditional feminine roles, as homemaker and as object of desire. Alternatively, the farmhouse, as warm interior space could signify the womb and a regression to an infantile sexuality that holds the promise of total satisfaction. The crucial factor here is the relationship between the reader and the text. If the text is understood in terms of the reader's identification with Sorrel, then the symbolic spaces of the kitchen and the bedroom appear to stereotype the social role of femininity. In this interpretation, the feminine reader/heroine assumes a passive function in relation to the active male hero. However, if the act of identification is not fixed, then the exchange between reader and text becomes more complicated. Readings that have explored the partial and temporary identifications made within the scene of fantasy take their cue from Freud's essay, 'A Child is Being Beaten'. Freud describes how, in this fantasy, the sex of the child and the figure of the beater are not fixed, but instead are changeable.[42] If the reader does not identify solely with Sorrel as trapped victim, but instead reads metaphorically, then it might be possible to participate in a fantasy where Sorrel actually wants to be trapped with a man she desires. Equally if the reader does not only see things through Sorrel's eyes, then the text might provide a setting in which the reader can shift perspective to the active position of the man. That these kinds of identifications are made possible by the romance text is illustrated by the following passage from *Valentine's Night*, which occurs after Sorrel has drunk too much of her mother's home-made wine. When she falls asleep Val puts her to bed and then joins her.

> The sensation of the soft, warm body burrowing against his own so closely mirrored his own brief fantasy that at first he wasn't sure if he was merely imagining it ... but, no, he acknowledged, grinning to himself, this was definitely real!
>
> Obligingly he turned round to face Sorrel, and saw that she was deeply asleep. He supposed it was only natural that she should seek the warmth she had just left, and the dip in the centre of the bed had caused her to roll naturally against him. (54)

The scene represents experience on the borderline between fantasy and reality. There is a realistic explanation for Sorrel's movement – the dip in the bed – but the reader is also told that this reality enacts Val's wish. Subsequently, he responds to Sorrel's movement:

> He reached to slip his arm around her and make himself more comfortable, and his fingers brushed against the silky fabric of her bra. He wondered what she normally wore in bed. A starched cotton nightdress with lots of Victorian lace and a high neck, perhaps; but certainly not her bra and panties. Deftly he reached for the catch of her bra and eased it away from her ...

While Val clearly takes an active, 'masculine' role, compared to Sorrel's passive 'feminine' one, the position of the subject (who desires) and the object (who is desired) of desire are not clear in the passage. The active reader can and will shift the point of identification from Sorrel's unconscious and therefore 'guiltless' pleasure to Val's conscious reaction. Neither position is without its problems. Sorrel is dangerously vulnerable, making it difficult to identify comfortably with her, while Val is culpable in having joined her in bed and then taken advantage of her situation. The setting of fantasy means, however, that the reader can project selectively on to the scene, making temporary, partial identifications, or withdrawing altogether and assuming the position of a voyeur. The scene of romance thus problematises the relationship between reality and representation in a way that destabilises, if only temporarily, fixed gender positions. Masculinity and femininity are represented as fixed poles in formula romance, but these poles act as symbolic positions which the reader can position her/himself with or between. There is no essential or universal identity from which the reader starts; nor is one found in the text. Rather, temporary, partial identifications are a product of a negotiation or exchange between reader and text.

A utopian reading of formula romance might argue that narrative closure occurs when both hero and heroine have shown themselves to be out of place in the symbolic order: the heroine through her problematic femininity and the man in his display of vulnerability. Love is the utopian state in which both lovers transgress the restrictive boundaries of their 'lawful' gender identities and enter into a relationship that supplies mutual, total satisfaction, the abolition of lack. However, while there is clearly a utopian element to all romance narratives, the repetitive nature of formula romances and their repeated consumption by readers suggests that the reader's participation in utopia is partial and short-lived. This suggests one limitation of psychoanalytic interpretations of popular fiction, because while psychoanalytic criticism can identify some of the narrative patterns of formula romance and relate these to moments of psychic development, it has a tendency to reduce those patterns to universal psychic structures. Psychoanalytic criticism provides some useful tools to analyse the relationship between the reader's self-identity and the text. It is less good at providing an account of that relationship in the context of the world.

One of the key problems with psychoanalytic criticism is that it does not question the structure of the nuclear family as a specific historical and cultural phenomenon. In addition, the focus within the nuclear family is on the father–son relationship, not the mother–daughter relationship. Consequently, feminine sexuality is not given as much attention as masculinity. While feminist critics have attempted to redress this balance, the focus on the nuclear family has meant that questions of class and 'race' have been neglected. Peter Stallybrass and Allon White point out that in his own family Freud's immediate carer was not his mother, but a servant. This has important consequences for the structure of childhood fantasies, but Freud displaces the position of the maid with that of the mother.[43] Following a similar line of criticism, Steph Lawler picks up an insight of

Carolyn Steedman's, that the childhood fantasies of alternative parents, which Freud called, 'The Family Romance', are usually of wealthier parents, not those of the same or a lower class than the child.[44] In her essay "'I never felt as though I fitted'", Lawler argues that class background and subsequent social mobility (or lack of it) will shape a sense of self as much as relations within the family. Lawler is equally critical of the assumption in much feminist psycho-analytic criticism that 'inadequate mothering' really does take place in the family. Instead, she argues that the figure of the inadequate mother is a fantasy that emerges in the context of the particular circumstances of lack associated with femininity and is especially clear amongst women who have a working-class background, but have achieved middle-class status through marriage or education. Fantasy, in other words, is not only structured through gender and sexuality, but by other social factors as well. In the final section of this chapter, I will try and relate psychological structures to historical change in a reading of Catherine Cookson's *The Golden Straw*.

The family saga as historical narrative

The Golden Straw was written by the veteran and indefatigable author of popular romance, Catherine Cookson. First published in hard-back in 1993, it reached the top ten of the paperback bestseller lists in early 1995. The family saga spans three generations in the period 1879–1941. The working-class heroine is Emily, and Book One, entitled 'Beginnings', opens with the break-up of her marriage. Her employer, Mrs Arkwright, then arranges a divorce. Subsequently, Mrs Arkwright has a heart attack and Emily takes over the running of her hat-making business. Mrs Arkwright dies, leaving the business to Emily, but she becomes ill from exhaustion and is looked after by Mrs Arkwright's doctor, Steve Montane. On his advice, she takes a holiday in France to recover. There she reads a letter he gave her on parting, which reveals his love, but she feels she cannot return it. In a French hotel she meets a married man Paul Anderson Steerman, to whom she is attracted. On returning to London, she agrees to become his mistress and soon finds herself pregnant. She loses the baby after a jealous physical attack by one of Steerman's other mistresses, and is looked after again by Dr Montane. While she is recovering, Steerman returns, drunk, and rapes her, leaving her pregnant with twins. Montane again appears to look after her and insists that Emily marry him. Book One ends with her agreement and realisation she has loved him all along.

'Beginnings' conforms to the formula romance. Emily starts 'out of place' as a result of her first marriage, and ends married to her 'true love'. The narrative tells of the misunderstandings that prevent a direct route to that love. The setting of desire consists of a series of situations in which she is reduced to dependency on Steve Montane; but the affair with Paul Anderson Steerman adds an extra dimension to the fantasy, where a love triangle that includes illicit, adulterous love and pregnancy outside marriage allows the active reader to make a number of different, partial identifications. Unlike the formula romance, Book One does not end with total love. Emily is left with her feelings still confused: 'She really was a stupid woman, because she had been aware of her own attraction to him from the first, yet she had been foolish enough to do everything in her power to stifle it with cheap and terse repartee.'[45] This sense of incompleteness is embodied in the damaging consequences of the rape, which are fully disclosed in the story of the next generation.

The lack of closure at the end of Book One leaves the question of Emily's feminine identity unresolved; and an indication that this is the central element in the narrative is given by the symbolic nature of the hat that gives the book its title. The untrimmed 'Golden Straw' is found in an attic. Emily takes to it and wears it, still untrimmed, to France, where it attracts the attention of Steerman. Gradually, Emily recognises the 'fated' hat as the symbol of her downfall. When she realises Steerman is going to pursue her in London she feels like destroying it: 'It was that hat that had caught his eye. She had a strong urge to pick it up and rip its brim apart' (203). After Steerman rapes her, she does tear off the brim and is only prevented from doing further damage by her maid.

From the perspective of a feminist psychoanalytical critique, the hat is representative of Emily's femininity. The Golden Straw appears after her divorce, at a time when she is 'out of place' in relation to the symbolic order. Untrimmed, the hat is described as 'naked', in a way that points to Emily's own vulnerability. In psychoanalytic terms it is a sign of her castration. That it draws the attention of men further suggests that it marks out her gender difference. Emily's ambivalent attitude to the hat represents her ambivalent attitude to her own feminine identity. At times, she 'performs' her femininity – wearing the hat, she is open about her desires – but the consequences make her justifiably resentful at the way her gender makes her vulnerable to male violence. The partial destruction of the hat at the end of 'Beginnings' is an act of attempted self-mutilation, where Emily turns the violence of the masculine symbolic order on herself. In this light, her marriage to Steve is in some ways a surrender, a subordination of her femininity to the patriarchal (and middle-class) institution of marriage, even as it frees her temporarily from confusion about her identity:

> 'Oh Steve, I've never really known you, but I want to so much. Oh, how I want to.' And now her arms went about him and she stroked the back of his head, while he, his voice thick with emotion, replied, 'You will, my love. You will.' (317)

Whether we take this knowledge as surrender or a fulfilment of identity depends very much on the context in which the text is read. One of the reasons Cookson's novel can be read in the context of the world more easily than a formula romance is because the historical narrative structures the reader's interpretation of the fantasy settings. The key element of contemporary popular romance, the representation of the feminine position within culture, thus becomes a way of telling history through the fragmented and damaged perspective of the feminine position. However, it is important to note that class is as important a factor as gender in the fantasy's structure.[46] The opportunity to get a divorce was, to say the least, unlikely for a working-class woman in the late nineteenth century. Emily's subsequent freedom and upward mobility is offset by an insecurity that leaves her ambivalent about her relationships with middle-class men. Where Montane represents the possibility of security, Steerman (whose name suggests a masculine will to power) represents the danger of exploitation by a more powerful man. Thus, the masculine symbolic order is not a universal fact, but a particular construction of the historical moment.

Book Two of the novel is entitled 'Passions', and Book Three 'Consequences', but the passions of Book Two are equally the consequences of Emily's history as documented in Book One. One of the twins, her daughter Janice, falls in love with Robert Anderson, who turns out to be her half-brother, the son of the man who raped her mother. Janice's symbolic inheritance of Emily's feminine history is represented by the Golden Straw, which she finds in the attic and patches up so as to hide the damage done by her mother. Thus, she repeats her mother's mistake: 'the past was to be brought into the open again, the past that had begun with that hat ... There was something bad about it; it was evil' (384). In the context of a new generation, Emily's role changes and she becomes the parent who is most emphatically against Janice and Robert's relationship. The role of transgressive femininity is passed on to Janice, while the married Emily defends the symbolic order, with its taboo against incest, even more strongly than her husband. Dr Montane's more secure place within respectable, middle-class society operates here to make him more tolerant: 'Professionally he would have had to forbid it; but the man of two worlds that he had become over the years would have closed his eyes to it' (406). Janice agrees to accept the law, but when she and Robert meet again after the collective trauma of the First World War (she is a nurse and he a soldier; thus another formula is incorporated into the historical narrative) they decide to marry and to adopt children. Emily's reaction to their marriage is to destroy the Golden Straw and to refuse to have anything more to do with her daughter. In effect, she effaces the mark of her femininity, denying her own history and choosing to become the staunchest defender of the symbolic order.

However, the consequences, as depicted in Book Three, do not support Emily's choice. The year of 1936 sees the once happy Montane family divided between the increasingly distant Emily and her husband and son, who prefer to associate with the new large, happy, adopted family of Janice and Robert. The novel ends in 1941, with Emily in the Blitz, alone except for her faithful lady's maid, Alice. Naturally, she returns to the hat:

> Lives start from an incident, don't they, Alice? Just an incident. The finding of a hat. Because that was the beginning of it, the finding of the hat up in the attic. Somebody had either been afraid of it or cherished it, because it had been carefully put away. It had a power, had that hat, and I burnt it. (607)

The historical narrative told by the family saga suggests the kinds of interpretative strategies that are needed to understand the formula romance in the context of modernity. While many of the narrative patterns that mark formula romance are contained within *The Golden Straw*, the historical narrative serves to contextualise them, so that the repeated drama that constructs the feminine position in relation to the symbolic order can be understood in relation to the changing nature of modern society. While Emily remains a prisoner of her own history, Janice is able to live a freer life and to combine marriage with her passion for Robert. Even the possibility that their incestuous relationship will be exposed is less of a threat by Book Three because of the more tolerant social conventions of the inter-war period.

The narrative of modernity that *The Golden Straw* tells is, in part at least, an optimistic one. Its story is of a changing relationship between a less exclusive feminine position and a more inclusive and flexible symbolic and social order. The most radical expression of this optimism comes in Book Three with the story of Janice's adopted son, Andrew. Andrew, who is an artist, has a mysterious disease that causes internal bleeding, and that often puts him in a weakened and dependent position akin to that often experienced by the heroines of formula romance. In this, and in the form of the disease, which might be interpreted as a kind of masculine menstruation, Andrew's character invokes a transgression of the binary divide between masculinity and femininity. It is as if, in the third generation, the mark of femininity has been passed to a man. Moreover, Andrew's life appears to repeat that of Emily, but in reverse. He seeks and finds his biological mother in the slums of London, an act whereby he returns to Emily's working-class roots, but this time as part of a virtuous rather than a vicious circle, where the experience of 'real life' improves his art. The adopted and rejected (by Emily) grandson, thus acts to remake her history. Andrew's voyage of self-discovery has another 'incestuous' consequence, a marriage between the son of Janice's twin, Freddie, and Andrew's biological sister, Betty. When Betty goes for Christmas to the Anderson's house, Emily's working-class past meets her prosperous present, even though she is absent.

The narrative is less progressive in the way it stigmatises Emily as an example of inadequate mothering. She becomes the object of a kind of 'matrophobia'.[47] Subsequent generations learn how to avoid her mistakes by rebelling against her, while she moves from marginal figure to becoming the symbol of a decaying set of moral values. Thus, the narrative gives no opportunity for a historical recovery of her social situation. Instead, in Lawler's words, 'working-class desire is constructed as trivial, as petty, as the "politics of envy"'.[48]

Conclusion

In this chapter I have introduced the genre of the romance and concentrated on two of its most popular contemporary forms: the formula romance and the family saga. I have analysed these forms in relation to the concepts of gender and some of the basic concepts of psychoanalytic criticism. Psychoanalytic criticism is an important tool in the study of popular fiction, but it does not provide all the answers. In particular it has a tendency to reduce psychological structures to universal truths. As we shall see in subsequent chapters, it is best used in the context of social and historical cultural criticism. In the case of *The Golden Straw*, despite the representation of the elder Emily, the historical narrative that contextualises the acts of repetition found in the family saga enables the reader to order a series of partial and temporary identifications into a sense of a developing or historical identity. A radical function of the family saga is to put the contradictions of femininity at the centre rather than at the margins of a historical narrative. It might be argued that the same could not be said of the individual formula romance, where there is no narrative progression from one historically situated scene of desire to another. However, once again, this is only true if the texts are separated from the context in which they are read. The serial reading of formula romances, where one is consumed after another, means that it is unrealistic to treat each as separate. Rather, they should be read as one long saga, where the happy ending is constantly rejected for a new, unhappy beginning. Each new beginning then reactivates the search for an explanation of the marginalised feminine position in contemporary society. The experience of reading formula romances might then be understood in the context of an ongoing rather than a circular dynamic between femininity and the symbolic order. The active, critical reader historicises each text, both in terms of other formula romances and in terms of her own life. A properly historical account of formula romance would need to chart the changing relationship between the construction of femininity and the symbolic order in the texts over a period of time. As I discussed above, several recent studies of popular romance have noted the increasing influence of feminism.[49] In this context, popular romance can be understood to mediate one of the most complex social relationships of modern society.

In the next chapter, I look at the more varied possibilities presented by fantasy in science fiction. In Chapter 5 I will return to and develop the uses and criticisms of psychoanalytic criticism in the context of gothic horror; and in Chapter 6 I will look at the importance of concepts of 'race' and cultural difference in the formation of fantasy and stereotypes.

Notes

1   See Terry Lovell, *Consuming Fictions* (London, Verso, 1987); and Laurie Langbauer, *Women and Romance: The Consolations of Gender in the English Novel* (Ithaca and London, Cornell University Press, 1990).

2   For an account of the Family Saga, see Christine Bridgewood, 'Family Romances: The Contemporary Popular Family Saga', in Jean Radford (ed.), *The Progress of Romance: The Politics of Popular Fiction* (London, Routledge & Kegan Paul, 1986), pp. 167–93.

3   Elaine Showalter, *Sexual Anarchy* (London, Bloomsbury, 1991), pp. 76–104.

4   Mikhail M. Bakhtin, *The Dialogic Imagination* (Austin: Texas University Press, 1981), pp. 87–110.

5   *Ibid.*, pp. 89, 111; Margaret Williamson, 'The Greek Romance', in Radford (ed.), *The Progress of Romance*, p. 35.

6   Martin de Riquer, 'Cervantes and the Romances of Chivalry', in Miguel de Cervantes Saavedra, *Don Quixote*, ed. Joseph R. Jones and Kenneth Douglas (New York, W. W. Norton, [1973] 1981), pp. 905–8.

7   Gillian Beer, *The Romance* (London, Methuen, 1970), p. 17.

8   Northrop Frye, *Anatomy of Criticism: Four Essays* (Princeton, Princeton University Press, 1957), pp. 186–7.

9   *Ibid.*, p. 189.

10 *Ibid.*, p. 186.

11 *Ibid.*, pp. 198, 208.

12 For example, *The Return of Caine O'Halloran*, by JoAnn Ross, is in the 'Temptations' series, but is also part of a sub-grouping, 'Lost Loves' (Richmond, Mills & Boon, 1994); and Sarah Westleigh, *A Lady of Independent Means* (Richmond, Mills & Boon, 1995) is in the 'Legacy of Love' series.

13 Saranne Dawson, *In Self Defence* (Richmond, Silhouette, 1994).

14 Mills & Boon Press Release, 'Passions Progress: The Changing Face of Mills and Boon' (Richmond, Mills & Boon, 1995).

15 Penny Jordan, *Valentine's Night* (Richmond, Mills & Boon [first published in 1989] reprinted in the 'Favourites' series in 1995) p. 37

(henceforth page numbers given in text).

16 Charlotte Lamb, 'Red Riding Hood and the Dirty Old Wolf', *Guardian*, 13 September 1982, p. 8; Ann Rosalind Jones, 'Mills and Boon Meets Feminism', in Radford (ed.), *The Progress of Romance*.

17 Giddens argues that the twentieth century has seen a move towards the 'pure relationship' in which two partners seek fulfilment in interpersonal intimacy. Anthony Giddens, *The Transformation of Intimacy: Sexuality, Love and Eroticism in Modern Societies* (Cambridge, Polity Press, 1992).

18 Michèle Barrett and Anne Philips (eds), *Destabilizing Theory: Contemporary Feminist Debates* (Cambridge, Polity Press, 1992), pp. 2–3.

19 Ann Barr Snitow, 'Mass Market Romance: Pornography for Women is Different', in Ann Barr Snitow, Christine Stansell and Sharon Thompson (eds), *Powers of Desire* (London, Virago, 1983), p. 260.

20 Janet Radway, *Reading the Romance: Women, Patriarchy and Popular Literature* (Chapel Hill, North Carolina University Press, 1984), p. 9.

21 *Ibid.*, p. 95.

22 For a concise account of Lacan's idea of the symbolic order see Cora Kaplan, *Sea Changes: Essays on Culture and Feminism* (London, Verso, 1986), p. 73.

23 Jacqueline Rose, *Sexuality in the Field of Vision* (London, Verso, 1986), pp. 64–6.

24 Juliet Mitchell, *Women: The Longest Revolution, Essays in Feminism, Literature and Psychoanalysis* (London, Virago, 1984), p. 250.

25 *Ibid.*, p. 230.

26 J. Laplanche and J.-B. Pontalis, *The Language of Psychoanalysis* (New York, W. W. Norton, 1973), p. 335.

27 Elizabeth Power, *Seed of Vengeance* (Richmond, Mills & Boon, 1990), p. 5. (henceforth page numbers given in text).

28 Snitow, 'Mass Market Romance', p. 248.

29 Tania Modleski, *Loving With a Vengeance: Mass-Produced Fantasies for Women* (London, Methuen, 1982), p. 34.

30 *Ibid.*, p. 48.

31 Radway, *Reading the Romance*, p. 136.

32 Emma Richmond, *A Wayward Love* (Richmond, Mills & Boon, 1994).

33 Snitow, 'Mass Market Romance', p. 256.

34 *Ibid.*, p. 259.

35 Helen Taylor, 'Romantic Readers', in Helen Carr (ed.), *From My Guy to Sci-Fi: Genre and Women's Writing in the Postmodern World* (London, Pandora, 1989), p. 66.

36 Tony Bennett and Jane Woollacott, quoted in Taylor, 'Romantic Readers', p. 66.

37 Kaplan, *Sea Changes*, pp. 127–8.

38 *Ibid.*, p. 131.

39 Mitchell, *Women: The Longest Revolution*, pp. 242–3.

40 *Ibid.*

41 The followers of Jacques Lacan are most critical of the idea of a fixed and stable identity.

42 For a full account of how Freud's essay has been used to understand the incomplete identifications available in fantasy, see Jean Laplanche and Jean-Bertrand Pontalis, 'Fantasy and the Origins of Sexuality', in V. Burgin, J. Donald, and C. Kaplan (eds), *Formations of Fantasy* (London, Routledge, 1989), pp. 5–34. For an outstanding reading of a popular text that employs this approach see '*The Thorn Birds*: Fiction, Fantasy, Femininity', Chapter 6 of Kaplan, *Sea Changes*.

43 Peter Stallybrass and Allon White, *The Poetics and Politics of Transgression* (London, Methuen, 1986), p. 157.

44 Steph Lawler, '"I never felt as though I fitted": Family Romances and the Mother–Daughter Relationship', in Lynne Pearce and Jackie Stacey (eds), *Romance Revisited* (London, Lawrence & Wishart, 1995); Carolyn Steedman, *Landscape for a Good Woman* (London, Virago, 1986).

45 Catherine Cookson, *The Golden Straw* (London, Corgi, 1994), p. 316 (henceforth page numbers given in text).

46 Bridget Fowler suggests that much of Cookson's attraction is 'her positive evaluation of the direct and pithy nature of "lower-class" speech, championing these qualities against the gentility and power of dominant languages'. 'Literature Beyond Modernism: Middlebrow and Popular Romance', in Pearce and Stacey (eds), *Romance Revisited*, p. 97.

47 Lawler, '"I never felt as though I fitted"', p. 270.

48 *Ibid.*, p. 274.

49 In her essay on Colleen McCullough's family saga, *The Thorn Birds* (cited above, n.42), Cora Kaplan suggests that popular romances are sensitive to movements in gender politics. See also Lamb, 'Red Riding Hood'; and Jones, 'Mills and Boon Meets Feminism'.

four
Science fiction

At the root of all science fiction lies the fantasy of alien encounter. The meeting of self with other is perhaps the most fearful, most exciting and most erotic encounter of all. It offers new possibilities of being and the exploration of new alternative realities: unknown lands, strange planets, alien visitations, and the discovery of new dimensions. Science fiction is enormously popular. It accounts for one in ten books sold in Britain; and in the United States the number is as high as one in four.[1] For much of the nineteenth and twentieth centuries the genre has supplied narratives of modernity which attempt to map the shifting cultural boundaries brought about by rapid social change. Recent innovations have gone further and questioned the project of modernity itself. The image of the enlightened scientist has given way to developments like cyberpunk, where the triumph of 'man' over nature has been replaced with a new uncertainty about the boundaries between the human and the inhuman. Cyberpunk's 'cyborg' fictions represent the increasingly complex relationship between humanity and technology.

In this chapter, I explore some of the ways science fiction probes and questions the changing borderlines between humanity and nature, testing the limits of time and space that appear to be normal and natural. In a comparison of two utopias, Edward Bellamy's *Looking Backward: 2000–1887* (1888) and William Morris's *News from Nowhere* (1891), I examine the difference between determinate and conditional futures. I consider the complicated relationship between science fiction and modernist artistic movements, and the ambivalent position of the genre in relation to the divide between high and low culture. However, I devote most of the chapter to the dominant trend in current science fiction: the cyborg fictions that tell us the stories that relate identity to new technologies. Implants, transplants, prostheses, hormonal treatment, cosmetic surgery and genetic engineering have all blurred the boundary between body and machine. My examples are taken from works by J. G. Ballard, Octavia Butler, William Gibson and Marge Piercy.

Contemporary science fiction has many antecedents. The development of the genre can be divided into four main periods: (1) Pre-nineteenth century: travel and fantasy literature, tales of other lands; (2) nineteenth century: reactions to the Industrial Revolution; (3) late nineteenth century to mid-twentieth century: the 'modernist' visions of the Scientific Enlightenment; (4) late twentieth century: the 'postmodern' visions of a post-industrial, often post-holocaust age, including feminist futures and cyberpunk.

Science fiction developed from the romance and fantasy elements of early European travel literature. The encounter with other lands, often in acts of imperial conquest, was a key determinant in the definition of modern European identities. Thomas More's *Utopia* (1516), inspired by voyages to the New World, was an early example of a narrative which attempted to represent an alternative perfect society, implicitly criticising sixteenth-century England. Francis Bacon's *New Atlantis* (1627) was one of the first attempts to imagine a new society brought about by technological innovation. In 1726, Jonathan Swift's *Gulliver's Travels* came closer to modern science fiction in its fantastic worlds of the very small (Lilliput) and the very large (Brobdingnag). The third part of the tale contains one of the first satires of modern science. It describes a flying island, Laputa, on which 'Projectors' engage in ridiculous schemes, for example the extraction of sunbeams from cucumbers. Swift addressed two of the issues that remain central to science fiction narratives: utopian and dystopian (unhappy) alternatives and the opportunities and dangers of scientific experimentation. Darko Suvin writes that utopia is 'not only historically, one of the roots of science fiction, it is also, logically if retroactively, one of its forms'.[2]

Utopia and utopianism

The word 'utopia' is a neologism invented by Thomas More, combining the Greek *eutopia* (a happy place) and *outopia* (no place). This combination neatly defines the distinction between a utopia and utopianism. A utopia is a blueprint of a better society, a happy place, but has the disadvantage of closing down other possible ways of imagining improvement. Utopianism, by contrast, is less specific; it offers no place in particular. Instead, it defines a sense of lack that stimulates a 'desire for a better way of being'.[3] As we have seen in earlier chapters, the sense that 'something is missing'[4] is an important element in all popular fiction. The popular text participates in a transaction with the incomplete sense of self described above in the Introduction. As we saw in the discussion of psychoanalysis in Chapter 3, the subject is never whole; it is always questing for 'an impossible particular object'.[5] That quest is the impulse for science fiction; but hope has its foundation in lack of hope, the desire for utopia has its beginning in despair or dystopia.

Two classic utopian narratives that explored the disruptive impact of social change on notions of identity are Edward Bellamy's *Looking Backward: 2000–1887* and William Morris's *News from Nowhere*. The latter was a response to the former's version of socialism, and the two texts represent contrasting perspectives on the Victorian ideal of progress. They are examples of two different types of science fiction, representing what we might call determinate and conditional futures respectively. Bellamy's determinate future can be seen as following the Scientific Enlightenment, discussed below. He saw technological progress as the solution to humanity's problems. Unable to marry because persistent labour disputes are delaying the completion of his matrimonial home, the hero of *Looking Backward*, Julian West, falls asleep in the nineteenth century and wakes up in the year 2000 when the labour 'problem' has been solved by machinery and the organisation of work along military lines. In the utopian future, West falls in love with his fiancée's great-granddaughter. She, it turns out, has already fallen in love with him after reading her great-grandmother's love letters. Thus, desires denied in the past are fulfilled in a future utopia. The narrative secures the boundaries of a self that had felt insecure, rather than questioning the boundaries themselves. It corresponds to what is sometimes called a modernist 'grand narrative': a narrative that charts progress towards a clear and certain goal.

By contrast, in *News from Nowhere*, William Morris offers a possible rather than a definite future. In his alternative version of a socialist utopia happiness is achieved through fulfilling work, not by its regulation. Elsewhere, Morris wrote: 'I believe that the ideal of the future does not point to the lessening of men's energy by the reduction of labour to a minimum, but rather to the reduction of pain in labour to a minimum, so small that it will cease to be pain'.[6] However, self-fulfilment is not available to Morris's hero, William Guest. He is only a temporary visitor to the future and cannot participate fully in its pleasures. Instead, he feels a sense of lack: he is 'stripped bare of every habitual thought and way of acting'.[7] While a potential better place is suggested, it is inaccessible: 'nowhere'. The gap between desire and satisfaction persists. At the end of the novel, the future and the object of his desire fade away: 'I turned to Ellen, and she *did* seem to recognise me for an instant; but her bright face turned sad directly, and she shook her head with a mournful look, and the next moment all consciousness of my presence had faded from her face.'[8] In contrast to Bellamy's utopia, Morris's utopianism represents the boundaries of the self as uncertain. They are not clearly fixed in time and space.

The determinate future offered in *Looking Backward* explores the possibilities of extrapolating the technology of the present. This can portend dystopia as well as utopia.[9] The conditional future offered in *News from Nowhere* explores the contradictions of the present, pursuing their complexity, and offers a future that is conditional or possible rather than a predetermined outcome. As the last sentence of Morris's novel has it: 'if others can see it as I have seen it, then it may be called a vision rather than a dream' (401). Narratives of conditional futures resist technological determination and concentrate more on the complex interaction of social relations and technological change.

Science fiction, modernism, mass culture

As with detective fiction, it was not until the mid-nineteenth century that science fiction assumed its contemporary guise. The genre started to become popular with the works of Jules Verne in France, for example *Voyage to the Centre of the Earth* (1864) and *Twenty Thousand Leagues Under the Sea* (1869), and in England with H. G. Wells, *The Time Machine* (1895), *The War of the Worlds* (1898) and *The First Men in the Moon* (1901). Science fiction from the latter half of the nineteenth century to the mid-twentieth century was informed by what Patrick Parrinder has called the 'Scientific Enlightenment': 'Modern scientific materialism, like the eighteenth-century Enlightenment, defined the good society as one which was organised on rational lines, free of the superstitions and religious dogmas of the past.'[10] The 'golden age' of 'Enlightenment' science fiction was the 1930s and 1940s. Prominent authors of the period, writers like Isaac Asimov and Robert Heinlein, were driven by this philosophy, which corresponds to one of the definitions of modernism – the active and enthusiastic participation in the modern age and modern ideas – discussed in the Introduction.

Fredric Jameson relates the emergence of science fiction in the second half of the nineteenth century to a shift in 'our relationship to historical time'.[11] Novels of the future succeed the historical novels of the early nineteenth century: 'SF as a form … now registers some nascent sense of the future, and does so in the space on which a sense of the past had once been inscribed.'[12] For Jameson, then, science fiction is about the difficulty of coming to terms with the present. It dramatises our 'incapacity to imagine the future', and as such is 'a contemplation of our own absolute limits'.[13] Its narratives perform what Darko Suvin describes as 'cognitive estrangement':[14] the ability to 'defamiliarise' the present (and implicitly to criticise it) through the representation of an other world.

Like all popular fiction, science fiction has a relationship with high culture that establishes its separate, but related, history as a genre.[15] Jules Verne's novels were published at the same time as the emergence of modernist fiction and poetry in France: for example, the novels of Gustave Flaubert (1821–80) and the poetry of Charles Baudelaire (1821–67). In England, H. G. Wells published his first novels in the 1890s when aesthetes like Oscar Wilde and novelists like Joseph Conrad pioneered modernist traits. The stylistic traits of modernism were the abandonment of realism; innovation in form; a distinction between the work of art and everyday life; and self-referentiality. The modernist work of art draws attention to its own conditions of production. In literature, for example, this might mean a self-consciousness about language, in painting about the materials involved – the canvas and the paint itself.

The relationship between modernism and science fiction is complicated by modernism's inauguration of a divide between high culture, which moves towards elitist, difficult art, and mass culture, which would include popular fiction. The diversity of different modernisms also makes it difficult to generalise about modernism as a whole. However, it is possible to see some connections between modernism's experimental nature and early science fiction's enthusiasm for technical innovation as the path to the future. Modernist movements like futurism and constructivism were clearly motivated by similar concerns, while surrealism's interest in dreams and the unconscious has its counterpart in many science fiction stories. The cultural historian Stephen Kern sees a clear causal connection between new technologies (railways, telegraph, steamships, telephone, radio, cinema) and modernist art. According to Kern, the increasing speed of transport and communication meant that the world shrank and became contemporaneous.[16] In other words, multiple points of communication and vision could be achieved at the same time. This is expressed in Delauney's picture of the Eiffel Tower (1911), which shows a fragmented vision, as if it is being viewed from different places at the same time. To achieve a comparable affect, James Joyce's *Ulysses* (1922) and Virginia Woolf's *Mrs Dalloway* (1925) describe the events of a single day. It can be argued that science fiction was the popular counterpart to modernism's enthusiasm for new possibilities in perception. While the scientist as hero popularises a version of creative genius comparable to the mythic status of the modernist artist as ahead of her or his time.

An example of this kind of science fiction is Isaac Asimov's *Foundation* trilogy (1949–1953). A small group of scientists manage to predict the collapse of their interplanetary civilisation, the Empire. They set up a small, secret, isolated community, which can survive the catastrophe and guide the fragments towards a new order. The novels exemplify the idea of an advanced, elite group with specialist, superior knowledge. They suggest history conforms to a logical pattern that can be understood and controlled. However, the anti-democratic, authoritarian implications of what came to be called 'hard' science fiction – where the white-coated scientist had sole control of an array of gleaming technology – became increasingly subject to criticism after the Second World War.

The post-war period saw a gradual disillusion with the enthusiasms of the Scientific Enlightenment, fed by fears of nuclear war and an increasing awareness of the role of technology in the destruction of the environment. In the 1960s an earlier generation of writers was confronted by the 'New Wave'. The movement began in Britain with writers like J. G. Ballard, Brian Aldiss and Michael Moorcock, but soon spread to the United States. The New Wave was characterised by a more critical, even apocalyptic, approach to science and technological innovation. Feminist science fiction has been a part of the genre's history since Mary Shelley's *Frankenstein* (1818). Charlotte Perkins Gilman's *Herland* (1915) was both a feminist utopia and a satire on male claims to rationality. In the 1960s and 1970s, feminist novels by writers like Ursula Le Guin, Joanna Russ and Marge Piercy were, in common with the resurgent women's movement, directly critical of contemporary gender relations.[17] The 1980s saw something of a reaction to the 'eco-feminist' utopias of Le Guin and Piercy with the much-publicised launch of cyberpunk, led by William Gibson and Bruce Sterling. The 1990s have seen something of an integration of the various strands, with Piercy writing her own cyberpunk novel, *Body of Glass*. These developments have been described as postmodern science fiction.

Postmodern science fiction

We have already encountered the idea of the postmodern in previous chapters. If modernism is a rather general term for a number of different artistic movements that took off between the middle of the nineteenth century and the middle of the twentieth, then postmodernism is even more difficult to define.[18] Several definitions are relevant to a discussion of contemporary science fiction: (1) a cultural epoch, already described in Chapter 1, which comes after modernism and is sometimes called the information age or the society of the spectacle; (2) the cultural logic of late-twentieth-century capitalism, with its global impact;[19] (3) a (philosophical) 'condition', a suspicion of the grand, rational, progressive narratives of modernity;[20] (4) an aesthetic sensibility, the formal characteristics of new movements in art, architecture and literature;[21] (5) a new political pluralism, the decline of the middle-class, masculine, Eurocentric, rational subject and the growth of feminist, lesbian and gay and other marginalised voices.[22]

Postmodern science fiction has emerged at the end of the twentieth century in the wake of the Scientific Enlightenment. This can be seen as a shift in cultural hegemony, as described in Chapter 1. Modernism and postmodernism might be regarded as 'cultural dominants'. The characteristics of each are not necessarily present or absent in particular epochs; rather, modernist formal characteristics were more dominant from the mid-nineteenth century to the mid-twentieth, while postmodernist forms have been dominant in the late twentieth century.[23] Thus, while *News from Nowhere*, published in 1891, demonstrates what we might now describe as a postmodern uncertainty about the future, this uncertainty was less common then, but has become more common in science fiction since the 1960s.

This shift in cultural hegemony has been the product of a number of social changes. The 'globalisation' of the world's economy, the growth in population movements, and the speed and quantity of information exchanges have been fertile ground for science fictions. In her essay 'A Manifesto for Cyborgs', Donna Haraway outlines these developments as paving the way for two possible futures: a terrifying vision of social control or new, emancipatory possibilities:

> From one perspective, a cyborg world is about the final imposition of a grid of control on the planet, about the final abdication embodied in the Star Wars apocalypse waged in the name of defence, about the final appropriation of women's bodies in a masculinist orgy of war. From another perspective, a cyborg world might be about lived social and bodily realities in which people are not afraid of their joint kinship with animals and machines, not afraid of permanently partial identities and contradictory standpoints.[24]

This opposition takes us back to the dialectic between determinate and conditional futures. Where a determinate future promises fixed and controlled identities, an alternative, and perhaps equally frightening, prospect is the lack of any unified identity at all. Despite the fact that cyborgs are frequently cited as a postmodern phenomenon, cyborg metaphors have appeared regularly in one form or another at moments of social crisis from the Industrial Revolution to the present day.[25] Perhaps the most influential text of the industrial age to take up the possibilities and dangers of scientific innovation was

Mary Shelley's *Frankenstein*, where the scientist's (although we would now call Frankenstein a scientist, the word itself was not coined until 1840) creation has equal capacity for good or evil. As we will see, this remains the basic plot of numerous science fictions. From Shelley's monster to Thomas Carlyle's image of the shuttle that 'drops from fingers of the weaver, and falls into iron fingers that ply it faster', to Marx's description of the proletariat as 'an appendage of the machine',[26] cyborg fictions have mediated the evolving relationship between humanity and technology. Rita Felski has found examples of male cyborgs during the last *fin de siècle* in the work of Rathchilde. Andreas Huyssen has written of the robot's use as a figure for feminised mass culture in Fritz Lang's film *Metropolis* (1927).[27]

In the 1990s, most cyborg fictions have been reactionary rather than revolutionary. At the end of the twentieth century, the absence of socialist alternatives has seen a conservative version of the techno-logical fix run rampant. The unseen hand of the free market is advocated as the inhuman machinery that will resolve all economic problems. A catalogue of cyberconcepts – the information super-highway, the Internet, artificial intelligence, virtual reality, interactive programs, cyberspace, cybersex – function as happy endings to the problems that an untrammelled capitalism is building up for the twenty-first century. They are the cheerful recourse of films like *Mission Impossible* (1996) or thrillers like Tom Clancy's *Debt of Honour* (1995), where the search always provides an instant answer, the tech-nology always works and the smart weapon always hits its target. The science fictions of political discourse are Newt Gingrich's idea of universal access to the Internet, Bill Clinton's slogan 'a computer in every classroom', or Al Gore's global network of fibre-optic cables as the solution to economic development.[28]

In an increasingly uncertain world, these conservative visions offer the hope that, after all, progress and human happiness are not mutually exclusive. They function because they have a powerful utopian impetus and, despite their limitations, even the most facile provide an imaginative space in which new forms of consciousness can be explored. But, like all popular fictions, they would not work if they did not first arouse the anxieties they are designed to quell. To be successful, each must provide the means through which a workable, coherent identity can be put together in the context of social and economic forces that fragment the rational self.

By contrast, progressive cyborg fictions problematise the question of identity. They give precedence neither to inhuman machinery, nor to a conservative version of human nature. Instead, they explore the transformations of what it means to be human. The impact of globalisation is an important factor here. In the latter half of the twentieth century the speed of global interactions, both human and economic, has been unprecedented. This has had real cultural effects. Global population movements and information networks have created a new environment in which the sense of self is radically different to earlier phases of capitalism. The levels of dislocation and alienation currently experienced by large numbers of people mean that identity has become a focus for popular culture. Cyborg fictions explore the kinds of identities needed to live in the new world. They attempt to think through the problem of the self in a context where the cultural boundaries are constantly shifting.

A pioneering example of a cyborg fiction is J. G. Ballard's novel *Crash* (1975). Ballard was a member of the British new wave of science fiction, and *Crash* has been described as 'the *de facto* founding manifesto of postmodern SF'.[29] Ballard himself describes it as 'the first pornographic novel based on technology'. Yet he makes it clear that his aim is political and 'cautionary' rather than sensational: 'In a sense, pornography is the most political of form of fiction, dealing with how we use and exploit each other, in the most urgent and ruthless way.'[30] The reason the text has fascinated is that it blurs the boundaries of sexual desire, so that the horrific interpenetration of the human body and the car in a motorway crash becomes the object of perverse interest:

> mechanisms of passenger ejection, the geometry of kneecap and hip-joint injuries, deformation of passenger compartments in head-on and rear-end collisions, injuries sustained in accidents at roundabouts, at trunk-road intersections, at the junctions between access roads and motorway intersections, the telescoping mechanisms of car-bodies in front-end collisions, abrasive injuries formed in roll-overs, the amputation of limbs by roof assemblies and door sills during roll-over, facial injuries caused by dashboard and window trim, scalp and cranial injuries caused by rear view mirrors and sunvisors, whiplash injuries in rear-end collisions, first and second-degree burns in accidents involving the rupture and detonation of fuel tanks.[31]

This passage combines a list of technical features which could come from a car manual, but it also contains some of the excitement inspired by a car advertisement with its inventory of 'features'. The introduction of the body into the passage makes explicit the already implicit erotic charge contained in the marketing of technology in a consumer society. The way the body is introduced, as a list of injuries inflicted by the 'features', creates a horrific reflection on the power of the machine to damage as well as enhance human life. The text suggests that the power to control and do harm is as much part of the pleasure of the car as the aesthetics of body parts and speed.

This revelation signals a world in which the modernist dream of solving social problems through technology no longer holds. One of the protagonists, Vaughan, is a scientist who lost his faith in the utopia of the Scientific Enlightenment: 'Literate, ambitious and adept at self-publicity, he was saved from being no more than a pushy careerist with a PhD. by a strain of naive idealism, his strange vision of the automobile and its real role in our lives.'[32] This 'strange vision' is replaced after a motorcycle accident by an obsession with car crashes. The physical relationship between humanity and cars becomes a metaphor for his disillusion with technological utopianism. One powerful image in *Crash* is the steadily increasing amount of traffic on the roads, something that signifies the apparently unstoppable movement towards urbanisation and the conquest of nature. This image is contrasted, in the later parts of the text, with moments of eerie silence, when the roads are deserted: moments that seem to prefigure an apocalyptic end to modern civilisation.

In *Crash*, images of apocalypse put into question the foundational truths and realities that we take for granted. According to Jean Baudrillard, in the postmodern world reality has been replaced with simulation: 'paradoxically, it is the real which has become our true utopia – but a utopia that is no longer a possibility, a utopia we can do no more than dream about, like a lost object'.[33] Baudrillard argues that '*Crash* is the first great novel of the universe of simulation, the world that we will be dealing with from now on: a non-symbolic universe but one which, by a kind of reversal of its mass-mediated substance (neon, concrete, cars, mechanical eroticism) seems truly saturated with an intense initiatory power.'[34] In this extreme version of postmodernism there is no foundational truth or reality and, as a consequence, none of the boundaries or limits that would define those states. Baudrillard sees in *Crash* the possibilities of a postmodern sexuality, one that is utopian, desiring rather than a vision of utopia: 'a body with neither organs nor organ pleasures, entirely dominated by gash marks, excisions, and technical scars – all under the gleaming sign of a sensuality that is without referentiality and without limits.'[35]

Unsurprisingly, not everyone has accepted this version. Baudrillard has been criticised for representing the body as an object rather than a subject. Vivian Sobchack accuses him of feminising the 'techno-body as full of orifices and without organs'.[36] Her article, 'Baudrillard's Obscenity', demonstrates that while the absence of limits or boundaries may appear liberating, it may be, as with the postmodernist criticism discussed in Chapter 1, that a passion for the utopian possibilities of the text obscures the ideological limitations of the critique. As Roger Luckhurst has argued, in postmodern science fiction the transgression of boundaries becomes the focus of the text, but this does not mean that the boundaries themselves become any less important.[37] One way in which recent science fiction has played with cultural boundaries has been through an exploration of the boundaries of 'race' and gender. Feminist writers have explored the possibility of going beyond the usually accepted definitions of masculinity and femininity. Science fiction is peculiarly well suited to this kind of exploration because of the imaginative possibilities of the genre. Perhaps the best-known example of an eco-feminist narrative is Marge Piercy's *Woman on the Edge of Time* (1976). The novel provides several interpretations for the alternative states of reality it projects. Connie Ramos, a Hispanic American, has been forcibly confined to a mental asylum, so one explanation for her narrative is that she is mentally ill and her experiences are delusions. But another explanation is that she is able to see beyond the limitations of the world which has confined her to better or, in one case, worse alternatives. There are sufficient similarities between the people Connie has known in her life and in the alternative societies she visits to encourage the reader to question how far the utopian and dystopian futures represented are hallucinations and how far realistic possibilities.

In one future, Connie visits Mattapoiset, an ecologically balanced community where women have given up bearing children and babies are gestated in machines. Child care is performed by three parents, and men as well as women are able to breast-feed. Connie is initially shocked and repelled by this apparent perversion of nature. However, when she compares the tolerance and equality with the treatment she has received as a Hispanic woman in twentieth-century America, the alternative begins to look more attractive. Whereas Connie has been denied a place in contemporary society because of a combination of poverty, gender and ethnicity, Mattapoiset has taken the best of several cultures, allows individual freedom and expression and has arranged a system of reproduction and child-rearing that makes for equality between men and women. The shock of the encounter with an alternative reality where the boundaries of gender have been redrawn provokes a sense of the possibilities of alternative ways of being.

One of the most productive scenarios for creating this kind of 'cognitive estrangement' is alien contact. The encounter with a life form from another planet produces a conflict, sometimes physical but always cultural, which forces a reflection on the limits of human culture. The passage below is an example of a first encounter with an alien from Octavia Butler's *Xenogenesis* (1987). Butler's novel undermines the foundations of human experience because it is set, like much post-war science fiction, after a nuclear holocaust. It explores the consequent loss in belief in humanity's ability to have a future. The effect of this is to question the reader's faith in the values usually held to be 'humanist'. The humans that remain show themselves to be incapable of rational co-operation, and the only realistic future for humanity appears to be to interbreed with the aliens who have rescued them from Earth. This can be seen as a metaphor for cultural exchanges that transform identity.

'When you can,' he said, 'come closer and look at me. I've had humans believe they saw human sensory organs on my head – and then get angry with me when they realized they were wrong.'

'I can't,' she whispered, though now she wanted to. Could she have been so wrong, so deceived by her own eyes?

'You will,' he said. 'My sensory organs aren't dangerous to you. You'll have to get used to them.'

'No!'

The tentacles were elastic. At her shout, some of them lengthened, stretching towards her. She imagined big slowly writhing, dying night crawlers stretched along the sidewalk after a rain. She imagined small, tentacled sea slugs – nudibranchs – grown impossibly to human size and shape, and, obscenely, sounding more like a human being than some humans. Yet she needed to hear him speak. Silent, he was utterly alien.[38]

Contact with an alien provokes feelings of horror of the unfamiliar, which Butler goes on to represent in relation to knowledge and ignorance, understanding and misunderstanding, power and power-lessness. The alien encounter thus becomes a metaphor for cultural conflict in contemporary society. Estrangement can, and in the novel does, lead to violence, but it can also open up the possibility of other ways of thinking and being. The consequent change in what it means to be human can be compared with the redrawing of boundaries explored in *Crash*. The novels of both Ballard and Butler are anti-foundationalist: they question the norms and foundations we rely on to make sense of the world.

Butler's novels include graphic descriptions of sexual relations with the, initially repugnant, aliens. The representation of new and strange sexual encounters is one of the pleasures of science fiction. In Gwyneth Jones's novel *North Wind* (1994) the representation of sex with an alien defamiliarises the gendered roles of feminine passivity and masculine activity to break down gendered boundaries: 'Sid forgot entirely that she was not a human woman. His prick slid inside a moist cleft that did nothing to dispel the illusion … and was *met* there, by something that clasped it with a wild grip, so terrifying and delightful he almost died.'[39]

Fantastic new experiences delight in science fiction, multiplying the possibilities of pleasure; but the new pluralism suggested by postmodernism is often difficult to reconcile with the twentieth century's tendency towards globalisation and standardisation. Some of the contradictions of the new constellation are explored in a science fiction movement which can be traced back to writers like Philip K. Dick who were writing in the 1960s,[40] but which emerged fully in the 1980s: cyberpunk. Fredric Jameson has described cyberpunk as 'a new type of science fiction … which is fully as much an expression of transnational corporate realities as it is of global paranoia itself'.[41] The movement is true to its name in its skilful self-promotion. It extrapolates from the cut-throat consumer society of the 1980s and that decade's increasing divide between rich and poor. The fictional world of the best-known proponent of cyberpunk, William Gibson, describes a recognisable geo-political system, characterised by weak nation-states and dominant transnationals. Its inequalities reflect the long-term tendencies of the global economy predicted by David Harvey: 'heightened international and inter-regional competition, with the least advantaged countries and regions suffering the severest conse-quences'.[42] Yet, although inspired by the development of new tech-nologies like virtual reality, personal computers and the Internet, Gibson's narratives focus as much on the social contradictions thrown up by technology as the machinery itself. On the one hand, cyberpunk is resolutely posthumanist. It delights in the transformation of what is meant by being human: Gibson's characters employ genetic engineer-ing, drugs and advanced forms of surgery to transform themselves. On the other hand, the cyberworld is peopled with the descendants of post-war countercultures, who represent a persistent romanticism.

Gibson's style is influenced by hard-boiled detective fiction in the tradition of Raymond Chandler.[43] A consequence is that the most marked aspect of his world is a sense of lack or unfulfilled potential. His novels and short stories explore the forms of hybrid, 'cyber' consciousness that arise from the employment of new technologies as a means of domination. His most famous contribution to the genre is the idea of 'jacking in'. Using a plug into their central nervous system, his characters are able to connect directly to the 'matrix' (an enhanced form of the Internet) and explore a virtual world of infor-mation, described as 'A graphic representation of data abstracted from the banks of every computer in the human system. Unthinkable complexity. Lines of light ranged in the nonspace of the mind, clusters and constellations of data. Like city lights, receding ...'[44] The matrix acts as a metaphor for the kinds of cultural collisions and re-inventions of the self made possible by new technologies.

Some of Gibson's best writing is in his shorter fiction. A character-istic example is 'The Winter Market' (1986), a short story in his collection *Burning Chrome*. On the first page, we are given an aestheti-cised description of a futuristic cityscape: 'False Creek water. City lights, that same gray bowl of sky smaller now, illuminated by neon and mercury-vapor arcs. And it was snowing, big flakes but not many, and when they touched black water, they were gone, no trace at all.'[45] The snow acts as a romantic metaphor for the sense of loss experienced by the narrator. The next few sentences introduce the other side of the dialectic the story explores, universal commodi-fication: 'I was wearing Japanese shoes, new and expensive, glove-leather Ginza monkey boots with rubber-capped toes.'

The story is set in the typical cyberpunk world, run by huge transnationals, where life for most people is reduced to an impoverished existence and for whom the only escape is the mass entertainment provided by virtual reality. The contradiction between the romance of hope and the degradation of everyday life is expressed almost humorously in the mysterious words of the first page: 'Because she was dead, and I'd let her go. Because, now, she was immortal, and I'd helped her get that way. And because I knew she'd phone me, in the morning' (140). The 'she' of this passage is Lise, a hybrid creature, supported by a polycarbon exoskeleton that allows her to move despite a wasting disease. As a robot, Lise belongs to an earlier era of science fiction. Her other more up-to-date talents are not revealed until Casey takes her home. Lise's unconscious creates the kind of raw material which, through 'jacking in', can be recorded and used as mass-market entertainment. Casey is a skilled editor of the kind of dreams she can produce. He fashions the raw material into a saleable commodity: 'The stuff we get out to the consumer, you see, has been structured, balanced, turned into art' (147). Lise's dreams turn out to be the most powerful he has ever encountered. The resulting product is a huge success because Lise's unconscious speaks to the unconscious dreams and hopes of her audience. Despite, or perhaps because of, her physical disability she feels the sense of lack felt by the millions who are excluded in Gibson's futuristic world: 'She's big because she was what they are, only more so. She knew Man. No dreams, no hope' (158).

The narrative works over some of the aesthetic binaries that characterise discussions of modernism and postmodernism: for example, the modernist divide between high and low cultures. Lise's mass-market talents are compared to the modernist artist, Rubin. His raw material is *gomi*, the Japanese word for rubbish: we are told that islands have been built out of *gomi* in Tokyo bay. In Rubin's studio, 'One box is filled with the severed heads of hundreds of Barbie dolls, another with armored industrial safety gauntlets that look like space suit gloves' (150). Rubin makes his art from physical detritus, while Casey makes his with the waste products of people's minds. For Rubin, 'everything he drags home must have been new and shiny once, must have meant something, however briefly, to someone' (161). The suggestion is that Lise's mind contains similar waste; she and it are cast-offs of a society that is extraordinarily wasteful, both of goods and people. But, where Rubin's art-works are displayed in galleries, Casey's editions of Lise's dreams become mass-produced commodities. Modernism's elitism is transformed into a direct relationship with the desires of mass society. Her hunger becomes not just her own. It now belongs to all the dispossessed: 'Those kids back down the Market, warming their butts around the fires and wondering if they'll find someplace to sleep tonight, they believe it' (158).

In the story, Lise escapes from the limitations of her physical existence by downloading her mind into a computer: 'she'd merged with the net, crossed over for good' (140). In one way, this can be seen as a utopian act. It frees her mind from her body, so that she becomes pure consciousness. Her escape is a metaphor for a post-modern utopia, where the self can be 'translated' into something new through any number of different media 'codes'. However, the act also imposes new limitations, in that she becomes part of a machine. The ability to construct new selves is shown to be controlled and manipulated by the inhuman forces of the entertainment industry. Thus, one way of reading the story is to see the relationship between Lise and Casey as a metaphor for the workings of mass culture, which must tap into the unconscious desires and hopes of its audience, but then represents those drives in a structured way that distracts rather than threatens the social order. For example, Julian Stallabrass sees the video game (the form that comes closest to Gibson's vision of Lise's products) as overwhelming the agency of the player: it is a 'phantasmagoric experience of total immersion'.[46] Stallabrass suggests that computer games simply reflect the economics of late capitalism: 'The operation of desire in these games is simply an acute form of the normal procedure of the market in a fashion-driven culture: there is always a sense of something beyond the present experience, of some unused potential within the machine, of a task never quite finished, of a realism not quite complete.'[47]

However, Stallabrass's image of 'immersion' is symptomatic of the tendency in negative theories of mass culture to conceive of the subject as powerless in the face of a great wave of pap. It denies the crucial role of fantasy in the formation of a critical subjectivity, where, as described in Chapter 3, the active 'reader's' needs and desires are projected onto the setting provided by the popular text. The 'text' of a computer game permits the player to project a self or selves who participate in the game. This fantasy is the basis for many cyberpunk narratives. In Gibson's prose, the use of 'cutting' or 'montage', where the narrative breaks and moves to another time or perspective, is akin to moving on to a new level in the computer game, which then represents the possibility of new fantastic experiences. In 'The Winter Market', it also allows a critical approach to the kinds of transaction that occur between the reader and contemporary popular texts. The dialectic then becomes a question of how far the possible selves are predetermined by the text as mechanism and how far a product of a reading that is itself productive.

One criticism that has been made of cyberpunk is that it is literature for boys,[48] and certainly 'The Winter Market' is structured as a kind of masculine romance, where Lise is the object of desire for the narrator. Casey and she first meet at a party, where he sees her as a sexual threat: '…she found me again. Came after me two hours later, weaving through the bodies and junk with that terrible grace programmed into the exoskeleton' (144). Despite his initial recoil, she insists that they go back to his flat, where they engage in a kind of sex-act through a computer: 'we jacked straight across'; and it is through this act that Casey becomes aware of the power of Lise's desires. These are expressed in sexually charged imagery:

> There's a segment on *King's of Sleep*; it's like you're on a motorcycle at midnight, no lights but somehow you don't need them, blasting along a cliff-high stretch of coast highway, so fast that you hang there in a cone of silence, the bike's thunder lost behind you …
> … What I got was the big daddy version of that, raw rush, the king hell killer uncut real thing, exploding eight ways from Sunday into a void that stank of poverty and lovelessness and obscurity. (148)

Thus, conventional codes of masculinity and femininity structure the relationship between Casey and Lise. Lise has a feminine access to the popular unconscious, but it is Casey's masculine job to structure and control the raw material she supplies. Moreover, despite his first reaction to her, Lise becomes the object of his desire and life. He begins to fear her loss: 'suddenly it hit me that it really was over, that I was done with Lise, and that now she'd be sucked off to Hollywood as inexorably as if she'd poked her toe into a black hole, drawn down by the unthinkable gravitic tug of Big Money' (160). As much as for the consumers of her dreams, Casey finds Lise gives his life a meaning it wouldn't otherwise have. He begins to see his flat as anonymous: 'there are moments when I see that anyone could be

living there, could own those things, and it all seems sort of interchangeable, my life and yours, my life and anybody's' (161). The
gender politics of masculine control are further enhanced by the
narrative, which is told by one man, Casey, to another, Rubin. Lise
becomes an object that is exchanged between men.

Ultimately, however, both Lise and Casey are shown to be trapped.
As a program she cannot escape from the dictates of the industry
she has sold herself to. She becomes more dependent on it. But
Casey is also caught in a continuing relationship governed by the
laws of market capitalism:

> you have to edit her next release. Which will almost certainly be soon,
> because she needs money bad. She's taking up a lot of ROM on some
> corporate mainframe, and her share of *Kings* won't come close to paying
> for what they had to do to put her there. And you're her editor Casey, I
> mean, who else? (166)

This brings us back to the original conceit of an immortal being who
is as ordinary and as strange as a morning phone call. At the end
of the short story, Casey is left, like the reader, waiting for a voice
of uncertain status. For Lise and Casey, artist and editor, the future
holds no clear borderline between creativity and the machine. Their
future selves will both be, to different degrees, posthuman cyberselves.
Thus, Gibson's short story maintains the element of ambivalence that
is essential to a creative encounter with the future, exploring the new
boundary positions that are emerging. The transformative metaphor
of the cyborg permits a different, more complex understanding of
the relationship between reader and text than that provided by earlier
theories of mass culture. In 'The Winter Market' the narrative un-
settles the opposition between human agency and the dehumanising
effects of the culture industry. Lise's fate provokes a reflection on the
reader's imaginative relationship with the popular text.[49] Gibson's
science fiction alternates between the transcendent utopian freedom
of the matrix and the banal ordinariness of everyday life. Even
Stallabrass's pessimistic (and somewhat mechanical) view of the
relationship between computer games and market economics suggests something of the utopian nature of fantasy, which, as we have
seen, must fill the gap created by 'unused potential'.

While much of Gibson's fiction is indeed structured around a
masculinist desire, as is shown by our next example, Marge Piercy's

Body of Glass,[50] this is not intrinsic to the form. *Body of Glass* is also set in a cyberpunk world, but the shifting boundaries of that world are used to explore, amongst other cultural borders, the limits and definitions of gender. In her acknowledgements, Piercy recognises the influence of Donna Haraway's essay, 'A Manifesto for Cyborgs'. Haraway argues that the boundaries between human and animal and human and machine were always and will always be fictional because our interaction with technology will always change what it means to be human. Central to Haraway's argument is the Marxist idea that what is important about machines is the way they fit into social organisation. It is not the technology itself but the way the machines relate to and re-create relations between people. This is one of the themes of *Body of Glass*.

The novel alternates two narratives, one historical and one of the future; both are concerned with boundaries. A historical narrative about seventeenth-century Prague tells the story of the Golem, a giant made out of clay by the Rabbi Judah Loew to protect the inhabitants of the Jewish ghetto. The parallel story of the twenty-first century also concerns a ghetto, Tikva. Tikva exists at a time when transnational corporations rule most of the globe, leaving the parts they do not need to administer to violence, poverty and anarchy. In Gibson's stories these areas are called the 'sprawl'. Piercy calls them the 'glop'. The stories of the Prague ghetto and Tikva tell of the boundaries that define a particular culture against the threatening world beyond. The ghetto has only its wall and the ingenuity of its rabbi. Tikva survives as an independent 'free town' by selling its innovative high-tech products to the corporations and protecting itself from the pollution and radiation that exist beyond its limits. Both Tikva and the ghetto are prisons as well as protected zones. The protection they afford is a reminder of the limits put on the lives of their inhabitants. Those limits are defined by the dominant power outside the ghetto: in Prague the Christian state, for Tikva the hegemony of the transnationals. However, while in the seventeenth century the boundaries are fairly fixed, in the twenty-first they have become more fluid, defined by the shifting space of the glop and the possibility of jacking in and moving through cyberspace. In each case, the ghetto is a metaphor for the vulnerability as well as the creativity of minority cultures that allow the possibility of different kinds of *self*-determination.

When the borders of Tikva are threatened, the scientist Avram creates a modern-day Golem, Yod. Yod is part machine, part genetically engineered cyborg and a strange hybrid of masculine and feminine attributes. His predecessors, starting with Alef (the first letter of the Hebrew alphabet; Yod is the tenth) all turned violent and had to be destroyed. Yod has been half-programmed by a woman, and has a more balanced personality. He is a constructed hybrid self, created, like the Golem, to police boundaries, but is not himself of the place he protects or the place that threatens. As a cyborg he has no essential identity. He is the border. Haraway writes of the relationship between bodies and machines as a 'border war'.[51] Science fiction, speculative fiction and fantasy are useful modes in this context because their subject is the point at which the boundaries between what is 'real' and what is possible are drawn (201). Cyborg fictions are ways of theorising and narrating these boundaries. The consequence is monster stories: 'Monsters have always defined the limits of community in Western imaginations' (180). Cyborgs are the monsters that populate the margins of discourse: 'These boundary creatures are, literally, monsters, a word that shares more than its root with the word to *demonstrate*. Monsters signify' (2). At this point, analysis of the narrative, of the fiction, becomes as important as the discovery of the facts, which have themselves been constituted as a story. Science, as the 'most respectable legitimator of new realities' (78), can provide the narratives society needs to resolve 'the contradiction between, or the gap between, human reality and human possibility in history' (42). But Haraway is not content to let those narratives be authoritative. They are always fictions, mediating social reality.

Body of Glass describes a process whereby machines are becoming more human and humans more like machines. As Yod says: 'I'm a fusion of machine and lab-created biological components – much as humans frequently are fusions of flesh and machine' (96). Yod's counterpart is a human, Nili, who has been genetically enhanced to give her superhuman powers. This corresponds to Haraway's new world of 'partial identities and contradictory standpoints'. Yod combines aspects of human and machine, masculinity and femininity, in a way that is genuinely utopian in its transgression of old boundaries and the creation of something new: 'Creation is always perilous, for it gives true life to what has been inchoate and voice to what has been dumb. It makes known what has been unknown, that perhaps we were more comfortable with not knowing. The new is necessarily dangerous' (91).

Like Gibson's 'The Winter Market', *Body of Glass* is also a romance, but this time the traditional gender relationship in Gibson's tale is reversed and questioned. The two narratives are told not from man to man, but through two feminine voices, Shira and her grandmother, Malkah, who tells Yod the story of the Golem. Inverting the structure of 'The Winter Market', Yod becomes the object of Shira's desire. Yod offers the fantasy of creating a being who is perfectly suited to one*self*. But because he has been manufactured, Shira's relationship with him is unnerving. She can never be sure whether what she experiences with him is genuine or pre-programmed.

> Her deep and almost violent sexual pleasure not only disturbed but confused her. She had imagined that it was her love for Gadi, that early emotional bonding, that had made the sex with him much more satisfying and engaging than anything in her life since. But what she was responding to in Yod was simply technique. He had been programmed to satisfy, and he satisfied. She had to admit she was perhaps a little disappointed in herself that she could indeed be pleased by what was programmed to do just that. (241)

This is the same dilemma as in 'The Winter Market'. Sleeping with Yod confuses Shira's sense of self, which she had believed was based on experiences that were particular to certain relationships, times and places. The utopian promise of perfect satisfaction is again compromised by the uncanny sense that what she is experiencing is an inhuman, mechanical repetition. We will return to the sense of the uncanny in Chapter 5. For now it is enough to mark how, in science fiction, the shock of alien encounter produces two contradictory possibilities: one of a better place, the other of our worst nightmare. The cyberpunk narratives of Gibson and Piercy negotiate the dialectic between new pleasures, and the 'grid of control' directs how we experience them.

Conclusion

Science fiction is perhaps the most innovative of popular forms. It is also one of the most critical. The representation of all new worlds involves a process of reflection and comparison with society as it is now. This means that science fiction can have a consciously utopian function; but it can also extrapolate the worst social trends, warning of terrifying futures. Cyborg fictions do both. Not all cyborgs are as challenging as Gibson's or Piercy's, but it is significant that new technologies are now ubiquitous in popular fiction. Tom Clancy's recent thriller, *Debt of Honour*, is a paranoid fantasy that sees a weakened United States overcome a military threat from an aggressive Japan using a variety of smart weapons co-ordinated through the use of satellites and computer technology. Satellites that are able to track fugitives and carry laser weapons turn up in a contemporary horror novel, Dean Koontz's *Dark Rivers of the Heart* (1994). In Clive Barker's fantastic tale of parallel universes, *Everville* (1994), the forces of evil are tracked with a computer database that receives information from every possible source. Even Michael Crichton's bestseller about sexual harassment, *Disclosure* (1994), involves a scene where the protagonist enters a virtual world to retrieve the information he needs to prove his 'innocence'. This constitutes a quantifiable shift, comparable with earlier moments in the post-war period that demonstrate that popular culture is not about standardised products but is subject to process. Cyborg fictions, whether in paperbacks, films or political rhetoric, provide the means through which visions of the future are fought over. Simplistic accounts of their function under capitalism fail to explain their range and scope. Narratives are now emerging that do, however inadequately, give structure to the new identities created in process with the inhuman, alien world of machines.

Notes

1 Philip John Davies, 'Science Fiction and Conflict', in P. J. Davies (ed.), *Science Fiction, Social Conflict and War* (Manchester, Manchester University Press, 1990), p. 2.

2 Darko Suvin, 'Counter-Projects: William Morris and Science Fiction of the 1880s', in Rhys Garnett and R. J. Ellis (eds), *Science Fiction Roots and Branches* (London, Macmillan, 1990), p. 7.

3 Ruth Levitas, *The Concept of Utopia* (London, Philip Allan, 1990), p. 8.

4 Theodor Adorno and Ernst Bloch, 'Something's Missing: A Discussion between Ernst Bloch and Theodor W. Adorno on the Contradictions of Utopian Longing', in E. Bloch, *The Utopian Function of Art and Literature* (Cambridge, MA and London, MIT Press, 1988).

5 Peter Dews, *Logics of Disintegration* (London, Verso, 1987), p. 82.

6 William Morris, 'Looking Backward', in *Political Writings of William Morris*, ed. A. L. Morton (London, Lawrence & Wishart, [1888] 1984), p. 252.

7 William Morris, *News from Nowhere*, in *Three Works by William Morris* (London, Lawrence & Wishart, [1891] 1986), pp. 286–7.

8 *Ibid.*, p. 399 (henceforth page numbers given in text).

9 Dystopian novels include Jack London's *The Iron Heel* (1908); Aldous Huxley's *Brave New World* (1932); and George Orwell's *Nineteen Eighty-four* (1949).

10 Patrick Parrinder, 'Scientists in Science Fiction: Enlightenment and After', in Garrett and Ellis (eds), *Science Fiction Roots and Branches*, p. 58.

11 Fredric Jameson, 'Progress Versus Utopia; or, Can We Imagine the Future?', *Science Fiction Studies*, 9:27:2 (July 1982) 149.

12 *Ibid.*, 150.

13 *Ibid.*, 153.

14 Darko Suvin, *Metamorphoses in Science Fiction* (London, Yale University Press, 1979), pp. 3–15.

15 Jameson, 'Progress Versus Utopia', p. 149.

16 Stephen Kern, *The Culture of Time and Space, 1880–1918* (London, Harvard University Press, 1983).

17 See Lucie Armitt (ed.), *Where No Man Has Gone Before: Women and Science Fiction* (London, Routledge, 1991).

18 See Scott McCracken, 'Postmodernism, a *Chance* to Reread?', in Sally Ledger and Scott McCracken (eds), *The Cultural Politics of the Fin de Siècle* (Cambridge, Cambridge University Press, 1995).

19 Fredric Jameson, *Postmodernism, or, The Cultural Logic of Late Capitalism* (London, Verso, 1991).

20 Jean-François Lyotard, *The Postmodern Condition* (Manchester, Manchester University Press, 1984).

21 See Jameson, *Postmodernism*, pp. 6–16.

22 bell hooks, 'Postmodern Blackness', in *Yearning: Race, Gender, and Cultural Politics* (London, Turnaround, 1991); Angela McRobbie, 'New Times in Cultural Studies', *New Formations*, 13 (Spring 1992) 1–17; Meaghan Morris, 'The Man in the Mirror: David Harvey's "Condition" of Postmodernity', in Mike Featherstone (ed.), *Cultural Theory and Cultural Change*, London, Sage, 1992.

23 Jameson, *Postmodernism*, p. 4; see also David Harvey, *The Condition of Postmodernity* (Oxford, Blackwell, 1989).

24 Donna J. Haraway, *Simians, Cyborgs and Women: The Reinvention of Nature* (New York, Routledge, 1991), p. 154.

25 For an expanded discussion of the use of cyborg fictions and politics, see Scott McCracken, 'Cyborg Fictions: The Cultural Logic of Posthumanism', *Socialist Register 1997* (London, Merlin Press, 1997), 288–301.

26 Thomas Carlyle, 'Signs of the Times', in *Selected Writings* (London, Penguin, 1971), p. 64; Karl Marx, *The Communist Manifesto*, in *The Port-*

able Karl Marx, ed. Eugene Kamenka (Harmondsworth, Penguin, 1983), p. 211.

27   Rita Felski, 'The Art of Perversion: Female Sadists and Male Cyborgs', in *The Gender of Modernity* (Cambridge MA, Harvard University Press, 1995); Andreas Huyssen, 'The Vamp and the Machine: Fritz Lang's *Metropolis*', in *After the Great Divide: Modernism, Mass Culture, Postmodernism* (Bloomington and Indianapolis, Indiana University Press, 1986).

28   On Al Gore's vision of the future, see Herbert I. Schiller, 'The Global Information Highway: Project for an Ungovernable World', in James Brook and Iain A. Boal (eds), *Resisting the Virtual Life: The Culture and Politics of Information* (San Francisco, City Lights, 1995). The collection as a whole provides an excellent survey of the political uses of cyber-culture.

29   Editorial, *Science Fiction and Postmodernism*, special edition of *Science Fiction Studies*, 18:55:3 (November 1991) 306.

30   J. G. Ballard, 'Introduction to the French Edition of *Crash*', reprinted in J. G. Ballard, *Crash* (London, TriadPaladin, [1973] 1990), p. 9.

31   Ballard, *Crash*, p. 103.

32   *Ibid.*, p. 53.

33   Jean Baudrillard, 'Simulacra and Science Fiction', *Science Fiction Studies*, 18:55:3 (November 1991) 310.

34   Jean Baudrillard, 'Ballard's *Crash*', *Science Fiction Studies*, 18:55:3 (November 1991) 319.

35   *Ibid.*, p. 313.

36   Vivian Sobchack, 'Baudrillard's Obscenity', *Science Fiction Studies*, 18:55:3 (November 1991) 327.

37   Roger Luckhurst, 'Border Policing, Postmodernism and Science Fiction', *Science Fiction Studies*, 18:55:3 (November 1991) 358–66.

38   Octavia Butler, *Xenogenesis* (London, Victor Gollancz, 1987), p. 13.

39   Gywneth Jones, *North Wind* (London, Victor Gollancz, 1994), p. 70.

40   The best known of Dick's influential novels and stories, *Do Androids Dream of Electric Sheep?* (1968) and 'We Can Remember it Wholesale' (1966), have made the transition to Hollywood cinema in the films *Blade Runner* and *Total Recall*.

41   Jameson, *Postmodernism*, p. 38.

42   Harvey, *The Condition of Postmodernity*, p. 183.

43   A recent novel, *Virtual Light* (1994), is a thriller set in the future.

44   William Gibson, *Neuromancer* (London, HarperCollins, [1984] 1986), p. 67.

45   William Gibson, 'The Winter Market', in *Burning Chrome* (London, HarperCollins, 1993), p. 140.

46   Julian Stallabrass, 'Just Gaming: Allegory and Economy in Computer Games', *New Left Review*, 198 (March/April 1993) 84.

47   *Ibid.*, 101.

48   See Neil Easterbrook, 'The Arc of Our Destruction: Reversal and Erasure in Cyberpunk', *Science Fiction Studies*, 19 (1992) 378–94; Nicola

Nixon, 'Cyberpunk: Preparing the Ground for Revolution or Keeping the Boys Satisfied?', *Science Fiction Studies*, 19 (1992) 219–35; Andrew Ross, *Strange Weather: Culture, Science, and Technology in the Age of Limits* (London, Verso, 1991).

49 The basic narrative structure of the story is taken from the myth of Orpheus who was a poet and marvellous player on the lyre. Orpheus rescued his wife from the Underworld, only to lose her again because he forgot his promise to the goddess Persephone not to look back on their return to the land of the living. The fundamental narrative trope is a critical one about the difficulty of defining what it is to be human in relation to the non-human, traditionally death, but in the modern period, what Marx called dead labour, machinery, which, in the information world, can be extended to include the simulations created with computers. It has been repeated in a more recent science fiction novel, Jeff Noon's *Vurt* (Stockport, Ringpull Press, 1993).

50 Marge Piercy, *Body of Glass* (Harmondsworth, Penguin, 1992); published in the USA by Alfred A. Knopf under the title, *He, She and It*, 1991 (henceforth, page numbers given in text).

51 Haraway, *Simians, Cyborgs and Women*, p. 150 (henceforth, page numbers given in text).

five
Gothic horror

The central and indispensable element of gothic horror is fear. In the words of Stephen King, 'I suppose the ultimate triumph would be to have somebody drop dead of a heart attack ... I'd say, 'Gee that's a shame,' but part of me would be thinking, Jesus, that really *worked*'.[1] At the centre of every horror narrative there is an emptiness which cannot be explained, or, to use a well-worn but serviceable phrase, a heart of darkness. The very effectiveness of the horror story depends upon the reader's inability to rationalise the source of the terror. Once explained or tamed, that which was monstrous is no longer terrible and, like the defeated King Kong, is more likely to appeal to our sympathies than to summon up our dread. This means that there is a fundamental contradiction between the reader-identity of the academic critic and the function of the horror narrative. Where the critic wishes to understand, the horror narrative resists interpretation, numbing the critical faculty with the spectacle of the unknown. Certainly, I do not like being scared. Horror stories have always given me sleepless nights and when I reluctantly immersed myself in horror fiction to research this chapter I found it impossible to read Peter Straub or James Herbert after dark and alone.

Yet to a greater or lesser extent, the experience of fear is a part of almost all popular fiction. Many bestsellers combine elements of horror with other genres. Suspense is employed in the thriller. The ghastly murder is an essential part of the detective story. The romantic heroine starts out afraid of the world, and fear of the hero is often compounded with desire. Fear and delight in equal measure characterise science fiction's encounters with the unknown. However, even in those narratives which are not primarily horror stories the horror element performs a distinct function, which it is worth discussing in detail. A useful way of defining that function is to compare it with the detective narrative. In the introduction, we encountered Benjamin's view that we use the popular text to escape the anxieties of modernity. But, while the crime story (Benjamin's example of the popular text) has disorder at its centre, the murder itself, the *sjuzet*, seeks to understand and control that disorder. In Chapter 2, I argued that the solution to the detective story does not so much allay those fears as provide a structure within which the reader can situate him- or herself in relation to modernity. Horror stories, by contrast, take apart a secure sense of self. They explore the fragile border between identity and non-identity and thus confront the frightening possibility of the self's destruction. Madness, disease and death, as well as those social and sexual bonds that reveal the limits of our autonomy, are all subjects of horror.

If I return to my own fears (and every horror story sooner or later suggests that what is monstrous is not outside but within[2]), then what is striking is that what I fear most is loss of control. Again, perhaps this reflects an academic mind, happier with order than disorder. Gothic horror explodes what we know to be certain and true so that anything imaginable may happen. All fears are not the same fear, however, and in tracking the monster to its lair it is useful to make some distinctions between different kinds of horror narrative and the different fears they provoke. In this chapter I look at three aspects of gothic horror. I begin with Freud's notion of the 'Uncanny' and its relationship with what Freud calls 'common reality'. Using extracts from two texts, Dennis Wheatley's *The Satanist* (1960) and James Herbert's *Moon* (1985), I examine the importance of 'reality-frames' in establishing the conventions that the gothic throws into doubt. I move on to a reading of Stephen King's *Carrie* (1974), where I look at horror as a kind of excess which transgresses and then overthrows the borders of convention. *Carrie* is a study in what Julia Kristeva calls 'abjection', by which she means the process whereby identity is defined against the risk of its collapse. Finally, in a reading of *Complicity* (1993), Iain Banks's tale in the tradition of the masculine gothic, I look at the role of the double in generating multiple, new 'posthuman' social identities.[3] To classify narratives, I use the term 'gothic horror' as a general definition of the genre – 'gothic' to describe eerie, uncanny or ambivalent texts, and 'horror' to describe excessive representations of destruction and gore. In all its versions I will be looking at the productive tension in gothic horror between our fears of the unknown and the desire to rationalise and explain. While, as already discussed in Chapter 3, I resist some of the more universalist claims of psychoanalytic criticism, I am also wary of neat, historically specific and usually unsatisfying interpretations of monsters. Gothic horror needs to be read in historical context, but the most successful narratives in the genre are able to draw on some of the most deeply embedded psychic and social structures in Western culture. These are particularly effective at exploiting the contradictions in gender and sexual identity; but modern horror has also drawn on the fears arising from class conflict and racist social structures. While I will suggest that there is always a political unconscious to gothic horror, I also argue that tales of fear tell of our inability to grasp the totality of the society that makes us what we are. In Kant's words: 'An object is *monstrous* where by its size it defeats the end that forms the concept'.[4] That which we cannot conceive is always frightening because it makes us doubt how much we know about ourselves.

Gothic horror emerges, like the detective novel, popular romance and science fiction, with modernity. David Punter ties its rise to the Industrial Revolution, but paradoxically in the midst of the eighteenth-century 'Enlightenment' the gothic harked back to an idea of the pre-modern. The term 'gothic', originally a medieval style of architecture, came to mean 'all things preceding about the middle of the seventeenth century'.[5] Early gothic novels include Ann Radcliffe's *The Mysteries of Udolpho* (1794) and M. G. Lewis's *The Monk* (1796). Mary Shelley's *Frankenstein* (1818), already mentioned in Chapter 4, shows the early links between the gothic and science fiction, links which continue up to the present.[6] In the nineteenth century, the German writer E. T. A. Hoffman and American gothic, including Charles Brockden Brown, Nathaniel Hawthorne and Edgar Allan Poe were important influences. The late nineteenth century saw a resurgence of gothic novels, most famously Robert Louis

Stevenson's *The Strange Case of Dr Jekyll and Mr Hyde* (1886) and Bram Stoker's *Dracula* (1897). The genre, from the early novels of Ann Radcliffe through to Shelley, *Dracula* and the horror films of the twentieth century, has always used a sense of the archaic juxtaposed with the modern to create a sense of terror from that which cannot be rationalised or quantified. The historical context of horror is vital to its understanding. For that reason, I return throughout the chapter to the importance of history.

Gothic conventions

In gothic horror the monster cannot exceed its concept unless it is first defined (albeit inadequately). Thus, all horror narratives rely heavily on convention for their effect. Normality must be established so that horror can prove itself by overthrowing the usual comforting patterns of life. Failure to create a convincing reality will lead not to terror but to comedy.[7] A horror narrative published in 1960, Dennis Wheatley's *The Satanist*, is a good example of horror's contingency. The world-view to which it subscribes now appears laughably dated. The following passage, from the point of view of Wheatley's daring young hero, Barney Sullivan, is typical:

> But now? Could one possibly love a girl who had been a prostitute?
>   To do so was against all a man's natural instincts. If one really loved a girl one wanted her for keeps. That meant marriage, and through the generations male mentality had been fashioned to demand that the future mother of a man's children should be chaste. Basically that was his own view, but he recognised that standards of morality had grown far more lax since women had claimed equal rights with men in almost every sphere of life and, like most men of his age, he would have been quite ready to ignore the past if, on asking a girl to marry him, she had confessed to having already had a lover, or even several, providing they had been genuine love affairs and she had not made herself cheap. But ... [8]

While the figure of the prostitute still has a problematic status in society, the demand for women's chastity before marriage is a long way from the taken-for-granted promiscuity of the bonkbuster. Changed gender relations have meant that more recent horror has had to be far more adventurous in its exploration of the limits of masculinity. In fact, in *The Satanist* (where the representation of masculinity is actually more conservative than classic nineteenth-century horror like *Jekyll and Hyde*) the very heroine who gives Barney pause for thought is by far the most interesting character. Mary Morden, *née* McCreedy, alias Margot Mauriac, was once indeed a 'fallen' woman, but is now the respectable widow of Agent Morden, who fell victim as a human sacrifice while investigating a Satanic Ring. Mary, as Margot, is able to infiltrate the Ring because she is not as respectable as she looks and indeed is prepared to sleep with a Satanist if it will lead to the discovery of her husband's murderer. As three women in one, prostitute, widow and pragmatic sexual agent, Mary embodies the contradictory ideologies surrounding the liberated young women of the post-war period. In fact, it is possible to see the whole Satanic ring as multicultural, post-1960s, New Left, postfeminist Britain in embryo. In addition to Mary it contains Bengalis, West Indians (including a lesbian Haitian priestess) and Africans, all of whom engage in 'orgies' and have sinister connections with a Communist trade-union conspiracy to sabotage British industry. In other words, the horror at the heart of *The Satanist* is a combination of all the traditional enemies of British imperial fiction and the *bêtes noires* of 1950s' suburbia. As exciting as these things might have been to the *Daily Mail*, which dubbed Wheatley 'the greatest adventure writer of our time', they fail to shock a quarter of a century later. Only one moment, the appearance of the 'black imp' during a 'black magic' ceremony, came close to inducing sleeplessness in this susceptible reader, but not close enough. The failure of *The Satanist* as horror narrative suggests that the demonisation of the cultural other forms an inadequate basis for the horror narrative. In this case it merely reinforces the prejudices of the assumed reader-identity. In order to be successful, horror must call that identity into question.

Freud discusses the ambivalent feelings aroused by gothic horror in his important essay 'The "Uncanny"'. 'Uncanny' is the English translation of the German word *unheimlich*, which has its etymological root in the German word for home, *Heim*. *Unheimlich* means unfamiliar, weird, eerie, creepy, dismal: in other words, the opposite of a familiar, domestic environment. However, Freud also notes some similarities between the word *unheimlich* and its opposite, *heimlich*, in that *heimlich* can also mean secret or concealed. The relationship between opposites which are also the same marks the starting point for a discussion of the difficulty of separating out the ego (self) from the external world (other). According to Freud, the fears provoked by the uncanny can be traced back to an early stage in child-hood when the ego has not yet achieved such a separation.[9] Thus, the uncanny achieves its effect by blurring the boundaries between identity and non-identity.

The Uncanny in literature appears when 'the writer pretends to operate in a world of common reality'.[10] Freud remarks that a sense of the Uncanny can be provoked more easily by a writer than by the coincidences of everyday life because fiction takes us into a fantasy world where we rely on the narrative for the frame which provides us with a sense of the 'real'. Once established the narrative can overstep the frame, upsetting our sense of proportion and giving us an uneasy sense that something is wrong. Freud makes a distinction between narratives that operate only in a fantasy world, like fairy tales where we accept magical events as part of the story's world, and tales of the Uncanny, where magical events provoke unease. As will be clear from earlier chapters, I am unwilling to accept that fantasy literature is ever totally cut-off from the world in which we live. Fantasy is always part of a transaction between world, text and reader. However, Freud is certainly right to distinguish uncanny tales from other kinds of narrative. The Uncanny interrupts the fantasy setting, calling into question its parameters. Elsewhere, Freud remarks that the moment we awaken ourselves from a nightmare is not when the dream becomes too fantastic, but when it comes too close to our own personal anxieties.[11] The Uncanny functions as a similar kind of awakening. The moment of unease is provoked when the fantasy's ability to evade or suture the gaps that constitute our fears is impaired. By foregrounding the limits of the frame, the Uncanny exposes the difficult time we have keeping a sense of self together. If effective, we are woken from our absorption in the text to wonder if the monster is in the fiction or in the room, under the bed or behind the chair.

Because narrative context and the situation of the reader are so important, it is difficult to re-create the sense of the Uncanny within a piece of academic prose. In fact, many horror tales begin by constructing a reader/listener scene – for example, a group of people gathered around a warming fire, while the wind whistles round the house.[12] The following passage opens James Herbert's *Moon* (1985). In order to achieve its full effect it needs to align the reader with the child in bed in the dark. So imagine yourself alone, late at night.

The boy had stopped crying.

He lay in his narrow bed, eyes closed, his face an alabaster mask in the moonlight. Occasionally a tremor would run the length of his body.

He clutched the bedsheets, pulling them tight under his chin. A dreadful heaviness inside weighed his body down, a feeling that his blood had turned into liquid lead: the burden was loss, and it had left him exhausted and weak.

The boy had rested there a long time – how many hours he had no way of knowing, for all of the last three days had been a timeless eternity – but his father had forbidden him to move from the bed again. So he lay there, enduring the loss, frightened by the new loneliness.

Until something caused him to open his red-rimmed eyes once more.

The figure stood near the end of the bed and she smiled at him. He felt her warmth, the momentary shedding of bereavement. But it was impossible. His father had told him it was impossible.

'You ... can't ... be ...' he said, his small voice a shivery intrusion on the night. 'He ... says ... you can't ... you can't ... be ...'

The sense of loss was renewed, for now it was also within her.

And then the startled boy looked elsewhere in the room, gazing upwards into a far corner as if suddenly aware of yet another presence, of someone else watching him, someone he could not see. The moment vanished when footsteps were heard along the corridor and the looked away, for the first time real fear in his eyes. The woman was gone.

In the doorway stood the swaying shadow of a man.

The boy's father stumbled towards the bed, the familiar reek of alcohol as much part of him as the perpetual sullenness of his features.

'I told you,' the man said, and there seemed to be guilt mixed with anger in the harsh words. 'No more! No more ...' His fist was raised as he approached and the boy cowered beneath the bedsheets.

Outside, the full moon was clear-edged and pure against the deep blackness of the night.[13]

Freud's 'common reality' is constructed here through a series of interlocking 'frames'. The boy's body forms the first border between self and not-self. Subsequently, the bedsheets, the edge of the bed, the walls of the room and the doorway to the rest of the house enclose the child in a series of projected reality-frames that create his relationship with the world. However, the darkness, which blurs boundaries, and the moonlight, which gives a strange light, disturb the potential for these frames to define a clear picture. This ambivalence raises questions about the status of what the child is experiencing. Is he asleep or awake, dreaming or seeing ghosts? On the one hand, the apparition at the end of his bed is maternal; it eases, temporarily, his sense of loss. On the other, its reality is in doubt:

it is 'impossible'. The second 'presence' heightens the sense of the Uncanny because it is unfamiliar and invisible. It is positioned in a 'far corner' of the room: on the edge of reality. Thus, the passage initiates a gradual breaking down of the reality-frames, creating the conditions where the boy's father's actual break-in – through the door, into the room, and over the edge of the bed – becomes an event of horror. The horror is more effective because it invites the participation of the reader, the violence itself – past the bedsheet, against the boy's body – is left to our imagination.

Ambivalence is the key term here. The Uncanny, while it must construct a convincing point of view, must then upset its security to produce contradictory feelings of love and hate. In the passage, it is uncertain whether the father is a real, violent authority figure or a projection of the boy's imagination. Leaving the, now monstrous, father above the bed with fist raised invites the reader to project his or her already awakened fears onto the outcome. According to Lucie Armitt:

> the space surrounded by the four walls of the gothic mansion is determined as an interior dream- (or rather nightmare-) space, while the space beyond that functions as the outer world of daylight order. But such three-dimensional constraints are by no means inviolable, for a gothic text *becomes* a gothic text only when such fixed demarcations are called into question by the presence of an interloper who interrogates the existence of such boundary demarcations.[14]

In the above passage, as the father moves through the frames constructed by the narrative he changes, growing more and more monstrous as each boundary is transgressed.

As Freud points out, in literature a sense of the Uncanny is easily dispelled, leaving a sense of dissatisfaction in the reader. This can occur in at least two ways. First, the strange events that give rise to the Uncanny are explained within the terms of the reality-frame. We might call this the Scooby-Doo ending, where the monster is unmasked as a scheming criminal, crying 'And I would have got away with it too, if it hadn't been for those pesky kids'. Mary Higgins Clark's recent novel *Remember Me* (1994) has just such an ending. After experiencing a series of uncanny events, the protagonist, Menley, discovers that her house is not haunted. She has been the victim of a plot by a woman, Elaine, who is in love with her husband. Using a secret chamber in her antiquated house, Elaine tries to exacerbate Menley's post-traumatic stress (after an accident in which her son was killed) to engineer a nervous breakdown. Second, the Uncanny's effects are undone when the narrative shifts out of the reality-frame into a fantasy world where acts of horror cease to inspire fear. This is the case for Clive Barker's *Everville* (1994), which, although it is chock-full of horrific happenings, has so many different frames, including historical shifts, doors between alternative universes and dead and living worlds, that the reader starts to take the shifts from one to another for granted and any sense of the Uncanny dwindles away. In order to sustain that sense the narrative must maintain its ambivalence. Ghost stories that do this effectively include Henry James's *Turn of the Screw* (1898) and Peter Straub's *Ghost Story* (1979). In the latter, a nightmare world gradually seeps into everyday life. The eerie tales told by a group of old men slowly meld into the main narrative until 'common reality' itself is haunted. It made me very scared indeed.

If Freud's analysis of the workings of the Uncanny is convincing, his account of the sources of our fear is less satisfying. He gives two separate explanations. First, unease is provoked by the revival of 'infantile complexes'. For example, tales of premature burial[15] evoke womb fantasies, tales of severed limbs fears of castration.[16] Second, a sense of the Uncanny arises when 'primitive beliefs we have surmounted seem once more to be confirmed'.[17] Freud's conclusions at first appear to be substantiated by the success of archetypes in horror narratives; for example, the common use of the haunted house or the persistence of certain types of monsters – vampires, werewolves, mummies. Freudian theory would suggest that the frequency of such archetypes is related to a basic psychological structure or a 'primitive' taboo. It is certainly true that a striking number of horror stories make a childhood trauma a 'primal scene' (as already discussed in Chapter 3), to which fear can be traced back or exploit the ambivalent feelings of love and hate in the parent–child relationship. Contemporary examples include *Moon* and *Remember Me*, referred to above; Dean Koontz's *Dark Rivers of the Heart* (1994), where a 'chase' narrative leads back to the hero's childhood discovery that his father was a serial killer; King's *Carrie*, and Bank's *Complicity*, both discussed below.

However, it can be argued that the horror relates not so much to particular psychic structures but to the multiplicity of different forms that primary relationships can take. We have already noted the multiplying effect of what I have called frames. This suggests that the success of the haunted house as horror trope is not the result of some single explanation, but the excess of meanings produced by its various enclosures, each of which discloses some new form of monstrosity. Judith Halberstam suggests that successful monsters are characterised by their ability to produce multiple monstrosities. Dracula, for example, is not reducible to one aspect of sexuality but to the multiple forms he embodies: 'the vampire is not lesbian, homosexual or heterosexual, the vampire represents the productions of sexuality itself'.[18] We could, for example, do a Freudian reading of the opening passage of *Moon*. It invites an Oedipal interpretation, where a castrating father is punishing the boy's love for the mother. However, to fit the passage into one interpretative structure can be to ignore the excess of meaning that horror produces.

The second problem with Freud's theory of the Uncanny relates to his discussion of 'primitive' cultures. Freud draws on a bewildering array of evidence, but even to accept his dubious anthropology does not help our understanding of the meaning of horror in the modern world. Placed historically it is difficult not to see Freud's explanation of the power of horror as a gothic narrative in itself. In describing the workings of the Uncanny, he sought its origins in an invented past, which, he claimed, was still evident in the 'primitive' rites of premodern cultures. Ironically in his discussion of taboos, Freud did not consider the taboo that structured most nineteenth-century anthropology: 'race'. The racism that structured the European empires of the period has influenced Western fears, so that many twentieth-century horror narratives are about an imagined threat to small, all-white communities. By contrast, many post-Freudian critics have tried to relate Freud's insights to questions of cultural difference as they arise at a particular historical moment.

We might conclude, then, that the clue to the use of the past in gothic horror lies more in the *projection* of our fears onto childhood or some originary historical event than in verifiable past experiences. David Punter's historical account of the rise of the gothic suggests that what is unearthed is not some primeval fear, but a terror that stems from current, modern preoccupations which is then projected back on an earlier time. This is, I think, a correct view of how horror works, but to suggest that horror's use of the past is entirely invention is misleading. Contemporary fears and anxieties are partly a legacy of history, and horror is able to be more effectively terrifying if it is able to evoke social and sexual contradictions which have a continuing relevance. This dialectic of projection and actual contradiction means that a psychoanalytic framework remains useful, albeit one that is more historicised than Freud's. For horror exploits some of the deep, psychic structures of subjectivity, which, while not unchanged by history, maintain a powerful grip on modern cultures. For Stephen Heath the critical problem lies in the need to articulate the relationship between 'the psychical and the social in the construction of sexuality and sexual identity'; this is the 'articulation that psychoanalysis lays the basis for and continually suggests but never makes'. He concludes laconically: 'Easier said than done'.[19] Notwithstanding I will attempt to take the discussion further with a socio-historical interpretation of Stephen King's *Carrie* that employs insights from psychoanalytic criticism.

Stephen King is probably the most successful author of contemporary popular fiction. Between 1979 and 1992 he had sixteen *New York Times* number one hardback bestsellers – one every 9.5 months.[20] *Carrie* was his first successful novel. The tale takes the deep-rooted social taboo around menstrual blood as its subject for horror, and this choice deserves some critical discussion. For Freud a taboo always arouses emotional ambivalence. To be taboo 'means, on the one hand, "sacred", "consecrated", and on the other "uncanny", "dangerous", "forbidden" and "unclean"'.[21] The meaning of menstruation is different in different cultures, but it is often associated with ideas of gender difference related to cleanliness and defilement. Julia Kristeva argues that, 'In societies where it occurs, ritualization of defilement is accompanied by a strong concern for separating the sexes, and this means giving men rights over women.'[22] This suggests that it is not menstrual blood *per se* which is horrifying, but the cluster of meanings that surround it in a particular society.[23] Menstruation acts as a strong central metaphor in *Carrie*, but the novel sites the taboo in several different narratives, each of which gives it a new and different meaning.

One of the novel's most striking effects is achieved by setting a familiar fairy-tale narrative in the context of a small New England town in the 1970s. Carrie is a latter-day Cinderella who does not expect to be invited to the High School Spring Ball; but like Cinders,

her true beauty is hidden. Descriptions of her are highly contradictory. As first she is 'a big chunky girl with pimples on her neck
and back and buttocks, her wet hair completely without color'.[24]
Later, when an unlikely fairy godmother, Susan Snell, persuades her
boyfriend Tommy Ross to invite Carrie to the Ball because she feels
remorse for her part in Carrie's persecution, Carrie is transformed
(by her own efforts) into her date's princess and they are voted the
event's King and Queen. Carrie's mother, who combines the functions of the ugly sisters, is similarly double. She is monstrous, 'a very
big woman ... lately her legs had begun to swell, and her feet always
seemed on the point of overflowing her shoes' (32); but we hear
conflicting reports of her looks as a young woman.

The fairy-tale structure does two things. It establishes a familiar
narrative about femininity as both beautiful and monstrous, a cultural
problem in a gendered social system, and it locates the narrative as
about one aspect of that problem, the transition from girlhood to
womanhood. This creates some familiar parameters for the reader,
easing us into the story. Far from establishing this transition as a
universal rite, however, the narrative is at pains to emphasise the
modernity and even the mundanity of the setting. The battles
between Carrie and her mother are exaggerated because her mother
adheres to a strict version of Christian fundamentalism; but the
arguments they have are the usual contest of parental prohibition
and adolescent transgression. The Spring Ball itself is an American
ritual familiar to everyone who has been exposed to Hollywood or
American television, but even this is given a specific time and place.
The crowning of the King and Queen is greeted by some members
of the audience as sexist and old-fashioned. Thus the ritual elements
of the tale, traditional and modern, are placed firmly within
contemporary history and society. Ritual and modernity, magic and
the mundane are the carefully balanced context for the emergence
of horror.

The horror begins with an unpleasant, but very familiar, incident
of bullying in the school showers. As class-victim, Carrie is represented as an abject figure.[25] Where the Uncanny describes an uneasy
anticipation in literature closely related to 'suspense', the condition
of abjection describes the horror itself, the collapse of identity.
Horror narratives usually postpone that collapse or operate on its
borders. Carrie, on the border between childhood and adulthood,

embarrassed about her body and ignorant about menstruation, is
pushed into abjection by her classmates.

> "PER-iod, PER-iod, PER-iod!"
> Carrie stood dumbly in the center of the forming circle, water rolling
> from her skin like beads. She stood like a patient ox, aware that the joke
> was on her (as always), dumbly embarrassed but unsurprised.
> Sue felt welling disgust as the first dark drops of menstrual blood
> struck the tile in dime-sized drops. "For God's sake, Carrie, you got your
> period!" she cried. "Clean yourself up!" (5)

The horror here is twofold: first what happens to Carrie, and
second the behaviour of the other girls. The passage represents the
collapse of Carrie's social identity. She lacks definition. Her wet body
is shapeless. The blood, in this context, is a sign of a lack of the
distinction between the inside of the body and the out, indicating a
lack of self-control. Kristeva argues that corporeal waste, menstrual
blood, excrement, even nail-parings, represent 'the objective frailty
of the symbolic order'.[26] Here what I described in Chapter 3 as the
symbolic order is endangered not so much because Carrie does not
know what is happening to her, but because she does not know
about the cultural meaning and rituals associated with menstrual
blood in contemporary American society. Earlier she had been ridi-
culed because she had used a tampon to blot her lipstick. Now the
girls humiliate her by throwing sanitary towels. Thus, it is the in-
appropriate nature of Carrie's actions rather than the bleeding itself
which horrifies her classmates.

One interpretation of their behaviour is that Carrie's shock provokes their own repressed fears. In her introduction to the 1991
edition, Tabitha King points out that the two girls identified in the
crowd, Susan who regrets her actions and Chris who does not, have
recently become sexually active (xiii). Having only recently achieved
puberty themselves, they are getting to grips with what it means to
be a young woman in the United States of the early 1970s. Seeing
in Carrie the embodiment of their fears, their violence towards her
can be understood as an attack upon the abjected part of themselves
of which they are in terror.

However, this interpretation is perhaps too neat a rationalisation
of the opening scene. It fails to explain the excess of emotions
provoked by the combination of social victimisation and personal
humiliation. It does not, for example, give much warning of the

disproportionate response Carrie inflicts upon the town. This is not to say that we cannot interpret horror, but that it puts tidy explanations into question. Its excessive nature begs a wider context. Why is Carrie the victim? Why are the other girls so insecure? The answers here are more resistant to socio-historic interpretation because the narrative strand that deals with Carrie's disproportionate response moves into a more fantastic mode. We learn of Carrie's 'telekinetic' powers: her ability to move physical objects just by thinking about them.

Where the fairy-tale narrative worked against the contemporary setting, the magical narrative is opposed to several other more realistic narratives. In the text, the supernatural is contrasted with a series of 'factual', retrospective accounts of the incidents preceding and following the Ball. These include a monograph, *The Shadow Exploded*; an autobiography by Susan Snell, *My Name is Susan Snell*; an official report, *The White Commission Report*; and numerous other academic and newspaper articles. In this, *Carrie* follows in the tradition of novels like *The Moonstone* and *Dracula*. The 'factual' accounts demonstrate the partial and incomplete nature of rational explanation. The mystery or horror that is at the heart of the narrative thus remains inexplicable – that is its power.

To maintain its power, the horror must continue to exceed any given explanation or potentially justifiable motive, like revenge. The trigger for mayhem comes in *Carrie* when she and Tommy are crowned King and Queen of the Ball. This moment is the high point in Carrie's gradual achievement of subjecthood after the process of abjection experienced in the shower scene, an achievement that is accompanied by her increasing telekinetic powers. The fairy-tale narrative (where Carrie is Cinderella emerging clean and beautiful from the filth) comes to a shocking end when she is soaked by a bucket of pig's blood which has been planted in the rafters above the throne. The effect is to return Carrie to an abject figure of fun, who stumbles from the stage, is tripped up and laughed at. This time, however, she responds. Using her telekinetic powers, Carrie burns down the school, murders her mother (becoming fatally wounded in the struggle) and destroys the town.

These excesses are minutely detailed from a variety of sources, each of which leaves the origins of the disaster open to question. To be effective, horror needs a highly structured narrative. In *Carrie*, fairy-tale archetypes, contemporary ritual, documentary reports and familiar common reality are skilfully combined to expose society's blind spots. The final destruction of the town evokes an almost revolutionary impulse: the overthrow of the existing order and a reconstitution of both society and psychic identity. The brutality of the bloody assault signifies the violence that enforces gender difference. Pigs represent the taboo, the dirty, the unacceptable; and the assault is engineered by the marginal elements of the society, those who have been excluded from the Ball.[27] Thus horror draws on the interrelationship between a personal and a political unconscious, the psychically and the socially repressed, overwhelming the rational self and the ordered society on which the presumption of reason is founded. If *Carrie* starts as a narrative about adolescence, once unleashed the horror threatens all the structures that make-up 'normality' in a small, white, North American community.

Doubling

We have seen how King's novel operates through a series of contrasting narratives. This has the effect of doubling, where the normal world is reflected back as a distorted, grotesque caricature of itself. Doubling is one of the most effective uncanny modes. Elisabeth Bronfen writes: 'The repeated event, action or term always contradicts its predecessor because, though similar, it is never identical, and through recalling the unique, singular and original quality of the former event, it emphasises that it is "more than one", a multiple duplicate, occurring at more than one site.'[28] Doubling in horror narratives is produced by the juxtaposition of the rational (common reality) with the irrational; and the effect is logarithmic rather than arithmetical. Whereas a rational explanation simply defines reason and unreason, horror shows a multiplicity of meanings and of selves.

One of the most common devices in gothic horror is the use of the double, or *Doppelgänger*.[29] In a discussion of Bram Stoker's *Dracula*, Franco Moretti comments that it is not the fact that the Count has no reflection that terrifies Jonathan Harker; the real fear comes not from what cannot be seen but from what can, himself.[30] Similarly, the supernatural beings in Peter Straub's *Ghost Story* claim eerily on being questioned, 'I am you'. In each case the reflection of the 'normal' self reveals fragmentation rather than coherence. This is the discovery in two of the most famous tales of doubles. In *The Strange Case of Dr Jekyll and Mr Hyde*, Jekyll finds that 'man is not truly one, but truly two' and projects that he 'will ultimately be known for a mere polity of multifarious, incongruous and independent denizens'.[31] In *The Picture of Dorian Gray* (1891), Dorian wonders 'at the shallow psychology of those who conceive the Ego in man as a thing single, permanent, reliable, and of one essence. To him, man was a being with myriad lives and myriad sensations, a complex multiform creature that bore within itself strange legacies of thought and passion.'[32]

Despite the genre's tendency towards multiplicity, the importance of normal self as the starting point for tales of doubles (the trope of the double is rooted in the conventions of the 'normal' self, just as the starting point for the Uncanny is common reality) means it is possible to talk about the feminine gothic or the masculine gothic as forms which explore the particular dynamics of 'normal' gendered identities. Feminine gothic usually opposes two kinds of femininity in much the same way as there are two Carries, one beautiful and one monstrous. In their book *The Madwoman in the Attic*, Sandra Gilbert and Susan Gubar argue that the gothic double is a common feature of women's writing in the nineteenth century.[33] For example, in Charlotte Brontë's *Jane Eyre*, Jane's good femininity is opposed by her alter ego, Rochester's mad wife, Bertha, who lives in the attic. This double femininity represents degrees of emotional ambivalence. First, Bertha's revolt against conventional femininity is counterpoised to Jane's apparent acceptance. Second, her murderous intentions towards Rochester show the unstable foundations of Jane's heterosexual desire. The narrative resolution is brought about when a fire started by Bertha kills her and blinds Rochester, opening the way for Jane, formerly a lowly governess, to be a second more powerful spouse to her disabled husband.

This narrative of female empowerment maintains its currency in contemporary popular fiction. In Catherine Cookson's *The Cultured Handmaiden*, Jinny is transferred from the typing pool to a position closer to power as the boss's secretary. Here, despite his fearsome reputation, she asserts herself and is well positioned to assume management of his home when a car crash inflicts a catalogue of injuries on his, the patriarch's, family. His wife and the wife of his eldest son are killed outright. The boss's physical injuries leave him paraplegic, while the mental trauma of the accident leaves him paralysed from the neck down. The eldest son is physically capable, too capable as Jinny discovers, but brain damage has destroyed his mind. When the prodigal younger son (who will, of course, inherit) returns home from a failed non-marital relationship, Jinny is the obvious partner. Glimpses of Jinny's other self are caught in the various 'monstrous' other women who haunt the text. She catches a potential boyfriend with a woman 'who looked like a mountain of wobbling flesh had metallic red hair, her breasts and stomach were enormous, and her thighs like those bursting out of bloomers on coarse seaside postcards'.[34] Another woman who was living with the younger son is soon discounted simply because she is living with a man before marriage.

While the car accident is out of all proportion to any reasonable achievement of Jinny's aims (two people dead, one bedridden and one a mindless zombie), perhaps reason cannot account for the strength of the feelings that had to be repressed in her original lowly position. In the feminine gothic the horror can be rationalised as a response to an oppressively masculine world;[35] but its manifestation always exceeds that logic. One of the functions of the gothic double is to upset the normality of acceptable desires, opening up other, transgressive possibilities. The most powerful of these is the desire to *be* the monstrous woman, who is both terrifying, disgusting and, at the same time, uncannily attractive. Queer identities lie beneath the conventional appearance of the gothic heroine, and at key moments that conventional appearance is exposed as a mask or masquerade.[36]

A comparable tradition of masculine gothic also exists, which explores masculinity as feminine gothic explores femininity.[37] The persistence of these two traditions is testimony to two aspects of horror. First, its continuing concern with social conventions and, second, the persistence of gender as one of the most fundamental forms of social organisation. A recent example, set in Edinburgh and following the Scottish tradition of James Hogg and Robert Louis Stevenson, is Iain Banks' *Complicity*, which reached number one in the *Sunday Times* bestseller list in October 1994. *Complicity* is both gothic horror and suspense thriller, a popular combination amongst contemporary bestsellers. Higgins Clark's *Remember Me* and Dean Koontz's *Dark Rivers of the Heart* both fall into this category. The narrative works best on a first reading (although it can take a second), when the reader has to work out the connections, and rule out the false trails, that link the protagonist, Cameron Colley, a journalist for the *Caledonian* (a thinly disguised *Scotsman*) to a series of politically motivated murders. As with all tales of doubling, *Complicity* invites multiple interpretations. To begin with, it has a double narrative. Cameron's narrative is in the first person, yet the novel opens in the second person, a device that leaves mysterious the identity of his other self: 'You hear the car after an hour and a half. During that time you've been here in the darkness, sitting on the small telephone seat near the front door, waiting.'[38] This opposition of 'I' and 'You' destabilises the relationship between self and other to the point where the reader is unsure whether or not 'You' is Cameron in another guise. The two narratives give us, on the one hand, an 'I' of internal dissension but relative external order: Cameron's 'I' keeps his life within certain limits, his life is complex and at times he seems to be preserving a precarious mental balance. On the other, 'You' has apparent internal coherence, but creates external disorder. The assaults are committed by 'You' in a state of perfect mental control, but the results of 'Your' violence have all the excessive paraphernalia of body-horror: penetrations, punctures, insides coming out, the drip of the terrified maid's urine on the floor, and the gory details of the victim's death: 'He falls onto the railings, hitting with his head, hip and leg; there is a surprisingly dry cracking, crunching noise; his head twists to one side and one of the railing spikes appears through the socket of his right eye' (8–9).

Cameron becomes implicated in the murders because a series of phone calls direct him to isolated spots when the crimes are being committed. The mystery caller promises leads on the kind of political conspiracy that Cameron loves: 'we're talking about a project with the code-name of the god of massacre, involving Iraq, a very secret deal and five dead men including at least three who had access to nuclear intelligence' (69). It is not until he is arrested and realises he has no alibis that Cameron wakes up to the fact that the only conspiracy is against himself. The police are even able to produce a piece of light-hearted television criticism he wrote in which he suggested the elimination of several of the victims by name.

Eve Kosofsky Sedgwick has argued that gothic narratives combine paranoia with a fear of homosexuality, a combination found in

Freud's case history of Dr Schreber.[39] In *Complicity*, the link between Cameron's paranoid belief in conspiracies and same-sex desire can be traced back to two childhood incidents, never far from his dreams. A psychoanalytic interpretation might read these incidents as 'primal scenes' that reveal the complexes structuring Cameron's unconscious self. Both involve his childhood friend Andy, who he refers to as 'my old soul-mate, my surrogate brother, my other me' (29), and who, as the reader has guessed by this time, is 'You': the not-I, non-self, Cameron's other. Both involve a betrayal of Andy by Cameron. In the first incident he fails to follow his friend and save him when he falls into a frozen river; but it is the second, an adolescent homosexual experience with Andy, that is more significant, revealing the queer desires that are masked by Cameron's performance of his 'normal' self. After experimenting with mutual masturbation, Andy and Cameron are caught by a passing hiker who has been watching them. The voyeur turns violent and sexually assaults Andy; but this time Cameron returns from flight and together they overpower and kill Andy's assailant, concealing his body in a disused railway tunnel.

This brings me to my first reading of *Complicity*, a Freudian interpretation of the masculine gothic that suggests that it reveals the transgressive desires that lie beneath the masquerade of 'normal' masculinity. In this reading, hiding the body can be read as a repression of Andy and Cameron's 'queer' desires, which have been externalised and made monstrous in their attacker. The act of hiding binds their friendship making each the other's double so that Cameron is always 'complicit' with Andy's aggression. In such an interpretation, Andy's violent career would represent a return of their repressed mutual attraction. The text is littered with homoerotic references which reinforce this reading. Cameron's married lover, Yvonne, has short hair and a 'sveltely muscular body', while in one of the assaults Andy uses a dildo to sodomise a judge who has been lenient on rapists. However, a Freudian interpretation of paranoid fears as homosexual desire not only reproduces a narrow and stereotyped version of same-sex relationships; it is too narrow in its understanding of horror's monstrous productivity. In my second reading of the novel, I want to suggest that a psychoanalytic reading, while useful in exploring the text's unconscious, can also close down the multiplying effects of gothic horror, offering a limited version of the Other as socially deviant. Instead I suggest that *Complicity* offers a postmodern version of a fragmented self. Cameron's identity, like Jekyll's or Dorian Gray's, is composed of fragments. He is not one self but multiple selves and these different identities are at war, threatening imminent dissolution. He uses drugs to control his emotional balance, taking endless cups of coffee, cigarettes and amphetamines as uppers, and alcohol and marijuana as downers. He projects a 'cyberself' into his favourite computer game, *Despot*, where he takes the role of an absolutist ruler, trying to keep order against the warring factions in his state as he builds up an empire: 'building roads, dredging ports, burning forests, digging mines and – using the very ironic Icon icon – opening more temples to myself' (55) (it comes as no surprise to learn that Banks writes science fiction novels under the name of Iain M. Banks). His sex-life with Yvonne is not reducible to a single desire. It involves an active fantasy element in which both act out dominant and submissive roles involving bondage and simulated rape.

A third reading might ask how the fragmented postmodern self could be related to a historical reading of the text. I want to suggest that Banks's gothic novel might also be read as a political allegory of Britain's Thatcherite decade, the 1980s. Each of Cameron's selves has some counterpart in the actions of 'You'. The political element of 'Your' crimes reflects the political tendencies of Cameron's journalism, but he is censored or censors himself to achieve articles that are what his editor calls 'nicely balanced; just hovering on the brink of editorialising, but never quite going over' (44). Where 'I' tests the limits of allowable dissent – playfully suggesting terrorism but only in the 'non-serious' style of television criticism – 'You' enacts political terrorism. 'I' uses drugs to the point of addiction, playing on the border between their ability to control his moods and their power over him. 'You', on the other hand, uses his knowledge of weapons and communications systems to exert power over others. Apart from the rape of the Judge, one other of the assaults involves a sexual element. 'You' ties up and makes a video of a child-pornographer in his death throes after 'You' has injected him with a mixture of infected semen from London rent boys. Where 'I' and Yvonne's sex games have rules – each is allowed to stop the other with a single, agreed word – 'Your' activities involve no such consent. 'I' plays the part of the rapist, while 'You' actually becomes one.

The double lives of Cameron and Andy create series of contrasting frames, each of which reinterprets the other, producing the excess of meaning that characterises gothic horror. Thus, homosexual desire is just one part of a constellation of different social and psychic bonds that make up their relationship. As Judith Halberstam has pointed out, 'Freud's interpretations of the cases of paranoia fix definitions of horror within a certain narrative, the narrative of psychosexuality. Fictions about fear which locate monstrosity in social, cultural, political, or national frames of reference are here superseded by the fiction of fear as desire or desire's disorder'.[40] Rather than providing evidence of a single narrative of identity, *Complicity* suggests the failure of the *despotic,* modern subject, which would, like Cameron's absolutist ruler, seek to subjugate its environment completely. Instead we see the fragmentation of the modernist self into multiple, postmodern selves.

'[S]kewering monstrosity on sexual perversion', in Halberstam's slashing phrase,[41] also misses the novel's larger political dimension: how the relationship between a modernist self and potential other selves is a product of a particular social and historic moment. Taking the central theme of the masculine gothic – masculinity and relations between men – *Complicity* also works as an allegory about the delicate relationship between coercion and consent in the context of the politics of Thatcherism.[42] The horror in *Complicity* does not come from a single, forbidden desire; it stems from a much more complex relationship between power and how we work within it. This complexity is suggested early on in the way Cameron plays *Despot*, where he has a 'long-term strategy of weakening the power of the regional lords and the Church by making the palace so luxuriantly, sumptuously, steeped in the pleasures of the flesh that the barons and the bishops become hopelessly decadent voluptuaries and hence ripe for the picking while my merchant classes prosper and I encourage cautious technological development' (55).

The point of these three possible readings is, first, to show the multiple interpretations invited by gothic horror and, second, to show the tension between this plurality of meanings and the text as the product of a particular time and place. In a comparable way both doubles are complicit with the political system: Andy, because he voted for Margaret Thatcher, fought in the Falklands/Malvinas war, made money in the consumer boom of the late 1980s and now employs his skills in methods that only involve coercion; Cameron, because he has consented to play his life as a series of games always staying within the rules, even when he disagrees with them. Andy uses the tactics of those he says he opposes. Cameron's attitude to life is to treat it as a game. He flirts with danger, testing the limits of power. But the boundary that separates each from their double is a fragile one. It is the boundary between a coercive self, one that 'identifies with the power that is belaboring him'[43] and the possibility of performing different, postmodern selves. The recognition that you do not make the rules in the games in which you play is a recognition that the balance between the two is extremely delicate. Andy, as Cameron's Nemesis, destroys his precarious equilibrium, but it is the horror of that destruction that allows the narrative to explore the boundary between self and other. The monster reveals the mass of social and psychic relations that construct identity and the impossibility of ever knowing or finding an adequate concept for those relations. A consciousness of that impossibility is also a consciousness of the impotence and fragility of the self.

Arrest leads to the collapse of the elaborate life Cameron has constructed for himself. His façade of self-control becomes untenable, revealing the artificial, temporary nature of his masquerade of masculinity. His big story is in ruins. Barbarians overrun his cyberempire. He resumes smoking. Under pressure he denounces his closest friends, including Yvonne and her husband. Like Carrie, he undergoes a process of abjection, a process which, it is suggested, will be quickly followed by death. The novel's ending continues the uncertainty that characterises Cameron's complicity. Cameron is captured by Andy but each lets the other go. Andy oversees this denouement, leaving Cameron with a mobile phone, but asking him for an hour to escape. In granting the request, Cameron's unconscious complicity is made manifest. In the final chapter, he has crossed over and become 'You': 'And so you sit on Salisbury Crags, remembering that still-present darkness and looking out over the city, feeling sorry for yourself and cursing your own stupidity' (310). His otherness is embodied in a cancerous growth the size of a tennis ball, the result of his addiction to cigarettes; but the ending maintains the text's ambivalence: 'You light another cigarette, shake your head as you look out over the grey-enthroned city, and laugh' (313).

On the one hand, Cameron has become a figure for death. In this sense he has become Andy, who suggested the name Ares, the god of massacre for his conspiracy. But, at the same time, the confrontation with death brings together everything about Andy's life that made it worth living. Elisabeth Bronfen argues that 'the presence of death in life' is 'what is most resistantly and universally repressed'[44] because death reveals limitations of the 'narcissistic' self, which believes itself to be self-sufficient. In a state of abjection, Cameron has lost his narcissism, but he is aware not only of the possibility of death, but also of his own otherness, the way his self is constructed in relation to the society in which he lives. His self has been coerced by powerful forces in society, 'institutionalised thoughtlessness, the sanctioned legal, lethal greed of the companies, the governments, the shareholders: all of them', but against this there is Cameron's affirmation of life, his self-destructive defiance of the forces that would make him something he does not want to be.

Conclusion

This chapter has examined some of the ways that gothic horror explores the limits of identity. Where some critics see the resolution of horror narrative as, in effect, frightening the reader back into a safe and conventional identity,[45] it is also possible to read Cameron's laughter (and the laughter that often follows in the wake of fear) as an affirmation. Laughter is itself an ambivalent reaction, expressing both relief and an engagement with that which we fear. In the words of Mikhail Bakhtin, 'laughter degrades and materializes'.[46] It breaks down a narcissistic sense of the classical body or the autonomous self. The grotesque, the partial and the excessive are not only self-destructive; they are productive. They formulate new possible ways of being despite the norms and conventions that are a coercive force on identity. Horror can terrify us into hiding under the bedclothes or it can reveal the ridiculousness of cowering beneath self-imposed limits. The monster can reveal the mass of social and psychic relations that construct identity, and if it makes us aware of the impossibility of ever fully understanding that mass, we can at least learn the impotence and relative fragility of the self. This can be liberating, and in the next chapter I will explore further the transgressive, utopian potential of popular fiction.

Notes

1 Cited in John Bear, *The #1 New York Times Bestseller* (Berkeley CA, Ten Speed Press, 1992), p. 209.
2 'The literature of terror is studded with passages where the protagonists brush against the awareness – described by Freud – that the perturbing element is *within them*.' Franco Moretti, 'Dialectic of Fear', in *Signs Taken for Wonders* (London, Verso, 1983), p. 102.
3 'The queer tendency of horror film ... lies in its ability to reconfigure gender not simply through inversion but by literally creating new categories.' Judith Halberstam, *Skin Shows: Gothic Horror and the Technology of Monsters* (Durham NC, Duke University Press, 1995), p. 139.
4 Immanuel Kant, cited in Moretti, *Signs Taken for Wonders*, p. 288 n.12.
5 David Punter, *The Literature of Terror* (London, Longman, 1980), p. 5.
6 Fred Botting, *Gothic* (London, Routledge, 1996), pp. 162–8.
7 In his essay on the Uncanny, Freud suggests these two emotions are closely connected. Sigmund Freud, 'The Uncanny', in *On Creativity and the Unconscious: Papers on the Psychology of Art, Literature, Love, Religion* (New York, Harper & Row, 1958).
8 Dennis Wheatley, *The Satanist* (London, Mandarin, [1960] 1995), p. 321.
9 See Avril Horner, '*Unheimlich*', in M. M. Roberts (ed.), *The Gothic Handbook* (London, Macmillan, 1997).
10 Freud, 'The Uncanny', p. 159.
11 Sigmund Freud, *Introductory Lectures on Psychoanalysis*, Pelican Freud Library vol. 1 (Harmondsworth, Penguin, 1973), pp. 254–5.
12 See, for example, Charles Dickens's semi-comic opening to *The Chimes* (1845); Henry James's *Turn of the Screw* (1898); or even the beginning of Joseph Conrad's *Heart of Darkness* (1899), which begins at dusk on a ship.
13 James Herbert, *Moon* (New York, Onyx, [1985] 1987), pp. 5–6.
14 Lucie Armitt, 'The Fragile Frames of *The Bloody Chamber*', in Treva Broughton and Joe Bristow (eds), *The Infernal Desires of Angela Carter* (London, Longman, 1997).
15 Examples would include two tales by Edgar Allan Poe: 'The Fall of the House of Usher' (1839) and 'The Cask of Amontillado' (1846).
16 Freud, 'The Uncanny', p. 151.
17 *Ibid.*, p. 157.
18 Judith Halberstam, 'Technologies of Monstrosity: Bram Stoker's *Dracula*', in Sally Ledger and Scott McCracken (eds), *Cultural Politics at the Fin de Siècle* (Cambridge, Cambridge University Press, 1995), p. 257.
19 Stephen Heath, 'Joan Riviere and the Masquerade', in Victor Burgin, James Donald and Cora Kaplan (eds), *Formations of Fantasy* (London, Routledge, 1989), p. 57.
20 Bear, *The #1 New York Times Bestseller*, p. 234. See, as examples, *The Dead Zone* (London, Futura, 1980) and *Insomnia* (New York, Signet, 1995).

21 Sigmund Freud, 'Taboo and Emotional Ambivalence', in *Totem and Taboo: Some Points of Agreement between the Mental Lives of Savages and Neurotics* (London, Norton, 1950), p. 24.

22 Julia Kristeva, *Powers of Horror: An Essay on Abjection* (New York, Columbia University Press, 1982), p. 70.

23 For a discussion of the cultural meaning of menstruation in twentieth-century American society, see Verena Lovett, 'Bodily Symbolism and the Fiction of Stephen King', in Derek Longhurst (ed.), *Gender, Genre and Narrative Pleasure* (London, Unwin Hyman, 1989).

24 Stephen King, *Carrie* (New York, Plume, [1974] 1991) p. 4 (henceforth, page numbers given in text).

25 Julia Kristeva describes abjection as that which is 'opposed to *I*', literally that which is thrown away. She differentiates abjection from the Uncanny as more violent: 'elaborated through a failure to recognize its kin; nothing is familiar, not even the shadow of memory'. *Powers of Horror*, p. 5.

26 *Ibid.*, p. 70.

27 Peter Stallybrass and Allon White, 'The Fair, the Pig, Authorship', in *The Poetics and Politics of Transgression* (London, Methuen, 1986).

28 Elisabeth Bronfen, *Over Her Dead Body: Death, Femininity and the Aesthetic* (Manchester, Manchester University Press, 1992), p. 324.

29 Freud, 'The Uncanny', p. 156 n.1.

30 Moretti, 'Dialectic of Fear', p. 103.

31 Robert Louis Stevenson, *The Strange Case of Dr Jekyll and Mr Hyde and Other Stories* (Harmondsworth, Penguin, [1886] 1979), p. 82.

32 Oscar Wilde, *The Picture of Dorian Gray and Other Writings* (New York, Bantam, [1891] 1982), p. 124.

33 Sandra Gilbert and Susan Gubar, *The Madwoman in the Attic: The Woman Writer and the Nineteenth-Century Literary Imagination* (New Haven CT and London, Yale University Press, 1979).

34 Catherine Cookson, *The Cultured Handmaiden* (London, Corgi, 1988), p. 168.

35 Halberstam, *Skin Shows*, p. 125.

36 Joan Riviere, 'Womanliness as Masquerade', in V. Burgin, J. Donald and C. Kaplan (eds), *Formations of Fantasy* (London, Routledge, 1989).

37 In English, amongst the best known narratives in the tradition of the masculine gothic are: James Hogg, *The Private Memoirs and Confessions of a Justified Sinner* (1824); Edgar Allan Poe, 'William Williamson' (1839); Robert Louis Stevenson, *The Strange Case of Dr Jekyll and Mr Hyde*; and Oscar Wilde, *The Picture of Dorian Gray*.

38 Iain Banks, *Complicity* (London, Little, Brown, 1993), p. 3 (henceforth page numbers given in text).

39 Eve Kosofsky Sedgwick, *Between Men: English Literature and Male Homosocial Desire* (Baltimore, Johns Hopkins University Press, 1985), p. 91.

40 Halberstam, *Skin Shows*, p. 112.

41 *Ibid.*, p. 112.

42 On Thatcherism, see Stuart Hall and Martin Jacques (eds), *The Politics of Thatcherism* (London, Lawrence & Wishart, 1983).

43 Theodor Adorno and Max Horkheimer, *Dialectic of Enlightenment* (London, Verso, 1979), p. 153. See Chapter 1 on the Frankfurt School.

44 Bronfen, *Over Her Dead Body*, p. 114.

45 'it is a fear one *needs*: *the* price one pays for coming to terms with a social body based on irrationality and menace. Who says it is escapist?' Moretti, 'Dialectic of Fear', p. 108.

46 Mikhail Bakhtin, *Rabelais and His World* (Cambridge MA, MIT Press, 1968), p. 20.

six
Transgression and utopianism

Popular fiction would have little point if it weren't fun. We read it for pleasure, not line by line, paragraph by paragraph. In *The Pleasure of the Text*, Roland Barthes writes, 'our very avidity for knowledge impels us to skim or skip certain passages (anticipated as "boring") in order to get more quickly to the warmer parts of the anecdote (which are always its articulations: whatever furthers the solution of the riddle, the revelation of fate): we boldly skip (no one is watching) descriptions, explanations, analyses, conversations.'[1] This final chapter is devoted to the kinds of pleasures popular fiction affords. These pleasures are not uniform and, not surprisingly, there are many different critical accounts of the diversions of the text. Pleasure, *jouissance*, laughter, the carnivalesque, the 'erotics of reading' are some of the critical concepts which have been used to describe the various satisfactions on offer. My basic argument is that transgression always plays a part in our enjoyment. To transgress means to violate or infringe, to go beyond certain bounds. Pleasure is always transgressive because it oversteps convention, taking us out of the realm of conformity and into a more dangerous zone.

Yet the still dominant view of popular fiction is that it consists of standard products. It corresponds to what Barthes calls the text of pleasure, where the pleasure comes from the text's conventional structure and 'a *comfortable* practice of reading'.[2] For many critics the popular text does not challenge the reader. It can never be what

Barthes calls the text of *jouissance* (meaning equally joy, bliss and orgasm), which disrupts the reader's identity: 'the text that imposes a state of loss, the text that discomforts'. In this book however I have argued that the division between the pleasure that confirms identity and the bliss that is its disruption is never so clear. Detective fiction has a conventional structure and yet the solution never fully answers all the questions raised by the investigation. There is an excess which discomforts, problematising the reader's identity in relation to the world. The formula romance might seem the most conventional of all narratives, but the crucial role of fantasy creates an active reader who has to project a self in relation to a number of provisional subject positions provided by the fantasy setting. Science fiction's very purpose is to explore an encounter with the new, opening up the possibility of weird and novel identities. The root of horror's success is in reaching to the ambivalences that mark the limits of a secure self. Barthes argues that the 'anachronic' reader can keep both texts in 'his field' by reading classics and popular fiction: 'he enjoys the consistency of his selfhood (that is his pleasure) and seeks its loss (that is his bliss). He is a subject split twice over, doubly perverse.'[3] But against Barthes' false division, I will argue that the reader of popular fiction can enjoy both pleasure and bliss from the same text. He or she is indeed a subject split twice over.

While I have tried to argue for the centrality of transgression in popular fiction, it is important not to go to the other extreme and argue that everything in popular culture is transgressive. In this chapter I want to look at the specific ways in which transgression operates in texts and this requires that the moment of transgression be discussed in its historical context. It is important to know which boundaries are being crossed and when. The transgressive moment in popular fiction can then be taken as a starting point for an analysis of the kinds of social conflicts that provide the impetus for and the pleasure obtained from popular fiction. This might be described as the cultural politics of transgression; but I do not invoke the word 'politics' in order to value texts as 'good' or 'bad', 'progressive' or 'reactionary', 'right' or 'left'. Transgression involves the destabilisation of such categories. In this I follow Stuart Hall, who argues that '[c]lassic metaphors of transformation are modelled on the "revolutionary moment"', and assume a 'rough correspondence' between social hierarchy and cultural values so that, 'when social hierarchies are overthrown, a reversal of cultural values and symbols is certain sooner or later to follow.'[4] In recent years, such models, with their 'brutal simplicities and truncated correspondences', have been superseded by new ways of thinking through the relationship between the social and the symbolic. In what follows, I examine some of these new ways of thinking.

I begin with Bakhtin's notion of the carnivalesque and the use of the grotesque body as a transgressive form in popular fiction. However, in the following section I switch my focus to the limits of transgression in a discussion of the uses of stereotypes. I use the work of Homi Bhabha to argue that the stereotype is not so much a sign of standardisation as of anxiety. The transgressive qualities of popular fiction rely on a dialectical relationship with the social conventions the stereotype upholds. The cultural politics of the popular text emerge from the relationship between that interaction and the specific conditions of the text's production and reception.

The second part of the chapter explores some recent innovations in popular fiction. A proper charting of all the new trends would require not just a chapter but a book. Among the narratives that demonstrate the extent to which social change has influenced the recent history of popular culture are: gay detective stories and romances, feminist thrillers, lesbian vampire stories and Westerns, and the increasing presence of black and Asian writers in the publishing market.[5] Given the limited space available, I have chosen to concentrate on recent popular fiction by African-American authors. This choice risks two dangers. First, it might suggest that black fiction is *in itself* transgressive; and, second, that black popular fiction can be easily compared with feminist or lesbian and gay popular fiction. Neither of these two propositions holds true. Rather, black fiction is transgressive not because of any intrinsic characteristics but because of the relationship between it and the social context in which it is produced. Fiction by black authors is one example of the complex relationship between a particular reader constituency and the publishing industry. A market for books aimed specifically at black readers is a relatively new phenomenon in both Britain and the United States and publishers have been slow to recognise its potential. In the United States, black readers account for 160 million sales a year, with young black middle-class women a particularly important audience. In the week ending 23 June 1996, books by black writers occupied number two in the fiction and numbers one and five in the non-fiction bestseller lists of the *New York Times*. However, demand has not been matched by editorial support. African-Americans made up as little as 3.6 per cent of the publishing industry's workforce in 1994, compared to 21.9 per cent of the workforce in the New York area, the centre of the American publishing industry.[6] Writing by African-Americans has to negotiate a situation where, despite its popularity, the assertion of a black identity is at odds with the hegemonic culture and the structures of the culture industry.

My two main examples of transgression and utopianism in popular fiction are Walter Mosley, who has written a series of novels about an African-American detective, Easy Rawlins; and Terry McMillan, who has written bestselling novels like *Waiting to Exhale* (1992) and, more recently, *How Stella Got Her Groove Back* (1996). Mosley and McMillan's novels demonstrate the dynamic nature of popular culture, its protean ability to supply an imaginative space for new social formations. This, finally, is the root of the utopian potential in all popular fiction: its capacity to imagine new ways of being in the world.

Theories of transgression

Theories of transgression have been employed in cultural criticism to describe the destabilisation of cultural categories that occurs in popular cultural forms. Following the work of Mikhail Bakhtin, this destabilisation is sometimes called the carnivalesque. Carnival revels in the topsy-turvy, in reversal, the back-to-front, and inversion, the upside down. In the carnivalesque, high becomes low, the spiritual becomes the bodily, the refined becomes vulgar. Conventional identities are transgressed, the masculine is feminised, the feminine masculinised, and desire breaks free from its 'correct' object. The carnivalesque is kept alive in contemporary popular culture through a transgressive upsetting of society's norms. In this, it reveals the relationship between culture and power, making clear that, in Antonio Gramsci's words,

> A given socio-historical moment is never homogeneous; on the contrary, it is rich in contradictions. It acquires a 'personality' and is a 'moment' of

development in that a certain fundamental activity of life prevails over others and represents a historical 'peak': but this presupposes a hierarchy, a contrast, a struggle.[7]

This view of popular culture is markedly different from that given by most theories of mass culture. In Chapter 1, I described negative theories of mass culture as those which understand popular culture in modern societies as the production of standardised commodities, yielding only degraded pleasures, the passive pleasures of consumption rather than the active pleasures of agency. A theory of transgression, by contrast, draws attention to popular culture's role in struggles over meaning. It argues that the popular text is successful because it operates at the borders of what is socially acceptable; and, in order to provoke a widespread interest, the text must, at some level, breach the bounds of that acceptability. It must, in other words, challenge social standards and norms.

One of the problems in arbitrating between the claims of negative theories of mass culture and a theory of transgression is that both have some claims to truth. As we have seen in Chapter 1, contemporary popular culture *is* characterised by mass production for a mass market and its products *are* often formulaic. However, as described in Chapter 1, close analyses of popular texts also demonstrate levels of irony, satire and parody that show them to open to many different interpretations, not all of which reinforce a view of the world as a model of rationalised capitalist efficiency. Consequently, a theory of transgression has to recognise the logic of the market and to account for the dynamic relationship between that logic and the unpredictability and heterogeneity of people's needs and desires.[8] This requires a complex model of the relationship between culture and power, because it suggests that power is not concentrated in one place, for example in a ruling class or dominant sex. According to Michel Foucault, whose work has contributed much to theories of transgression, power permeates throughout the whole of society. For Foucault, 'there are as many different kinds of revolution ... as there are possible subversive recodifications of power.'[9]

Mikhail Bakhtin's work on the carnivalesque and 'dialogism' is of particular importance for a discussion of popular fiction because his work takes as its starting point a rethinking of the novel. The moment of carnival is a dialogic moment of freedom when meaning breaks free from 'monologism': in other words, a single authoritative voice is replaced by voices in dialogue. Where classic theories of the novel have seen it as a middle-class form that arose at the same time as capitalism,[10] Bakhtin traces its development back to early parodies of epic in the ancient world and to a 'folkloric' tradition of earthy humour. Significant here is his concept of 'uncrowning', by which he means the bringing low of symbols of power. He argues that the novel, like carnival, incorporates a dialogic principle into its structure. In the novel no statement goes unanswered, unquestioned or un-qualified. Every utterance is represented in relation to the specific context of the particular speech act. Thus meaning is achieved not through any intrinsic significance contained within the utterance itself but only in relation to its reception. While the carnivalesque does not necessarily challenge social power, it does disrupt its representations through a process of 'transcoding'.

One of the key areas for transcoding is the body. Concepts of social value are mapped on to the body, so that the upper part of the body signifies order and the lower part disorder and rebellion. Bakhtin charts a history of the 'grotesque' where the carnival body disrupts these neat distinctions. Peter Stallybrass and Allon White describe the 'carnival body' as follows:

> The openings and orifices of this carnival body are emphasized, not its closure and finish. It is an image of impure corporeal bulk with its orifices (mouth, flared nostrils, anus yawning wide and its lower regions (belly, legs, feet buttocks and genitals) giving priority over the upper regions (head 'spirit', reason).[11]

A good example of such transcoding is this 1980s' headline from the popular British tabloid newspaper the *Sun*:

SEX ROMPS
OF PHILIP'S
FRIEND
*Top horsewoman tells
of her lodger lovers*[12]

The headline, which is in effect a very short popular narrative, is typical of the tabloid front page in its lack of verbs, so that the order of the nouns gives a sequential or horizontal reading as described in Chapter 2. This sequence upsets the social hierarchy which descends from the royal family at the top to the propertyless lodger at the bottom of the social scale, by beginning with the bodily. The first two lines, read quickly, hint that Prince Philip himself was involved in sexual escapades, while the phrase itself, in a vertical reading, sparks associations which subvert the royal family's attempts to maintain a dignified image. The opening sentence of the article continues to 'carnivalise' the social hierarchy by transcoding it on to bodily images:

> A HORSEY woman chum of Prince Philip told yesterday of her amazing sex frolics with TWO lodgers she hired as odd-job men.

The upper-case 'HORSEY' signifies both aristocratic equestrianism and the popular jibe that upper-class riders resemble the animals they sit on. This involves one of the most common functions of the carnivalesque, where the superiority of human over beast is inverted. In the article the social order of landowner over tenant, and Prince over subject, is brought down (and here Bakhtin's term 'uncrowning' is peculiarly apt) by the transgressive intervention of the sexual act. Where the symbolism of power relies on images of dignity, its disruption glories in the grotesque – a woman who looks like a horse – and in the relish for the bodily summoned up in the hyphenated 'sex-romp'. It doesn't matter that the actual social connection between the Prince and the lodger may be very tenuous, the headline works (achieves its popularity) because it upsets the devaluation of the corporeal in the symbolism of power. Sue Townsend's comic novel *The Queen and I*, which reached number one in the British paperback bestseller lists in October 1993, works on a similar principle. It tells of the downfall of the house of Windsor thanks to the declaration of a republic. They are moved to a council estate, where the story of their adaptation to a new lifestyle unfolds.

Uncrowning is a common device in popular fiction and it does not always require royalty. Bakhtin traces a tradition of the popular grotesque which works through comic images of the body, sex and death, and exists in contradistinction to canonical literature. It is a tradition which continues in popular fiction. The novels of Jilly Cooper are packed with extraordinary grotesques. The list of characters of *Polo* (1991), her international tale of the rich and sporty, includes, amongst many others, Jackie Cosgrove, 'Hippie painter and art lecturer. Also proficient in the art of lechery'; Sharon Kaputnik, 'nymphomaniac night-club hostess'; and Lionel Mannering, 'goaty psychiatrist'. In one gloriously Bacchanalian scene in another of her novels, *Rivals*, a tale of competition over a television franchise, two characters commit adultery while drinking champagne and consuming a large coffee cake. The occasion is particularly satisfying because both participants are nagged by their respective spouses for being overweight. The sex act thus becomes a double transgression, against both the strictures of marriage and the constraints of the modern disciplined 'Californian' body. Pleasure is found in exceeding the limits imposed by social norms; and in some exceedingly bad jokes.

> 'You do say the loveliest fings,' said Freddie, drawing her close. His paunch slotted in below her splendid breasts, so it was very easy for them to kiss ...
>
> 'I'm so fat,' sighed Lizzie.
>
> 'You're not,' said Freddie. 'It's much more fun climbing Everest than the foothills.'
>
> Lizzie put her hand on his cock. 'And it's so nice to see software becoming hardware.'
>
> 'And I'm going to declare this an area of outstanding natural beauty,' said Freddie. Reaching for his glass of champagne on the bedside table, he emptied it into her bush and proceeded to lick it off. After Mousie's fragility, he reflected as he climbed on top of her, it was like having a wonderfully sturdy cob between your thighs.
>
> 'I hope you're using a Condom Perignon,' mumbled Lizzie half-laughing and half-crying with pleasure as he entered her ...
>
> Afterwards they had another bottle and ate all the coffee cake ...[13]

With food and sex, the other main figures through which the grotesque is represented are defecation, disease, injury and death. We have already seen in Chapter 5 how the abject body is used in horror to signify the limits of identity. But in all genres of popular fiction death marks the point where the individual self collapses to reveal identity as a social construction. Bakhtin's account of representations of death marks a somewhat different version of popular representations of violence than that given by media accounts of 'sex and violence'. Complaints about the 'body-count' in action movies such as *Die Hard II* or *Total Recall* centre on the de-individualisation involved in the serial killing of the faceless opponents of the hero. For Bakhtin, however, to see these figures as individuals would be to miss their function as images of decay and rebirth. As discussed in Chapter 5, laughter embraces the materiality of the body. He locates this tradition in the work of Rabelais: 'The nature of Rabelaisian laughter is revealed in its full vividness in the death series, at the points of intersection of this series with the eating, drinking and sexual series and in its direct association of death with the birth of new life.'[14] Death in popular culture often signifies not the end of the individual but the possibility of social change and renewal. What Bakhtin says about the poetry of Baudelaire is also true of popular fiction: death 'ceases to be an aspect of life itself and becomes again a phenomenon on the border between my life here-and-now and a potential other kind of life'.[15]

In the following passage, from Tom Clancy's bestselling thriller *Debt of Honour* (already mentioned in Chapters 1 and 4), two American agents break into a flat to rescue a kidnapped Japanese politician:

> One man was in view, just getting up from a chair in front of the TV, his face surprised and alarmed at the unannounced entry. There wasn't time for mercy. Clark brought the gun up in both hands and squeezed twice, both shots entering the man's forehead. John felt Ding's hand on his shoulder, which allowed him to move right, almost running now, down a hallway, looking into each room. *Kitchen*, he thought. *You always found people in the —*
>
> He did. This man was almost his height, and his gun was already out as he moved for the hallway that led to the foyer, calling out a name and a question, but he, too, was a little too slow, and his gun was still down, and he met a man with his pistol up and ready. It was the last thing he would ever see.[16]

The death of the villains marks the turning point in an (imagined) war with Japan. Their demise is important symbolically as a moment of triumph for the heroes and the rebirth of their hopes. The release of the Japanese politician signals the start of Japan's return to 'sense': that is, its subordinate role to the might of the USA. Although the agents stop briefly to consider the meaning of their actions, the morality of murder is not their main concern. Death relates to the eating, drinking and sexual series described by Bakhtin. The enemy agent is in the kitchen, presumably preparing food, and he is cut down in the midst of life's pleasures. His gun is down and he is vanquished by the hero whose 'pistol is up and ready'. The gun, as so often in popular representations, is a symbol of phallic power: killing is the victory of virility over impotence.

Such visual spectacles[17] and figures of excess persist in, amongst many others, the use of special effects in film and in a continuing delight in the bodily in all forms of popular fiction. However, while it is clear that the carnivalesque is a crucial element in popular fiction, it is important to emphasise that carnival does not necessarily involve a permanent upsetting of the social order. It may even have the opposite effect. Temporary license may allow a letting off of steam which then facilitates a return to the status quo.[18] In certain cases, carnival may be the occasion for public displays of prejudice against oppressed groups.[19] This is the case in the Clancy extract above, where the killing of the non-American foe is part of a long tradition of imperial adventure stories. The destruction of the Other is the excessive event which defines the identity of the heroic self. The carnivalesque moment is, however, one of liberation in the sense that it is a moment when meanings break free and new visions of what is possible come into being. An excess of meaning is produced which, as in science fiction, operates on the edge of the future. Figures of excess, whether, sex, food or death, suggest the utopian potential of the popular, the possibility that meaning may exceed the mundane norms of our lives.[20] Here the pleasure of the text is its promise of something else and something better.

Stereotypes

One aspect of popular fiction that would seem to contradict a theory of transgression is the widespread use of stereotypes. The word originally referred to the printing plate that is used to reproduce the same piece of type over and over again, and is thus peculiarly well suited to a discussion of popular fiction. It now refers to cultural representations which are reproduced with monotonous regularity. For Barthes,

> the stereotype is the word repeated without any magic, any enthusiasm, as though it were natural, as though by some miracle this recurring word were adequate on each occasion for different reasons, as though to imitate could no longer be sensed as an imitation: an unconstrained word that claims consistency and is unaware of its own insistence.[21]

As we have seen, the standardisation that exists in many popular texts is one of the targets of negative theories of mass culture.

Racist and sexist images are commonplace. The *Sun* headline above is a case in point. A masculine social hierarchy is disrupted by a grotesque feminine body: the horse-woman. It could be argued that, while the headline disrupts the British class system, it reinforces the symbolic order that sees feminine sexuality as abnormal. This combination of radicalism and conservatism is typical of the transgressive and makes the argument for its careful unpicking.

A good place to start is to question the common view of the stereotype as a function of an oppressive and unassailable value system. On the contrary, argues Homi Bhabha, the very fact that the stereotype needs to be repeated over and over again demonstrates its ambivalence (for more on ambivalence, see Chapter 5): 'the stereotype ... is a form of knowledge and identification that vacillates between what is always "in place", already known, and something that must be anxiously repeated'.[22] For Bhabha, an analysis of the stereotype shows its function in drawing the boundaries between self and other. The stereotype operates as a phobia or fetish, which, as described in Chapter 3, provides a setting of desire on to which the reader's fantasies can be projected. The fantasy involves a confirmation of the reader's wish that his or her identity is original and unalterable, rather than the product of an ongoing interaction between self and other:

> The stereotype is not a simplification because it is a false representation of a given reality. It is a simplification because it is an arrested, fixated form of representation that, in denying the play of difference (which the negation through the Other permits), constitutes a problem for the *representation* of the subject in significations of psychic and social relations.[23]

Seen as a problem of representation, an analysis of the stereotype as evidence of cultural anxiety makes for some productive readings of popular fiction.

Cultural stereotypes of 'race', class and gender abound in Jilly Cooper's novels and while some are comic, others are profoundly offensive. An example is the following use of the term 'nigger' in her novel *Polo*:

> Come on, Nigger,' said Perdita clamping her legs round her fat black pony. 'Why are you so fucking slow?'
> 'You better rename him Snowflake if he wins Best Playing Pony,' said Luke with a grin. 'It's being presented by some African prince ...'[24]

The word 'nigger' brings with it a history of racism dating back to the enslavement of Africans. Here the expression signifies the racist culture of its owners, in which a slow, stupid horse is named after a derogatory term for someone of African descent. That the term is so used, apparently without a second thought, is a denial of what Bhabha calls 'the play of difference'. Instead, it expresses a fantasy of essential whiteness: a society in which multiculturalism is not an issue. In this passage, however, that fantasy is broken by the presence of a problematic figure: an African who is taking part in the same social event as the white characters. This changes the dialogic context of the word. Used by one white European to another, the horse's name signifies a common identity, one which here bonds an American man, Luke, and an English woman. Applied to an African, the name becomes a direct (rather than an indirect) expression of a continued sense of white superiority.

Luke registers the new dialogic context through a joke. The joke indicates some recognition of a heterogeneous society and suggests the anxiety already existing in the stereotype: the fear that a secure white identity is not available.[25] The form of the joke, where a black horse is renamed 'Snowflake' performs the vacillation described by Bhabha between the 'knowledge' that blackness means an essential difference and the need to repeat the racist expression, which reveals that difference as cultural. Both 'nigger' and 'snowflake' are signs that only achieve meaning in a particular dialogic context. Both, in fact, are 'racial' epithets, used to describe the 'other' group. Their function is to establish the boundaries that are in danger of transgression. In this case, the utterance of the stereotype and the joke signify the cultural boundaries within which the text operates.

Cooper's novel is global in its scope, taking in the main (white) international centres of polo, but the home of the key characters is Rutshire, an imaginary English county. As with the cyberpunk novels discussed in Chapter 4, the bestseller negotiates between local identities and a global culture. Argentina, Florida and Singapore are just some of the novel's non-English locations. However, the international milieu and multiple cultural and sexual encounters of *Polo* have limits. Despite the fact that polo originates in Asia, it is represented exclusively as the game of the white super-rich. Rutshire is the home to many larger-than-life characters; but there is no indication that Britain is now a multicultural society. The use of the stereotype in that context signals the limits of transgression in the novel. The need to repeat the stereotype in the context of an international milieu suggests the ambivalent status of Middle England in relation to processes of globalisation and detraditionalisation in the late twentieth century, a process which brings both advantages and insecurity to the English middle class and for which, as Kevin Davey points out, 'black people risk serving as a convenient code'.[26]

The point of this discussion of the cultural politics of transgression is not, however, to point the finger at the narrow outlook of the white, English, upper-middle class. The point is to show that popular fiction relies on the definition and transgression of cultural boundaries to achieve its popularity. The racist stereotype establishes the limits of transgression in *Polo*. For Barthes the pleasure of the text is located at the point where convention (the stereotype) and transgression meet:

> Two edges are created: an obedient, conformist, plagiarizing edge (the language is to be copied in its canonical state, as it has been established by schooling, good usage, literature, culture), and *another edge*, mobile, blank (ready to assume any contours) ... These two edges, *the compromise they bring about*, are necessary. Neither culture nor its destruction is erotic; it is the seam between them, the fault, the flaw, which becomes so.[27]

Barthes' is a deliberately scandalous suggestion because it suggests that our pleasures are always transgressive, but that we rely on conventions to produce the effect of transgression. The other edge 'is never anything but the site of its effect: the place where the death of language is glimpsed'.[28] A theory of transgression developed from these insights suggests that the unconscious is structured around the fixed positions that cultural and sexual stereotypes reproduce. As in popular romance, where fixed poles of masculinity and femininity create a fantasy setting within which the reader's vacillating sense of his or her gender identity is experienced, so the pleasure of the text is gained from our ambivalent reaction to those fixed positions. This makes it difficult to have a 'politically correct' analysis of the workings of the transgressive text. Instead, criticism needs to give some account of a text's cultural politics, which will include a contradictory combination that will be difficult to categorise as right or left, right or wrong. For example, the cultural politics of the Jilly Cooper series of 'bonkbusters' (*Riders, Rivals, Polo*) might be analysed in terms of a licensed carnival tied in to the celebration of sport in the case of *Riders* and *Polo* and television entertainment in the case of *Rivals*. Cooper's carnivalesque is a celebration of bodily pleasures, but that celebration excludes those who are not part of the charmed social circle who participate in the worlds of sport and entertainment. This is not to say that you have to play polo to enjoy *Polo*. Generally speaking, the text is inclusive rather than exclusive, a process which is aided by the traditional novelistic device of making a less-well-off, fatherless girl, Perdita, the central character. However, the carnival has limits and the position of the reader in relation to those limits is a question of power. For a critical approach to popular fiction, this discovery means the uncomfortable realisation that some, and perhaps all, the pleasures of reading involve an identification which denies those it excludes an equal right to identity.

For this reason alone the context in which a text is read is important; but even if we know the exact circumstances of the reader's situation, it is difficult to be precise about how she or he uses the popular text. The power of the psychic structures of racism or homophobia is such that even those who are socially excluded by such structures may be attracted as well as repelled by racist or homophobic representations. The text's pleasures will be elicited by the kind of vacillations provided by the fantasy of a fixed and powerful identity. However, while it is not possible to define the audience of a popular text through an analysis of the text on its own, it is possible to identify certain reader constituencies which are attracted to certain kinds of texts.[29] This suggests a fragmented rather than a homogeneous account of the popular audience. Different genres attract different groups of readers. Bestsellers, which I described in Chapter 1 as hybrid genres, attract a coalition of reader groups, which will differ depending on the nature of the bestseller text. None of these audiences will be stable, but will instead be made and remade in a changing society.

Transgressive identities

One recent development in popular fiction has been the growth of new voices. As we have seen in previous chapters, women writers like Marcia Muller and Sarah Paretsky have entered the previously masculine world of the thriller and hard-boiled detective fiction.

Lesbian and gay detective fiction has emerged in the works of Mary Wings, Val McDermid, Barbara Wilson and Joseph Hansen. Black writers have tapped a market for popular fiction amongst readers in the United States and Britain. Writers like Octavia Butler use the genres of popular fiction to challenge the limits of social conventions. This in turn has an effect on the dominant forms of popular fiction, which must then engage these new voices in dialogue, even if it is to repudiate them.

Walter Mosley's African-American detective, Easy Rawlins, is a recent example of the capacity of popular culture to give expression to transgressive identities. Easy is a philosopher-detective, like those described in Chapter 2, who also serves as a historian, rewriting the experience of the African-American community in post-war Los Angeles. While Easy has to construct his conception of the world in relation to the violence of racism, his position as single parent and small businessman also locates his identity within a matrix of social contradictions in the city that has been seen as the epitome of postmodern culture. The Rawlins mysteries are an exploration of what Paul Gilroy, following W. E. B. DuBois, calls double-consciousness: the experience of the African diaspora, which, because of slavery and racism, is both inside and outside European modernity at the same time.[30]

The history of Easy's identity can be traced through three stages. First, his upbringing in the South: he was raised on a sharecropping farm in Texas, then orphaned and left to a violent and brutal childhood on the streets of Houston. Second, the channelling of some of that violence into army life during the Second World War, where his experience of war was one of sanctioned transgression. In Europe, he saw the breakdown of segregation in the US army under the pressure of battle. At the Battle of the Bulge, he fought alongside whites and Japanese-Americans. He experienced the different attitudes of Europeans to blacks. The Nazi death camps gave him a comparative sense of racism which contributed to his double-consciousness of a double-sided modernity of both civilisation and barbarism: 'in Europe the Jew had been a Negro for more than a thousand years'.[31] In an inversion of the 'racial' codes of the United States, he slept with white women and had state sanction to kill white German soldiers. One of the starkest images of *Devil in a Blue Dress* is his memory of blue-eyed German corpses piled up along the road (3, 21, 143). It is this memory, above all, which gives him the confidence to assert himself in the face of white authority after the war. Released from the army, Easy becomes part of the mass migration of African-Americans west to California to work in the defence industries that were the basis of Californian prosperity throughout the Cold War. Thus, Easy is a typical figure in the sense of being a contradictory character who represents the movement of a whole social group through a historical period. He becomes a detective in the context of that movement because, partly as a result of his wartime experiences, he refuses the 'racial' conventions of American industrial relations and loses his job because he won't apologise to the foreman.

As a detective, Easy operates on the edge, between the conformist structures of white society and the closed space of the black ghetto. He works at the seam between what a racist society defines as culture and non-culture. White politicians, the FBI, even the notoriously racist Los Angeles Police Department (LAPD) hire him. They need him because he has access to Watts, a predominantly African-American neighbourhood. He needs them because, like the character Albright who works for a white politician, they provide the money and the power he needs to hold on to his social status:

> When I was a poor man, and landless, all I worried about was a place to eat; you really didn't need much for that. A friend would always stand me a meal, and there were plenty of women who would let me sleep with them. But when I got that mortgage I found that I needed more than friendship. Mr Albright wasn't a friend but he had what I needed. (20)

Despite the nostalgia expressed here for the physical and sexual comforts of an earlier black community, Easy maintains his links with that past through his childhood friend and alter-ego, Raymond Alexander, known as Mouse. Mouse and Easy are examples of the kind of male doubles discussed in Chapter 5. They reflect Easy's double consciousness. On the one hand, as home-owner, businessman and family man, Easy has a respectable, proto-bourgeois identity. On the other, he has a quasi-criminal identity, formed by his childhood experiences and his continuing connections with the underworld, especially with Mouse. Easy's relationship to property is ambivalent. He takes his first detective job because he needs to pay his mortgage after he is fired. In later novels in the Easy Rawlins series,[32] he builds up a business of several properties in an attempt to become a bona fide member of the black middle class. However, the precarious position of the black property-owner forces him to keep his status secret, and he gives out that his is the cleaner of his own buildings. In the American context, property establishes his right to citizenship, and when his own house is threatened he is prepared to defend it with arms. But Easy's house is also a variation on the tradition of the detective's pad described in Chapter 2, which stretches from Baker Street to V. I. Warshawski's apartment. In that tradition the pad is emblematic of the detective's individuality, the limits of her or his identity, and in this case the extent of Easy's minimal stake in society. In this sense, Easy's house represents an achievement in the context of a specifically African-American struggle against dispossession and exclusion: 'I loved going home. Maybe it was that I was raised on a share cropper's farm' (12). His house acts as safe place. It marks the beginning of some autonomy for its owner.

The trope of Easy's double identity permits an exploration of the limits of identity in relation to a critical conception of the world. As a detective he works on the boundaries of 'race', class and, as we shall see, gender. The first novel, *Devil in a Blue Dress*, has at its centre a woman who passes as white, Daphne Monet/Ruby Hanks, whose double identity marks the cultural border which defines 'racial' categories.[33] The other side of Easy's bourgeois citizen self relates to the other side of modernity represented by the disorganised violence of the South and the organised violence of the Second World War. This other side is personified by his alter-ego, Mouse. Mouse lacks any clear limits. He corresponds to Barthes' other edge. Promiscuous, insatiable and with an infinite capacity to satisfy, he is everything Easy's aspirational bourgeois identity is not. Yet Easy is linked to Mouse through a primal scene like those described in Chapters 3 and 5, where he was an accomplice to the murder of Mouse's stepfather.[34] Where Mouse feels no guilt, Easy feels guilt by association. He is Mouse's conscience, but he wishes for Mouse's lack of conscience:

> Mouse is crazy, I thought, just crazy!
> But I wished for his insanity.[35]

Mouse's potency, violence and lack of remorse represent a carnivalesque celebration of everything that Easy is trying to leave behind.

On his own he might be read as a stereotype: representing a kind of essentialised 'blackness' that is more bodily and closer to nature than 'whiteness'. In a dialogic relationship with Easy, however, Mouse shows up the limits of Easy's social sphere. His is a voice that Easy does not fully believe in; but when Mouse compares Easy with Daphne/Ruby, an idea of 'authentic' blackness acts as a powerful criticism of respectability.

> Easy. You learn stuff and you be thinkin' like white be thinkin'. You be thinkin' that what's right fo' them is right fo' you. She look like she white and you think like you white But brother you don't know that you both poor niggers. And a nigger 'ain't never gonna be happy 'less he accept what he is. (180)

Mouse's street wisdom, spoken in Black English, succinctly encapsulates the dilemma of Easy's 'racialised' identity. Here the dialogic context of the term 'nigger' is very different to that in *Polo*. Mouse describes a situation which can never be a joke to him: white society's definition of African-Americans as outsiders. In that context, Mouse's advice can be understood not so much as a definition of Easy's essential nature but as the necessity of performing a black identity within and against the constraints of racism.[36]

The relationship between Easy and Mouse is one where each defines the other. In the tradition of the masculine gothic discussed in Chapter 5, the double explores the limits of masculinity, as well as here the limits of 'racial' categories. The relationship between Easy and Mouse is a classic example of what Eve Kosofsky Sedgwick calls 'male homosocial desire'; that is, a strong social bond between men not overtly sexual, but which incorporates an undercover homoeroticism.[37] Mouse's sexuality is infectious; his sexual exploits overheard in another room cause other men to become aroused. Easy and Mouse have a history of sharing lovers, in Easy's words, 'what was a woman compared to the love of two friends' (42); and in the second novel in the Easy Rawlins series, *Red Death*, Easy has an affair with Mouse's wife, Etta-Mae, when she and Mouse are estranged.

Easy's need for Mouse is an essential part of the narrative structure of Mosley's novels. There is always a dramatic moment when Mouse rescues Easy from imminent danger. The moment usually occurs when Easy is being squeezed between two kinds of white authority.

In *Devil in a Blue Dress* these are Albright and the LAPD. In order
to extricate himself, Easy needs Mouse's infinite capacity for violence. Mouse's talent for murder is linked to his sexual potency, and
both contrast with Easy's reserve. As in *Debt of Honour*, the connection between phallic power and violence is symbolised in their guns.
Where Mouse has a long-barrelled .41, Easy has a snub-nosed .38.

The relationship between Easy and his double is an exploration
of the relationship between violence and desire in black masculinity.
Easy is connected to Mouse's violence through their shared childhood; it is a violence that has grown up in the racially structured
society of the South. Easy calls upon Mouse in times of need created
as a result of the continuing structural violence of a racist society.
The need for Mouse always occurs when Easy is at his most vulnerable. Thus Mouse represents both a kind of justice of last resort and
a solidarity which Easy cannot find anywhere else. In all the Easy
Rawlins novels, Easy goes through a pattern of first rejecting Mouse
then finding that he cannot do without him. In the climactic scene
of both *Devil in a Blue Dress* and *A Red Death*, it is Mouse's enormous pistol which, unexpectedly, comes to the rescue:

> I heard a shot, and something else, something that seemed almost impos-
> sible: Dewitt Albright grunted, 'Wha?'
> Then I saw Mouse! The smoking pistol in his hand! (*Devil in a Blue
> Dress*, 174)

In the second novel, Easy has planned for Mouse to be there:

> I tried to bring my gun around but couldn't. Lawrence ran down and
> kicked my shoulder. He grinned at me as he yanked awkwardly at the
> pistol in his pocket.
> 'Don't do it, man!' I shouted in warning. But he had the pistol out.
> He said the word, nigger, and then he flew backwards about six feet.
> When he was in the air I heard the cannonlike pistol shot from down
> among the trees. I was running before the echoes were through shouting
> my name.
> As fast as I ran, Mouse was already in the car by the time I got there.
> (*A Red Death*, 416)

In the second passage, the word 'nigger' appears again in the context
of a joke, but this time at the expense of the man who uses it. The
word is designed to reduce Easy to nothing just before he is killed.
In that dialogic context, Mouse's action is a punchline which is also

a revenge for the negation of Easy's black identity. As in *Debt of Honour*, death is also a rebirth, a moment of terror and laughter. The shot from Mouse's .41 is a moment of *jouissance*. It is a kind of ejaculation which shatters the oppressive social convention of racism and allows Easy to be reborn.

In the third novel, *White Butterfly*, Mouse bails Easy out of prison just as he is about to be murdered by a fellow prisoner. In the fourth, *Black Betty*, he nearly kills Easy, believing that he has betrayed him, but, at the last minute, Easy manages to convince him of his innocence. Mouse's friendship represents a sense of fierce community he cannot afford to give up, even if the price of his loyalty is high.

As Easy gains more of a foothold in society in the later novels, he finds more barriers are set in his way – the police, politicians, tax men, unscrupulous developers – and hence more of a need to call on Mouse. Gradually he recognises the similarity between his participation in business – the ruthless nature of capitalism – and Mouse's violence, which in many ways is far less hypocritical than his own. In *A Red Death*, Easy feels that his responsibility for the death of a tenant who cannot pay her rent is comparable with murder. One of the resolutions to this dilemma (which emerges over six novels) is Easy's creation of an alternative community which requires an alternative conception of masculinity. At the end of *A Red Death*, Mouse and Etta-Mae get back together. In a scene which is again heavy with symbolism, Easy arrives in time to hear the noisy consummation of their reunion:

> And she made a sound that I cannot duplicate. It was deep and guttural and so charged with pleasure that I got dizzy and lowered myself to the floor.
> The sounds Etta-Mae made got louder and ever more passionate. She never made those sounds because of me; no woman ever had. (422)

The scene reduces Easy to abjection and this time Mouse is not available to help him up. Consequently, Easy has to give up the fantasy he had of running off to Mexico with Etta-Mae and Mouse's son, LaMarque. In that fantasy his masculinity and Etta-Mae's femininity would have been frozen into the traditional roles of the nuclear family. Instead, he reassumes responsibility for the boy, Jesus, he rescued from an abusive white politician in *Devil in a Blue Dress*. *White Butterfly* sees him with a wife and daughter, but by the beginning of *Black Betty* he is again a single parent, now bringing up two adopted children in the house he has always defended. In this way, the Rawlins narratives operate to break down any fixed sense of identity. While stereotypical positions are offered, they are not given as final. Instead, an alternative community and therefore an alternative conception of both society and identity are possible because of the text's critical engagement with modernity. Any sense of progress is disrupted by the novels' double time scheme, where historical events are viewed from the perspective of the 1990s. This introduces the final mystery that has to be solved. How did the hopes that came first from migration and then through the Civil Rights Movement end up in the catastrophe of America's inner cities now? In the case of Watts in Los Angeles, how did an area with respectable black neighbourhoods become the war-zone of crack, gangs and urban devastation it is today?

The Rawlins novels are deliberately transgressive. They are an attempt to write black history through the popular narrative of the hard-boiled detective; but it is important to note that Mosley isn't using the detective story as a vehicle. The detective form already has within it the critical framework for the kind of historical narrative he is writing. Mosley's innovation is to focus on a particular social contradiction, racism against African-Americans in the context of post-war American society. At this point, content does alter form in the sense that the narrative achieves a far more sophisticated account of the issue of 'race' than the detective novel has ever achieved before; but the form provides the basic elements for this development. The elaboration of the traditional role of the helper into the exploration of black masculinity in Mouse and Easy is just the best example of this.[38] The transgressive element in popular fiction means that it always has a subversive potential; but the use of that potential for a particular political project requires a sophisticated narrative which can relate the symbolic and the social for liberation rather than domination.

Utopianism

One of the driving forces of popular fiction is a sense of lack. As I have already discussed in Chapter 4, this utopian element is characterised not so much by the presentation of alternative realities as blue-prints or ready-made perfect societies, but by a sense of longing or yearning for something other than what is. In the Easy Rawlins narratives, the hope is embodied in embryo in Easy's adopted family. This mixed 'race' community offers an alternative to the racist, violent society beyond the boundaries of his home. Similarly, in Sarah Paretsky's novels, V. I. Warshawski resists the binds of the nuclear family and builds up an alternative community in the face of an unforgiving city. Such better worlds turn up in unexpected places in popular fiction. In the Caribbean-British gangster novel *Yardie*, Jamaica acts as a nostalgic homeland for the novel's criminal heroes. In this the novel mimics the nostalgia for Sicily of Mario Puzo's mafia novels. In each case, Britain or the United States stand as a figure for a new, exciting, but dangerous modernity in comparison with an impoverished original community back home. While he commits horrific acts of violence, it is suggested that the main character, D., was driven to a life of crime in London by the economic situation at home. Nostalgic on the one hand, the novel also maps out the new geographical space of the Jamaican diaspora. A community that stretches from Kingston to London, Miami, New York and Toronto enables D.'s business activities. This kind of global reach again brings senses of both loss and opportunity. While Jilly Cooper's novels map one kind of international community, *Yardie* maps another. The success of the original publishers of the novel, X Press, demonstrated the existence of a British audience for popular fiction that had been untapped by mainstream publishing. Part of *Yardie*'s appeal was its hero's multiple identity: a Jamaican, operating in London on a false passport with international links through the drug trade. But the novel achieves popularity because it draws on the wider sense of cultural change in the whole of British society, exploiting anxieties that are common to much contemporary British popular fiction. D.'s character is at once that of the traditional picaresque hero, the rogue who works at society's margins, and that of an up-to-date media bugbear. Scares about the operation of 'Yardie' gangs preceded the novel and continue to crop up in the press,[39] while the novel itself helped to glamorise the idea of a criminal underworld of shebeens and reggae dancehalls. D. thus has an ambivalent and transgressive status as representative of both the worst fears and the new possibilities of global population movements. A dialogue in the last few pages demonstrates the novel's strong romantic element:

Donna knew Leroy spoke the truth. All her friends who had gone back
[to Kingston, Jamaica] had told her the same thing. Within herself she
wanted to hold on to the vision of the town she had left behind, the way
it was then ... She looked at Leroy thoughtfully.
'All demn man deh, it's drugs mash dem up.'
'Drugs, yes! But hear dis: if you grow up poor in Jamaica, with no
education, drugs is the only t'ing that will take you out of the trap. Either
you take a chance or you stay and suffer ...'
'... D. grow up downtown and him know seh the only way out of the
ghetto, out of poverty, is the rough way. Him make up his mind a long
time ago – it's too late for him to change now.'[40]

Yardie marks a moment of change in British popular culture. The
book achieved its status as scandalous because it exploited current
anxieties about immigration and crime. Its success amongst black
readers suggests that, despite its use of stereotypes in the character
of D., the novel operated as what has been called (in the context of
same-sex sexualities) a 'reverse discourse', a return of the 'demonised
other' to challenge power through the 'appropriation and negation'
of the same dominant notions of identity and human nature, 'by
which it was initially excluded and defined'.[41] Following this reading,
readers of *Yardie* can appropriate D. as a contradictory figure, both
criminal and rebel, corrupted and corrupter.

Not surprisingly, given the larger black community, fiction by
African-American writers exists in a more developed tradition than
in Britain. One recent example is the author Terry McMillan, who,
in an interesting illustration of 'low' culture following 'high', has
followed critically acclaimed authors like Alice Walker and Toni
Morrison into the marketplace to write bestselling fictions about
black women. *Waiting to Exhale* was first published in 1992 and was
released as a film with Whitney Houston in 1996.

The novel follows the structure of a television soap opera, taking
the lives of four women who live in Phoenix, Arizona. Unlike most
soap operas, the narrative has a political edge. It develops some of
the themes of black feminism that arose out of the American Civil
Rights Movement and inspired novels like Walker's *The Color Purple*
and Morrison's *Beloved*. The narrative structure mixes first-person
and third-person narration which shifts from character to character.
Each is an identifiable type. Savannah is a level-headed, single career
woman, who is trying to break into television production. Bernadine
has sacrificed her own career to her children and her husband's

business only to have him leave her for his white assistant at the beginning of the novel. Robin is a successful insurance underwriter, but is 'dizzy', susceptible to men who are chronically unfaithful and financially untrustworthy. Gloria is an overweight single mother with a teenage son, who owns a thriving hairdresser's business.

All are successful, upwardly mobile, professional women. In contrast with McMillan's earlier novel, *Mama*, which is about a single mother bringing up her children on welfare, the problems these women encounter are related to their social mobility. This means that 'social' issues like racism and sexism are seen through the prism of increased expectations of a black middle class. One of the functions of the novel is to create a sense of distinction (in Bourdieu's sense of the word discussed in Chapter 1) for that class. This is defined by both artistic and personal tastes. We are told that Savannah collects art by black artists and that, when she arrives in Phoenix, Bernadine produces 'a large bottle of Perrier and two goblets' (151). Both these details represent as distinct a culture of class as Joanna Trollope's 'aga-sagas', set in the English home counties. However, the novel preserves a link between an individualist pursuit of success and a sense of a black community informed by the Civil Rights Movement and feminism through the female community represented by the four women themselves and their participation in social movements like the organisation Black Women on the Move. It thus relates the individual self to a politicised social group.

Despite their independence, all the characters want, but lack, a relationship with a man. Thus, all start in the position of the heroine of popular romance as described in Chapter 3, and part of *Waiting to Exhale*'s utopian impulse is the desire for the perfect relationship. However, the novel is not just about the exploration of the limits of gender identity. It is also about the limits of the black community in the United States, where an oppressive ideology of 'race' makes 'black' synonymous with urban poverty, drugs and crime. Arizona is an expanding part of the United States economy, but Phoenix does not have a large African-American population. Gloria's son, Tarik, claims they make up less than 3 per cent of the state's population.[42] When Savannah decides to move there, she is met with a variety of social and political objections from friends and family: 'isn't that where that governor rescinded the [Martin Luther] King holiday after it had already been passed?' (3); 'Not many of *us* out there', says her partner at a New Year's Eve party (22). Thus, the experience of all the characters is transgressive in several senses. As successful black women, they are breaking codes of gender, class and 'race'. Their presence in prosperous Phoenix creates a new sense of space, disrupting a white and masculine public sphere. Driving through fields of cotton, Robin thinks 'it's ironic that it's Mexicans now who pick it' (158). The narrative gives form to a new kind of social experience. While it preserves in its structure sufficient elements of other popular genres to make it generally accessible to a wide popular audience, it interacts with a reader constituency that can identify with and/or aspire to the social experience represented. The social base of this reader constituency is indicated by the fact that economic and political pressures have combined to give African-American women more economic success than African-American men in the United States.[43]

What the critic bell hooks calls 'yearning' is a crucial part of the text. In the introduction to her book of essays of that title, hooks writes of the black community in the States: 'I was struck by the depths of longing in many of us. Those without money long to find a way to get rid of the endless sense of deprivation. Those with money wonder why so much feels so meaningless and long to find the site of "meaning".'[44] Hooks argues that such utopian yearning is not confined to political struggles: 'Surely our desire for radical social change is intimately linked with the desire to experience pleasure, erotic fulfilment, and a host of other passions'.[45] These links become clear in a key scene where all the women gather to celebrate Gloria's birthday. The episode ends in a carnivalesque tableau of overeating and drunkenness; but, before they all collapse, each articulates a sense of unfulfilled potential. Their declarations are first inspired by a sense of nostalgia evoked by black music: 'Robin had put on Teddy Pendergrass, singing "Turn Off the Lights"' (342). A sense of something lost becomes a desire for a different future. Bernadine says: 'I want to roll all these songs up and feel like this for the next thirty years. Is that asking too much? If it is, why do they make these damn songs to make you think and believe and dream that you *can* feel like this? Huh?' (344). The present is rejected in terms of the lack of suitable men available, although we get the sense that this lack is indicative of a larger sense of something missing:

'They're ugly.'
　'Stupid.'
　'In prison.'
　'Unemployed.'
　'Crackheads.'
　'Short.'
　'Liars.'
　'Unreliable.'
　'Irresponsible.'
　'Too possessive.'
　'Dogs.'
　'Shallow.'
　'Boring.'
　'Stuck in the sixties.'
　'Arrogant.'
　'Childish.'
　'Wimps.'
　'Too goddamn old and set in their ways.'
　'Can't fuck.'
　'Stop!' Savannah said.
　'Well shit, you asked.' Robin said. (351–2)

This combined attraction to and disillusion with the heterosexual ideal is partly overcome by the alternative community of women represented at the birthday party.

> 'So what?' Gloria said. 'Men ain't everything. When are you going to realize that? I'm having a good time sitting here with you guys, and do you think if any of us had a man we'd be here doing this?'
> 'That's precisely my point,' Savannah said. 'If. But we don't. And let me say this up front. If I had a man and it was your birthday and you were going to be over here by yourself all lonely and shit and Robin and Bernie called me up to come over here to help you celebrate, I'd still be here, girl. So don't ever think a man would have that much power over me that I'd stop caring about my friends. And that's the truth, Ruth. (345)

While the novel ends up with one of the characters, Bernadine, apparently heading for a new relationship and a new career after winning half her divorced husband's assets, none of the women actually achieves her goals. Instead, the novel preserves its basic utopian hope for a better future in a sense of an unfulfilled present. The final paragraph of the book expresses this in a vision of food produced and sold by and for the black community:

> She'd had a better dream. One that would see the light. Since these white folks were making a fortune selling these damn chocolate chip cookies,

she'd open up her own little shop. Sell nothing but sweets, the kind black folks ate: blackberry cobbler, peach cobbler, sweet potato pie, bread pudding, banana pudding, rice pudding, lemon meringue pie, and pound cake ... She already had a name picked: Bernadine's Sweet Tooth. That sounded good. Yeah, she thought. It's got a real nice ring to it.

Conclusion

Bernadine's vision of food can be related to a long utopian tradition dating back to the medieval peasant ballads of the land of Cockagne, where peace and plenty reigned.[46] Here that vision offers a place in the world for a particular reader constituency in the face of a common experience of exclusion. In this chapter, I have argued that transgression is a necessary part of popular fiction, but that its results are unpredictable. Popular fiction can glory in the bodily, but the use of the grotesque can also confirm social conventions. Popular fiction can reinforce stereotypes even as it exploits the anxieties they raise. The cultural politics of transgression require that the popular text be placed in relation to the world and the reader. Only then will the full possibilities of its meaning become clear. In the best examples, the text will signify the excess envisioned by Bernadine as food, the potential that lies beyond the limitations of the reader's present position. At the very least it will signify a lack which stimulates the reader's desire for a better world.

Notes

1 Roland Barthes, *The Pleasure of the Text* (Oxford, Blackwell, 1975), p. 11.
2 *Ibid.*, p. 14.
3 *Ibid.*
4 Stuart Hall, 'For Allon White: Metaphors of Transformation', in introduction to Allon White, *Carnival, Hysteria and Writing*, ed. Stuart Hall *et al.* (Oxford, Oxford University Press, 1993), p. 2.
5 See, for example, Pam Keesey (ed.), *Daughters of Darkness: Lesbian Vampire Stories* (Pittsburgh, Cleis Press, 1993); Fiona Cooper, *Heartbreak on the High Sierra* (London, Virago, 1989).
6 Doreen Carvajal, 'An Emerging Prominence for Blacks in Publishing', *New York Times*, 24 June 1996, p. C1.
7 Antonio Gramsci, *Selections from Cultural Writings* (London, Lawrence & Wishart, 1985), p. 93.
8 See Hans Magnus Enzensberger, 'Constituents of a Theory of the Media', in *The Consciousness Industry: On Literature, Politics and the Media*

(New York, Seabury, 1974).

9　Michel Foucault, *The Foucault Reader*, ed. Paul Rabinow (Harmondsworth, Penguin, 1991), p. 67.

10　See Ian Watt, *The Rise of the Novel: Studies in Defoe, Richardson and Fielding* (Harmondsworth, Penguin, 1963).

11　Peter Stallybrass and Allon White, *The Poetics and Politics of Transgression* (London, Methuen, 1986), p. 9.

12　Kieron Saunders, 'Sex Romps of Philip's Friend', *Sun*, 16 January 1985, p. 1

13　Jilly Cooper, *Rivals* (London, Corgi, 1989), pp. 540–41.

14　Mikhail Bakhtin, *The Dialogic Imagination*, Austin, Texas University Press, p. 198.

15　*Ibid.*, p. 200.

16　Tom Clancy, *Debt of Honor* (New York, Berkley Books, 1995), p. 843.

17　Raymond Williams, *The Politics of Modernism*, ed. Tony Pinkney (London, Verso, 1989), p. 110.

18　Stallybrass and White, *The Poetics and Politics of Transgression*, pp. 13–16.

19　E. P. Thompson, 'Rough Music', in *Customs in Common* (London, Merlin Press, 1991).

20　Fredric Jameson, 'Reification and Utopia in Mass Culture', *Social Text*, 1 (1979) 130–48.

21　Barthes, *The Pleasure of the Text*, p. 42.

22　Homi Bhabha, 'The Other Question: Stereotype, Discrimination and the Discourse of Colonialism', in *The Location of Culture* (London, Routledge, 1994), p. 66.

23　Bhabha, 'The Other Question', p. 75.

24　Jilly Cooper, *Polo* (London, Corgi, 1992), p. 495.

25　For a psychoanalytic account of the joke, see Sigmund Freud, *Jokes and their Relation to the Unconscious*, Pelican Freud Library vol. 6 (Harmondsworth, Penguin, 1986).

26　Kevin Davey, 'The Impermanence of New Labour', in Mark Perryman (ed.), *The Blair Agenda* (London, Lawrence & Wishart, 1996), p. 94.

27　Barthes, *The Pleasure of the Text*, pp. 6–7.

28　*Ibid.*, p. 6.

29　Clive Bloom, *Cult Fiction: Popular Reading and Pulp Theory* (London, Macmillan, 1996), p. 84.

30　Paul Gilroy, *The Black Atlantic* (Cambridge MA, Harvard University Press, 1993).

31　Walter Mosley, *Devil in a Blue Dress*, in *The Walter Mosley Omnibus* (London, Picador, [1990] 1995), p. 123 (henceforth page numbers given in text).

32　The series includes *Devil in a Blue Dress* (1990); *A Red Death* (1991); *White Butterfly* (1992); *Black Betty* (1994); *Little Yellow Dog* (1996) and *Gone Fishin'* (1997).

33　Earlier in the century, 'passing' was a theme of the Harlem Renaissance, most famously in Nella Larsen's novel of that name (1929).

34 These events are narrated in the first Easy Rawlins mystery, which was the sixth to be published, *Gone Fishin'* (London, Serpent's Tail, 1997).

35 Walter Mosley, *A Red Death*, in *The Walter Mosley Omnibus*, p. 422.

36 'The paradox of subjectivation (*assujetissement*) is precisely that the subject who would resist such norms is itself enabled, if not produced, by such norms. Although this constitutive restraint does not foreclose the possibility of agency, it does locate agency as a reiterative or rearticulatory practice, immanent to power, and not a relation of external opposition to power'. Judith Butler, *Bodies That Matter: On the Discursive Limits of 'Sex'* (London, Routledge, 1993), p. 15.

37 Eve Kosofsky Sedgwick, *Between Men: English Literature and Male Homosocial Desire* (Baltimore, Johns Hopkins University Press, 1985).

38 It is interesting here to compare two other African-American novels. In both *Beloved* (1987) and *Jazz* (1992) by Toni Morrison, a murder serves as the mystery around which the narrative circulates, a violent act which can only be explained in relation to the violence of slavery and racism.

39 See Nick Davies, 'Police Yardie Scandal', *Guardian*, 3 February 1997, p. 1.

40 Victor Headley, *Yardie* (London, Pan, 1993), pp. 184–5 (first published London, X Press, 1992).

41 Jonathan Dollimore, *Sexual Dissidence* (Oxford, Oxford University Press, 1991), p. 225–6. The term 'reverse discourse' comes from Michel Foucault.

42 Terry McMillan, *Waiting to Exhale* (London, Black Swan, 1993), p. 195 (henceforth page numbers given in text).

43 There are similar statistics for black women in Britain: 'in a 1993 survey of GCSE results in the London borough of Lambeth, girls did almost twice as well as boys. And unemployment rates among young black women are nowhere near as high as those among men; in parts of the capital, over 60 per cent of black men aged between 16 and 24 are out of work.' Angela Neustatter, 'Winning the Race', *Guardian*, G2, 30 January 1997, p. 4.

44 bell hooks, *Yearning: Race, Gender, and Cultural Politics* (London, Turnaround, 1991), p. 12.

45 *Ibid.*, p. 13.

46 A. L. Morton, *The English Utopia* (London, Lawrence & Wishart, 1969).

Conclusion

The utopian element in popular fiction suggests the possibility of new and different selves. In this book I have suggested that the readers of popular fiction use the popular text to renegotiate a sense of self. I began with Walter Benjamin's image of the reader as traveller: someone whose identity is in flux, between destinations, but for whom the popular text supplies a structure within which she or he can fashion a workable self to manage the transition from here to there. I argued that the fantasies we participate in while reading are related to the world in which we live. However, in the preceding chapters I have shown that those fantasies take many different forms and that their relationship with the world is made up of a constellation of different relations between text and reader. An understanding of these relations requires a politics of reading that relates to an idea of a politics of the self. Only when reading popular fiction is placed in the context of the social conflicts that shape identity will its full impact be discerned.

As we saw in Chapter 1, understanding the world in which we live is of crucial importance to our understanding of popular fiction. In the late twentieth century our journeys of the self have become ever more complex. Refashioning identity means negotiating between the micro-politics of the personal and the macro-politics of the national, international and global institutions that govern our lives. In Chapter 1 we saw how, as a consequence, bestselling fiction varies enormously. Bestselling titles attract reader coalitions made up of widely differing social groups. The key to a successful title is its ability to relate the minutiae of everyday life with the powerful structures within which we live. In contrast, the bestselling genre attracts a more constant, although still changing, audience. While bestselling titles are hybrid forms, incorporating elements from many genres, the detective novel and the formula romance remain popular because they supply a familiar framework within which an identity can be created.

The study of narrative form, the text, should always be put in the context of our understanding of the world; but form also requires detailed study in its own right. Narrative conventions provide the structure within which our understanding of the world is made. Paradoxically, however, formula narrative can provide the most opportunity for fantasy because the conventional setting sets the co-ordinates for imaginative possibilities beyond the text. As we have seen, the solution dissatisfies the critical reader of detective fiction, and the questions raised by the investigation offer other interpretations of the world. Formula romance allows the reader to position herself or himself between two poles of masculinity and femininity, making multiple identifications and negotiating the limits and possibilities of a gendered identity. Different genres allow different prospects for the renegotiation of self-identity. Detective fiction permits particular kinds of self, emphasising the critical even where irrationality (both on the part of the murderer and the detective) is the subject of the investigation. Romance, by contrast, affirms the longing for a unified subjectivity where desire meets its object. The romance narrative explores the obstacles that impede desire and, ultimately, cannot satisfy the needs that drive it.

As we saw in Chapters 4 and 5, the narratives of science fiction and gothic horror are less formulaic, although each utilise familiar patterns and archetypes. Science fiction is perhaps the most innovative popular form. It is constantly seeking new scenarios and outlandish contexts in which to test the kinds of new identities that might now be possible. Gothic horror is more inward looking than outward looking. It explores the limits of identity rather than its metamorphoses: the point at which coherence cracks and crumbles and the reader is left struggling for rational explanations. Science fiction and horror play with narrative and social conventions, repeating or transgressing them in order to achieve the desired effect of wonder or terror. The skill or lack of skill with which narrative conventions are handled underpins the success of popular fiction. This means that such fiction will always be closely tied to the time in which it is written.

Popular fiction's dependence on convention makes it ephemeral. While 'classic' fiction is also dependent for its meaning on an understanding of its time and place, the speed at which the culture industry moves in the late twentieth century means that all cultural artefacts rapidly become outdated. Fashion would have it so. As we saw in Chapter 1, it has been argued that popular fiction's ephemerality means that it simply reflects the dominant ideology of the period. But, while it is prey to temporary fads, this is not necessarily a sign of superficiality. Popular narratives play a vital role in mediating social change, informing their audience of new currents and allowing the reader to insert him- or herself into new scenarios in a way that can be related to her or his own experience. Its engagement in the present, in now-time, means that the political nature of popular fiction is never in doubt. Only a very one-sided view of popular culture could see it as a kind of sop, serving up standard fare to a discriminating audience. The narratives can, must, and do change, not just because of the dictates of the culture industry, nor only because of the needs and desires of the audience, but because of a complex interaction between these two forces, which sometimes work in tandem, sometimes pull against one another. As readers we enjoy that interaction, but that enjoyment is seldom passive. There is a critical element to the way we read. We use fiction to help us refine our conception of the world. As critics our interest is raised to a further level of awareness, and one of the main concerns of criticism must be to place popular fiction in the context of its world. Inevitably, this is a political project and as such the study of popular culture is always controversial.

Since the 1960s, there has been in an increasing interest in what has been described as cultural politics. This interest has been most marked on the left and is without precedent since the work of the Frankfurt School in the first half this century. One of the most important aspects of this latest cultural turn has been the diverse forms it has taken. Feminist criticism, anti-racist and postcolonial, lesbian and gay, queer, as well as the continuing influence of Marxist criticism, all have established the important role of culture in the making of political identities. This has had an important effect on the understanding of how popular culture works. Movements like feminism, which exist both in the sphere of political activism and as an academic current, have been less disparaging of popular audiences than earlier forms of criticism. Lesbian and gay, anti-racist and postcolonial criticism also exist both inside and outside the academy. Two complementary approaches have been used. On the one hand, critiques of the dominant culture have demonstrated how cultural hegemony is maintained. On the other, these critiques have been accompanied by analyses which demonstrate how culture is used and subverted to sustain dissident positions.

The social movements that have led the way towards a more pluralist society have found unexpected resources in popular genres. As we saw in Chapter 3, feminist criticism has challenged the predominantly dismissive attitude to formula romance. It has also had a significant effect on mainstream popular fiction. Feminist thrillers are perhaps the best known example. For example, Susan R. Sloan's *Guilt By Association* (1995), which reached the *New York Times* top ten in 1996, is a good example of a plot informed by feminist critiques of male power. The protagonist, Karen Kern, waits thirty years, from 1962 to 1992, to have her revenge on the man who raped her and left her for dead. It is not, I think, a coincidence that those thirty years also mark the history of the post-war resurgence in feminist activism. Lesbian and gay criticism has questioned the normative understanding of sexuality in popular fiction. Its influence has been most marked in the study of gothic horror, where, as in my reading of Ian Banks's *Complicity*, it has focused on the 'queer' desires that emerge from horror's excesses. In Chapter 6, I showed how the relationship between Easy and Mouse in Walter Mosley's mysteries could be read using the same techniques. More generally, the growing number of titles in the new categories of lesbian and gay detective fiction demonstrates the popularity of the new detectives. Writers like Mosley and Terry McMillan also show signs of a new pluralism in popular culture. As Homi Bhabha shows, stereotypes signify the powerful forces that exclude through racism and discrimination, but their conventions are unstable and can be transgressed to produce new kinds of narratives that challenge the hegemonic culture.

To illustrate the popular concern with the cultural politics of identity, I end with *A Tangled Web* by Judith Michael, the novel I started with. On the final page, the twins, Sabrina and Stephanie, finally do the impossible. They go beyond the game where each plays at being the other, and actually assume the other's identity. Stephanie becomes Sabrina. She escapes her dull life as a housewife and mother and embraces a more exciting glamorous world. Sabrina, having lived with Garth when she thought that Stephanie was dead, decides to stay on with the man and children she has come to love. The final paragraphs underline the strange and unreal shifts that occur as each sister becomes the other.

> Garth put his arm around her. 'Time to go.' He kissed Stephanie's cheek. 'We'll talk to you soon. And see you soon.'
>
> His arm around Sabrina, they walked to the door and into the corridor without looking back. But Sabrina could not help it. She glanced quickly into the room as the door closed and saw Stephanie standing alone, one hand clutching the photo album, the other raised in farewell.
>
> Then she and Garth were in each other's arms for a long silent moment until, together, they turned to walk down the corridor. Hand in hand, Garth and Stephanie Andersen walked to the elevator, to the lobby, to the street, where a few blocks away, their children waited.[1]

Sabrina and Stephanie make the magical transition from the constraints of their real lives to new, more desirable identities. The reader of *A Tangled Web* does not, of course, have that option. But in the act of reading we can, at least, explore what it might be like to shift shape and become someone or (in the case of science fiction) some*thing* else. The possibilities offered by popular fiction are, of course, limited. The two sisters represent two stereotypical choices: the security of the nuclear family woman or individual freedom; but the reader, at least while reading, is not entirely constrained by either, and can enjoy the fantasy of both roles. Unlike the sisters, at the end of the book, having investigated everything it has to offer, we have to return to a real situation; but we do so in the knowledge of how things might, possibly, be different. Popular fiction feeds the desire for something beyond the limitations of our lives, for something new. At its most successful it is able to seep into the cracks of contradictions of social reality and demonstrate the possibility of a better world; but, having shown us everything it can, it leaves the achievement of that world up to us. In the end, we have to forsake the pleasures of the text, put down the book, get off the train, enter the station, and experience, to repeat Benjamin's gothic overstatement, the real 'horror of the unfamiliar arrival hall'.

Note

1   Judith Michael, *A Tangled Web* (New York, Pocket Books, 1995), p. 584.

Bibliography

Fiction

Archer, J. (1984), *First Among Equals*, London, HarperCollins, 1993.

Asimov, I. (1949), *Second Foundation*, London, Voyager, 1995.

Asimov, I. (1952), *Foundation and Empire*, London, Voyager, 1996.

Asimov, I. (1953), *Foundation*, London, Voyager, 1995.

Ballard, J. G. (1973), *Crash*, London, TriadPaladin, 1990.

Banks, I. (1993), *Complicity*, London, Little, Brown.

Barker, C. (1994), *Everville*, London, HarperCollins.

Bellamy, E. (1888), *Looking Backward*, Harmondsworth, Penguin, 1982.

Binchy, M. (1990), *Circle of Friends*, New York, Dell.

Burchill, J. (1990), *Ambition*, London, Corgi.

Butler, O. (1987), *Xenogenesis*, London, Victor Gollancz.

Chandler, R. (1939), *The Big Sleep*, Harmondsworth, Penguin, 1948.

Chang, J. (1993), *Wild Swans*, London, Flamingo.

Clancy, T. (1995), *Debt of Honour*, London, HarperCollins.

Clark, M. H. (1994), *Remember Me*, New York, Pocket Books.

Collins, J. (1984), *Hollywood Wives*, London, Pan.

Collins, J. (1987), *Hollywood Husbands*, London, Pan.

Collins, J. (1995), *Hollywood Kids*, London, Pan.

Collins, W. (1868), *The Moonstone*, London, Bantam Classics, 1982.

Cookson, C. (1988), *The Cultured Handmaiden*, London, Corgi.

Cookson, C. (1994), *The Golden Straw*, London, Corgi.

Cooper, F. (1989), *Heartbreak on the High Sierra*, London, Virago.

Cooper, J. (1986), *Riders*, London, Corgi.

Cooper, J. (1989), *Rivals*, London, Corgi.

Cooper, J. (1992), *Polo*, London, Corgi.

Cox, J. (1995), *More than Riches*, London, Headline.

Crichton, M. (1992), *Jurassic Park*, London, Arrow.

Crichton, M. (1994), *Disclosure*, London, Arrow.

Dawson, S. (1994), *In Self Defence*, Richmond, Silhouette.

Dexter, C. (1977), *The Last Bus to Woodstock*, London, Pan.

Dexter, C. (1979), *Service of the all the Dead*, London, Pan.

Dick, P. K. (1966), 'We Can Remember It Wholesale', in P. K. Dick, *We Can Remember It Wholesale*, vol. 5 of *The Collected Stories of Philip K. Dick*, London, Grafton, 1991.

Dick, P. K. (1968), *Do Androids Dream of Electric Sheep?*, London, Grafton, 1972.

Doyle, A. C. (1892), 'The Adventure of the Copper Beeches', in *The Complete Adventures of Sherlock Holmes*, ed. C. Morley, Harmondsworth, Penguin, 1985.

Du Maurier, D. (1938), *Rebecca*, London, Gollancz, 1996.

Francis, D. (1992), *Driving Force*, New York, Fawcett Crest.

Gibson, W. (1984), *Neuromancer*, London, HarperCollins, 1986.

Gibson, W. (1986), *Burning Chrome*, London, HarperCollins, 1993.

Gibson, W. (1990), *The Difference Engine*, London, Gollancz.

Gibson, W. (1994), *Virtual Light*, New York, Bantam.

Grafton, S. (1993), *I is for Innocent*, London, Pan.

Grisham, J. (1992), *A Time to Kill*, London, Arrow.

Hammett, D. (1932), *The Thin Man*, Harmondsworth, Penguin, 1935.

Hansen, J. (1986), *The Little Dog Laughed*, New York, Henry Holt.

Headley, V. (1992), *Yardie*, London, Pan, 1993.

Herbert, J. (1985) *Moon*, New York, Onyx, 1987.

James, P. D. (1962), *Cover Her Face*, Harmondsworth, Penguin, 1989.

Jones, G. (1994), *North Wind*, London, Victor Gollancz.

Jordan, P. (1989), *Valentine's Night*, Richmond, Mills & Boon, 1995.

Keesey, P. (ed.) (1993), *Daughters of Darkness: Lesbian Vampire Stories*, Pittsburgh, Cleis Press.

King, S. (1974), *Carrie*, New York, Plume, 1991.

King, S. (1995), *Insomnia*, New York, Signet.

King, S. (1980), *The Dead Zone*, London, Futura.

Koontz, D. (1994), *Dark Rivers of the Heart*, New York, Ballantine.

Le Guin, U. (1974), *The Dispossessed*, London, HarperCollins, 1996.

Leonard, E. (1992), *Rum Punch*, Harmondsworth, Penguin.

McMillan, T. (1993), *Waiting to Exhale*, London, Black Swan.

McMillan, T. (1996), *How Stella Got Her Groove Back*, London, Viking.

Michael, J. (1982), *Deceptions*, New York, Poseiden.

Michael, J. (1995), *A Tangled Web*, New York, Pocket Books.

Morris, W. (1891), *News from Nowhere*, in *Three Works by William Morris*, London, Lawrence & Wishart, 1986.

Morrison, T. (1987), *Beloved*, London, Chatto & Windus.

Morrison, T. (1992), *Jazz*, London, Chatto & Windus.

Mosley, W. (1990), *Devil in a Blue Dress*, in *The Walter Mosley Omnibus*, London, Picador, 1995.

Mosley, W. (1991), *A Red Death*, in *The Walter Mosley Omnibus*, London, Picador, 1995.

Mosley, W. (1992), *White Butterfly*, in *The Walter Mosley Omnibus*, London, Picador, 1995.

Mosley, W. (1994), *Black Betty*, London, Serpent's Tail.

Mosley, W. (1996), *Little Yellow Dog*, London, Serpent's Tail.

Mosley, W. (1997), *Gone Fishin'*, London, Serpent's Tail.

Muller, M. (1977), *Edwin of the Iron Shoes*, London, Women's Press, 1993.

Muller, M. (1990), *Trophies and Dead Things*, London, Women's Press, 1992.

Noon, J. (1993), *Vurt*, Stockport, Ringpull Press.

Paretsky, S. (1987), *Deadlock*, Harmondsworth, Penguin.

Paretsky, S. (1991), *Burn Marks*, London, Virago.

Paretsky, S. (1992), *Guardian Angel*, Harmondsworth, Penguin.

Piercy, M. (1979), *Woman on the Edge of Time*, London, Women's Press.

Piercy, M. (1992) *Body of Glass*, Harmondsworth, Penguin (first published in the USA by Alfred A. Knopf under the title *He, She and It*, 1991).

Poe, E. A. (1841), 'The Murders in the Rue Morgue', in *Selected Tales*, ed. J. Symons, Oxford, Oxford University Press, 1980.

Power, E. (1990), *Seed of Vengeance*, Richmond, Mills & Boon.

Rendell, R. (1966), *Vanity Dies Hard*, London, Arrow, 1984.

Rendell, R. (1972), *Murder Being Once Done*, London, Hutchinson, 1991.

Rice, A. (1977), *Interview with a Vampire*, London, Futura.

Rice, A. (1986), *The Vampire Lestat*, London, Futura.

Rice, A. (1995), *Taltos*, New York, Ballantine

Richmond, E. (1994), *A Wayward Love*, Richmond, Mills & Boon.

Robbins, H. (1961), *The Carpetbaggers*, New York, Simon & Schuster.

Robbins, H. (1995), *Raiders*, New York, Pocketbooks.

Ross, J. (1994), *The Return of Caine O'Halloran*, Richmond, Mills & Boon, 1994.

Sayers, D. L. (1934), *The Nine Tailors*, London, Coronet, 1988.

Sloan, S. R. (1995), *Guilt By Association*, New York, Warner.

Steel, D. (1993), *Jewels*, London, Corgi.

Steel, D. (1993), *Mixed Blessings*, London, Corgi.

Stevenson, R. L. (1886), *The Strange Case of Dr Jekyll and Mr Hyde and Other Stories*, Harmondsworth, Penguin, 1979.

Straub, P. (1979), *Ghost Story*, New York, Pocket Books, 1980.

Tan, A. (1990), *The Joy-Luck Club*, London, Minerva.
Townsend, S. (1993), *The Queen and I*, London, Mandarin.
Trollope, J. (1992), *The Rector's Wife*, London, Black Swan.
Westleigh, S. (1994), *A Lady of Independent Means*, Richmond, Mills & Boon.
Wheatley, D. (1960), *The Satanist*, London, Mandarin, 1995.
Wilde, O. (1891), *The Picture of Dorian Gray and Other Writings*, New York, Bantam, 1982.
Wilson, B. (1984), *Murder in the Collective*, London, Women's Press.
Wilson, B. (1987), *Sisters of the Road*, London, Women's Press.
Wilson, B. (1989), *The Dog Collar Murders*, London, Virago.
Wings, M. (1992), *Divine Victim*, London, Women's Press.
Wings, M. (1996), *She Came By the Book*, New York, Berkeley.

Secondary sources

Adorno, T. W. (1990), *Negative Dialectics*, London, Routledge.
Adorno, T. W. *et al.* (1977), *Aesthetics and Politics*, London, New Left Books.
Adorno, T. W. and E. Bloch (1988), 'Something's Missing: A Discussion between Ernst Bloch and Theodor W. Adorno on the Contradictions of Utopian Longing', in E. Bloch, *The Utopian Function of Art and Literature*, Cambridge MA and London, MIT Press.
Adorno, T. W. and M. Horkheimer (1979), *Dialectic of Enlightenment*, London, Verso.
Armitt, L. (1997), 'The Fragile Frames of *The Bloody Chamber*', in T. Broughton and J. Bristow (eds), *The Infernal Desires of Angela Carter*, London, Longman.
Armitt, L. (ed.) (1991), *Where No Man Has Gone Before: Women and Science Fiction*, London, Routledge.
Ashley, B. (ed.) (1989), *The Study of Popular Fiction: A Source Book*, London, Pinter.
Bakhtin, M. M. (1968), *Rabelais and His World*, Cambridge MA, MIT Press.
Bakhtin, M. M. (1981), *The Dialogic Imagination*, Austin, Texas University Press.
Barrett, M. and A. Philips (eds) (1991), *Destabilizing Theory: Contemporary Feminist Debates*, Cambridge, Polity Press.
Barthes, R. (1975), *The Pleasure of the Text*, Oxford, Blackwell.
Baudrillard, J. (1988), *Selected Writings*, ed. M. Poster, Stanford CA, Stanford University Press.
Baudrillard, J. (1991), 'Ballard's *Crash*', *Science Fiction Studies*, 18:55:3 (November), 313–20.
Baudrillard, J. (1991), 'Simulacra and Science Fiction', *Science Fiction Studies*, 18:55:3 (November), 309–13.
Bear, J. (1992), *The #1 New York Times Bestseller*, Berkeley CA, Ten Speed Press.

Beer, G. (1970), *The Romance*, London, Methuen.

Belsey, C. (1980), 'Critical Practice', in B. Ashley (ed.), *The Study of Popular Fiction: A Source Book*, London, Pinter, 1989.

Benjamin, W. (1969), *Illuminations*, New York, Schocken.

Benjamin, W. (1972), *Gesammelte Schriften*, Frankfurt am Main, Suhrkamp Verlag.

Benjamin, W. (1983), *Charles Baudelaire, A Lyric Poet in the Era of High Capitalism*, London, Verso.

Bennett, T. (ed.) (1990), *Popular Fiction*, London, Routledge.

Bennett, T., C. Mercer and J. Woollacott (eds) (1986), *Popular Culture and Social Relations*, Milton Keynes, Open University Press.

Bennett, T. and J. Woollacott (1987), *Bond and Beyond: The Political Career of a Popular Hero*, London, Macmillan.

Berman, M. (1982), *All That Is Solid Melts Into Air: The Experience of Modernity*, New York, Simon & Schuster.

Bernstein, R. (1991), *The New Constellation: The Ethical-Political Horizons of Modernity/Postmodernity*, Cambridge, Polity Press.

Bhabha, H. (1994), *The Location of Culture*, London, Routledge.

Billon, A. (1993), 'Getting Up on the Wrong Side of Bed', *Observer Review*, 3 January, pp. 2–3.

Bloch, E. (1988), *The Utopian Function of Art and Literature*, Cambridge MA and London, MIT Press.

Bloom, C. (1996), *Cult Fiction: Popular Reading and Pulp Theory*, London, Macmillan.

Botting, F. (1996), *Gothic*, London, Routledge.

Bourdieu, P. (1984), *Distinction: A Social Critique of the Judgement of Taste*, Cambridge MA, Harvard University Press.

Brecht, B. (1967), 'Über die Popularität des Kriminalromans', in *Gesammelte Werke* vol. 8., Frankfurt am Main, Suhrkamp Verlag.

Bridgewood, C. (1986), 'Family Romances: The Contemporary Popular Family Saga', in Jean Radford (ed.), *The Progress of Romance: The Politics of Popular Fiction*, London, Routledge & Kegan Paul.

Bronfen, E. (1992), *Over Her Dead Body: Death, Femininity and the Aesthetic*, Manchester, Manchester University Press.

Brook, J. and I. A. Boal (eds) (1995), *Resisting the Virtual Life: The Culture and Politics of Information*, San Francisco, City Lights.

Brunt, R. (1984), 'A Career in Love: The Romantic World of Barbara Cartland', in C. Pawling (ed.), *Popular Fiction and Social Change*, London, Macmillan.

Burgin, V., J. Donald and C. Kaplan (eds) (1989) *Formations of Fantasy*, London, Routledge.

Butler, J. (1993), *Bodies That Matter: On the Discursive Limits of 'Sex'*, London, Routledge.

Carlyle, T. (1971), 'Signs of the Times', in *Selected Writings*, Harmondsworth, Penguin.

Carr, H. (ed.) (1989), *From My Guy to Sci-Fi: Genre and Women's Writing in the Postmodern World*, London, Pandora.

Carvajal, D. (1996), 'An Emerging Prominence for Blacks in Publishing', *New York Times* (24 June), pp. C1, C4.

Cawelti, J. G. (1976), *Adventure, Mystery and Romance: Formula Stories as Art and Popular Culture*, Chicago, Chicago University Press.

Davey, K. (1996), 'The Impermanence of New Labour', in M. Perryman (ed.), *The Blair Agenda*, London, Lawrence & Wishart.

Davies, N. (1997), 'Police Yardie Scandal', *Guardian* (3 February), p. 1.

Davies, P. J. (ed.) (1990), *Science Fiction, Social Conflict and War*, Manchester, Manchester University Press.

Dews, P. (1987), *Logics of Disintegration*, London, Verso.

Docherty, T. (ed.) (1993), *Postmodernism: A Reader*, New York, Columbia University Press.

Dollimore, J. (1991), *Sexual Dissidence*, Oxford, Oxford University Press.

Easterbrook, N. (1992), 'The Arc of Our Destruction: Reversal and Erasure in Cyberpunk', *Science Fiction Studies*, 19, 378–94.

Eco, U. (1977), *The Bond Affair*, London, Macdonald.

Edgell, S., K. Heatherington and A. Warde (eds) (1996) *Consumption Matters*, Oxford, Blackwell.

Enzensberger, H. M. (1974), 'Constituents of a Theory of the Media', in *The Consciousness Industry: On Literature, Politics and the Media*, New York, Seabury.

Felski, R. (1995), *The Gender of Modernity* (Cambridge MA, Harvard University Press.

Foucault, M. (1991), *The Foucault Reader*, ed. Paul Rabinow, Harmondsworth, Penguin.

Fowler, B. (1995), 'Literature Beyond Modernism: Middlebrow and Popular Romance', in L. Pearce and J. Stacey (eds), *Romance Revisited*, London, Lawrence & Wishart.

Freud, S. (1950), *Totem and Taboo: Some Points of Agreement between the Mental Lives of Savages and Neurotics*, London, Norton.

Freud, S. (1958), *On Creativity and the Unconscious: Papers on the Psychology of Art, Literature, Love, Religion*, New York, Harper & Row.

Freud, S. (1973), *Introductory Lectures on Psychoanalysis*, Pelican Freud Library vol. 1, Harmondsworth, Penguin.

Freud, S. (1977), *On Sexuality*, Pelican Freud Library vol. 7, Harmondsworth, Penguin.

Freud, S. (1986), *Jokes and their Relation to the Unconscious*, Pelican Freud Library vol. 6, Harmondsworth, Penguin.

Frow, J. (1995), *Cultural Studies and Cultural Value*, Oxford, Clarendon Press.

Frye, N. (1957), *Anatomy of Criticism: Four Essays*, Princeton, Princeton University Press.

Garnett, R. and R. J. Ellis (eds) (1990), *Science Fiction Roots and Branches*, London, Macmillan.

Gibbs, L. (ed.) (1994), *Daring to Dissent: Lesbian Culture from Margin to Mainstream*, London, Cassell.

Giddens, A. (1991), *Modernity and Self-Identity: Self and Society in the Late Modern Age*, Cambridge, Polity Press.

Giddens, A. (1992), *The Transformation of Intimacy: Sexuality, Love and Eroticism in Modern Societies*, Cambridge, Polity Press.

Gilbert, S. and S. Gubar (1979), *The Madwoman in the Attic: The Woman Writer and the Nineteenth-Century Literary Imagination*, New Haven and London, Yale University Press.

Gilroy, P. (1993), *The Black Atlantic*, Cambridge MA, Harvard University Press.

Gramsci, A. (1971), *Selections from the Prison Notebooks*, London, Lawrence & Wishart.

Gramsci, A. (1985), *Selections from Cultural Writings*, London, Lawrence & Wishart.

Griffith, V. (1996), 'The Power of the Plug', *Financial Times*, 1 April.

Habermas, J. (1987), *The Philosophical Discourse of Modernity*, Cambridge MA, MIT Press.

Habermas, J. (1993), 'Modernity – An Incomplete Project', in T. Docherty (ed.), *Postmodernism: A Reader*, New York, Columbia University Press.

Halberstam, J. (1995), *Skin Shows: Gothic Horror and the Technology of Monsters*, Durham NC, Duke University Press.

Halberstam, J. (1995), 'Technologies of Monstrosity: Bram Stoker's *Dracula*', in S. Ledger and S. McCracken (eds), *Cultural Politics at the Fin de Siècle*, Cambridge, Cambridge University Press.

Hall, S. (1993), 'For Allon White: Metaphors of Transformation', introduction to Allon White, *Carnival, Hysteria and Writing*, ed. S. Hall *et al.*, Oxford, Oxford University Press.

Hall, S. and P. Whannel (1964), 'The Popular Arts', in B. Ashley (ed.), *The Study of Popular Fiction: A Source Book*, London, Pinter, 1989.

Hall, S. and M. Jacques (eds) (1983), *The Politics of Thatcherism*, London, Lawrence & Wishart.

Hamilton, A. (1991), 'Adrift on a Sea of Turtles', *Guardian*, 10 January.

Hamilton, A. (1994), 'Clogs by the Aga', *Guardian*, 11 January.

Hamilton, A. (1996), 'Titans and Terrors in a Troubled Industry', *Guardian*, 19 January.

Haraway, D. J. (1991), *Simians, Cyborgs and Women: The Reinvention of Nature*, New York, Routledge.

Harvey, D. (1989), *The Condition of Postmodernity*, Oxford, Blackwell.

Hawkes, T. (1977), *Structuralism and Semiotics*, London, Routledge.

Hawkins, H. (1990), *Classics and Trash: Traditions and Taboos in High Literature and Popular Modern Genres*, Toronto, Toronto University Press.

Heath, S. (1989), 'Joan Riviere and the Masquerade', in V. Burgin, J. Donald and C. Kaplan (eds), *Formations of Fantasy*, London, Routledge.

Heath, S. (1990), 'On Screen, in Frame: Film and Ideology', in T. Bennett (ed.), *Popular Fiction*, London, Routledge.

Hoggart, R. (1957), *The Uses of Literacy: Changing Patterns in English Mass Culture*, Fair Lawn NJ, Essential Books.

hooks, b. (1991), *Yearning: Race, Gender, and Cultural Politics*, London, Turnaround.

Horner, A. (1997), *Unheimlich*, in M. M. Roberts (ed.), *The Gothic Handbook*, London, Macmillan.

Horner, A. and S. Zlosnik (1997), '"Extremely Valuable Property": the Marketing of *Rebecca*', in J. Simons and K. Fullbrook (eds), *Writing: A Woman's Business. Women, Writing and the Market Place*, Manchester, Manchester University Press.

Huyssen, A. (1986), *After the Great Divide: Modernism, Mass Culture, Postmodernism*, Bloomington and Indianapolis, Indiana University Press.

Jameson, F. (1971), *Marxism and Form*, Princeton, Princeton University Press.

Jameson, F. (1972), *The Prison-House of Language*, Princeton, Princeton University Press.

Jameson, F. (1979), 'Reification and Utopia in Mass Culture', *Social Text*, 1, pp. 130–48.

Jameson, F. (1981), *The Political Unconscious: Narrative as Socially Symbolic Act*, London, Methuen.

Jameson, F. (1982), 'Progress Versus Utopia; or, Can We Imagine the Future?', *Science Fiction Studies*, 9:27:2 (July), pp. 147–58.

Jameson, F. (1991), *Postmodernism, or, The Cultural Logic of Late Capitalism*, London, Verso.

Jones, A. R. (1986), 'Mills and Boon meet Feminism', in J. Radford (ed.), *The Progress of Romance: The Politics of Popular Fiction*, London, Routledge & Kegan Paul.

Kaplan, C. (1986), *Sea Changes: Essays on Culture and Feminism*, London, Verso.

Kaplan, C. (1989), 'An Unsuitable Genre for a Feminist', in B. Ashley (ed.), *The Study of Popular Fiction: A Source Book*, London, Pinter.

Kern, S. (1983), *The Culture of Time and Space, 1880–1918*, London, Harvard University Press.

Kerr, P. (1990), 'The Making of (the) MTM (Show)', in T. Bennett (ed.), *Popular Fiction*, London, Routledge.

Knight, S. (1980), *Form and Ideology in Crime Fiction*, London, Macmillan.

Kristeva, J. (1982), *Powers of Horror: An Essay on Abjection*, New York, Columbia University Press.

Lamb, C. (1982), 'Red Riding Hood and the Dirty Old Wolf', *Guardian*, 13 September, p. 8.

Langbauer, L. (1990), *Women and Romance: The Consolations of Gender in the English Novel*, Ithaca and London, Cornell University Press.

Laplanche, J. and J.-B. Pontalis (1973), *The Language of Psychoanalysis*, New York, W. W. Norton.

Laplanche, J. and J.-B. Pontalis (1989), 'Fantasy and the Origins of Sexuality', in V. Burgin, J. Donald and C. Kaplan (eds), *Formations of Fantasy*, London, Routledge.

Lawler, S. (1995), 'I Never Felt as though I Fitted: Family Romances and the Mother–Daughter Relationship', in L. Pearce and J. Stacey (eds), *Romance Revisited*, London, Lawrence & Wishart.

Leavis, Q. D. (1932), *Fiction and the Reading Public*, London, Chatto & Windus.

Leavis, Q. D. (1937), 'The Case of Miss Dorothy Sayers', in B. Ashley (ed.), *The Study of Popular Fiction: A Source Book*, London, Pinter, 1989.

Ledger, S. and S. McCracken (eds) (1995), *Cultural Politics at the Fin de Siècle*, Cambridge, Cambridge University Press.

Levitas, R. (1990), *The Concept of Utopia*, London, Philip Allan.

Longhurst, B. and M. Savage (1996), 'Social Class, Consumption and the Influence of Bourdieu: Some Critical Issues', in S. Edgell, K. Heatherington and A. Warde (eds), *Consumption Matters*, Oxford, Blackwell.

Longhurst D. (ed.) (1989), *Gender, Genre and Narrative Pleasure*, London, Unwin Hyman.

Lovell, T. (1987), *Consuming Fiction*, London, Verso.

Lovett, V. (1989), 'Bodily Symbolism and the Fiction of Stephen King', in D. Longhurst (ed.), *Gender, Genre and Narrative Pleasure*, London, Unwin Hyman.

Luckhurst, R. (1991), 'Border Policing, Postmodernism and Science Fiction', *Science Fiction Studies*, 18:55:3 (November), 358–66.

Lyotard, J.-F. (1984), *The Postmodern Condition*, Manchester, Manchester University Press.

MacCabe, C. (1986), *High Theory/Low Culture*, Manchester, Manchester University Press.

McCracken, S. (1995), 'Postmodernism, a *Chance* to Reread?', in S. Ledger and S. McCracken (eds), *The Cultural Politics of the Fin de Siècle*, Cambridge, Cambridge University Press.

McCracken, S. (1997), 'Cyborg Fictions: The Cultural Logic of Posthumanism', *Socialist Register 1997*, London, Merlin Press.

Macdonald, M. and M. Streeter (1997), 'The Joy of Reading Leaves Men on the Shelf', *Independent*, 2 January.

McRobbie, A. (1992), 'New Times in Cultural Studies', *New Formations*, 13 (Spring), 1–17.

Mandel, E. (1984), *Delightful Murder: A Social History of the Crime Story*, London, Pluto, 1984.

Marx, K. (1967), *Capital* vol. 2, Moscow, Progress Publishers.

Marx, K. (1982), *The Communist Manifesto*, in *The Portable Karl Marx*, ed. Eugene Kamenka, Harmondsworth, Penguin.

Marx, K. and F. Engels (1976), *The German Ideology*, in *Collected Works* vol. 5, New York, International Publishers.

Massent, P. (ed.) (1997), *Criminal Proceedings: The Contemporary American Crime Novel*, London, Pluto.

Mills & Boon (1995), 'Passions Progress, The Changing Face of Mills and Boon', Press Release, Richmond, Mills & Boon.

Mitchell, J. (1984), *Women: The Longest Revolution, Essays in Feminism, Literature and Psychoanalysis*, London, Virago.

Modleski, T. (1982), *Loving with a Vengeance: Mass-Produced Fantasies for Women*, London, Methuen.

Modleski, T. (ed.) (1986), *Studies in Entertainment: Critical Theories of Mass Culture*, Bloomington and Indianapolis, Indiana University Press.

Moretti, F. (1983), *Signs Taken for Wonders*, London, Verso.

Morris, M. (1992), 'The Man in the Mirror: David Harvey's "Condition" of Postmodernity', in M. Featherstone (ed.), *Cultural Theory and Cultural Change*, London, Sage.

Morris, W. (1888), 'Looking Backward', in *Political Writings of William Morris*, ed. A. L. Morton, London, Lawrence & Wishart, 1984.

Morton, A. L. (1969), *The English Utopia*, London, Lawrence & Wishart.

Nash, W. (1990), *Language in Popular Fiction*, London, Routledge.

Neustatter, A. (1997), 'Winning the Race', *Guardian*, G2, 30 January, p. 4.

Nixon, N. (1992), 'Cyberpunk: Preparing the Ground for Revolution or Keeping the Boys Satisfied', *Science Fiction Studies*, 19, 219–35.

Palmer, J. (1978), *Thrillers*, London, Edward Arnold.

Palmer, J. (1991), *Potboilers: Methods, Concepts and Case Studies in Popular Fiction*, London, Routledge.

Palmer, P. (1997), 'The Lesbian Thriller: Transgressive Investigations', in Pete Massent (ed.), *Criminal Proceedings: The Contemporary American Crime Novel*, London, Pluto.

Parrinder, P. (1990), 'Scientists in Science Fiction: Enlightenment and After', in R. Garrett and R. J. Ellis (eds), *Science Fiction Roots and Branches*, London, Macmillan.

Pawling, C. (ed.) (1984), *Popular Fiction and Social Change*, London, Macmillan.

Pearce, L. and J. Stacey (eds) (1995), *Romance Revisited*, London, Lawrence &

Wishart.

Perryman, M. (ed.) (1996), *The Blair Agenda*, London, Lawrence & Wishart.

Polan, D. (1986), 'Brief Encounters: Mass Culture and the Evacuation of Sense', in T. Modleski (ed.), *Studies in Entertainment: Critical Theories of Mass Culture*, Bloomington and Indianapolis, Indiana University Press.

Propp, V. (1928), 'Morphology of the Folk Tale', in B. Ashley (ed.), *The Study of Popular Fiction: A Source Book*, London, Pinter, 1989.

Punter, D. (1980), *The Literature of Terror*, London, Longman.

Radford, J. (ed.) (1986), *The Progress of Romance: The Politics of Popular Fiction*, London, Routledge & Kegan Paul.

Radway, J. (1984), *Reading the Romance: Women, Patriarchy and Popular Literature*, Chapel Hill and London, North Carolina University Press.

Riquer, M. de (1973), 'Cervantes and the Romances of Chivalry', in Miguel de Cervantes Saavedra, *Don Quixote*, ed. J. R. Jones and K. Douglas, New York, W. W. Norton, 1981.

Riviere, J. (1989), 'Womanliness as Masquerade', in V. Burgin, J. Donald and C. Kaplan (eds), *Formations of Fantasy*, London, Routledge.

Roberts, T. J. (1990), *An Aesthetics of Junk Fiction*, Athens GA, University of Georgia Press.

Rose, J. (1986), *Sexuality in the Field of Vision*, London, Verso.

Ross, A. (1991), *Strange Weather: Culture, Science, and Technology in the Age of Limits*, London, Verso.

Rowlands, S. (1996), 'Detecting Society in the Novels of Sarah Paretsky', paper given at conference, 'Detective Fiction, Nostalgia, Progress and Doubt', Liverpool John Moores University (November).

Said, E. (1983), *The World, the Text and the Critic*, Cambridge MA, Harvard University Press.

Said, E. (1991), *Orientalism: Western Conceptions of the Orient*, Harmondsworth, Penguin.

Saunders, K. (1985), 'Sex Romps of Philip's Friend', *Sun* (16 January), pp. 1–2.

Schiller, H. I. (1995), 'The Global Information Highway: Project for an Ungovernable World', in J. Brook and I. A. Boal (eds), *Resisting the Virtual Life: The Culture and Politics of Information*, San Francisco, City Lights.

Schulhafer, J. (1993), 'Embracing the Niche', *Publishers Weekly*, 14 June.

Science Fiction Studies (1991), *Editorial, Science Fiction and Postmodernism*, special edition, 18:55:3 (November), 306.

Sedgwick, E. K. (1985), *Between Men: English Literature and Male Homosocial Desire*, Baltimore MD, Johns Hopkins University Press.

Shiach, M. (1989), *Discourse on Popular Culture: Class, Gender and History in Cultural Analysis, 1730 to the Present*, Oxford, Basil Blackwell, 1989.

Showalter, E. (1991) *Sexual Anarchy*, London, Bloomsbury.

Snitow, A. B. (1983), 'Mass Market Romance: Pornography for Women is Different', in A. B. Snitow, C. Stansell and S. Thompson (eds), *Powers of Desire*, London, Virago.

Sobchack, V. (1991), 'Baudrillard's Obscenity', *Science Fiction Studies*, 18:55:3 (November), 327–9.

Stallabrass, J. (1993), 'Just Gaming: Allegory and Economy in Computer Games', *New Left Review*, 198 (March/April), pp. 83–106.

Stallybrass, P. and A. White (1986), *The Poetics and Politics of Transgression*, London, Methuen.

Steedman, C. (1986), *Landscape for a Good Woman*, London, Virago.

Sutherland, J. (1978), *Fiction and the Fiction Industry*, London, Athlone Press.

Sutherland, J. (1981), *Bestsellers: Popular Fiction of the 1970s*, London, Routledge & Kegan Paul.

Sutherland, J. (1991), 'Fiction and the Erotic Cover', *Critical Quarterly*, 33:2, pp. 3–18.

Suvin, D. (1979), *Metamorphoses in Science Fiction*, London, Yale University Press.

Suvin, D. (1990), 'Counter-Projects: William Morris and Science Fiction of the 1880s', in R. Garnett and R. J. Ellis (eds), *Science Fiction Roots and Branches*, London, Macmillan.

Taylor, H. (1989), 'Romantic Readers', in H. Carr (ed.), *From My Guy to Sci-Fi: Genre and Women's Writing in the Postmodern World*, London, Pandora.

Thompson, E. P. (1991), 'Rough Music', in *Customs in Common*, London, Merlin Press.

Todorov, T. (1977), *The Poetics of Prose*, Oxford, Basil Blackwell.

Trotter, D. (1991), 'Theory and Detective Fiction', *Critical Quarterly*, 33:2, 66–79.

Warner, M. (1994), *From the Beast to the Blonde: On Fairy Tales and their Tellers*, London, Chatto & Windus.

Watt, I. (1963), *The Rise of the Novel: Studies in Defoe, Richardson and Fielding*, Harmondsworth, Penguin.

White, A. (1993), *Carnival, Hysteria and Writing*, ed. S. Hall *et al.*, Oxford, Oxford University Press.

Williams, R. (1976), *Keywords*, London, Fontana.

Williams, R. (1977), *Marxism and Literature*, Oxford, Oxford University Press.

Williams, R. (1989), *The Politics of Modernism*, ed. T. Pinkney, London, Verso.

Williams, R. (1986), 'An Interview with Raymond Williams' by Stephen Heath and Gillian Skirrow, in T. Modleski (ed.), *Studies in Entertainment: Critical Theories of Mass Culture*, Bloomington and Indianapolis, Indiana University Press.

Williamson, M. (1986), 'The Greek Romance', in J. Radford (ed.), *The Progress of Romance: The Politics of Popular Fiction*, London, Routledge & Kegan Paul.

Wings, M. (1994), 'Rebecca Redux: Tears on a Lesbian Pillow', in L. Gibbs (ed.), *Daring to Dissent: Lesbian Culture from Margin to Mainstream*, London, Cassell.

Woollacott, J. (1986), 'Fictions and Ideologies: The Case of Situation Comedy', in T. Bennett, C. Mercer and J. Woollacott (eds), *Popular Culture and Social Relations*, Milton Keynes, Open University Press.

Wright, W. (1975), *Sixguns and Society: A Structural Study of the Western*, Berkeley, California University Press.

Index